Advance praise for
Players and Issues in International Aid
Paula Hoy

❝Paula Hoy's *Players and Issues in International Aid* is an indispensable resource for students, scholars, and professionals in the field of international development. Hoy offers a clear-eyed and comprehensive survey of the major governmental and private actors in international aid. Statistics and portraits of leading players are nicely complemented by critical and constructive commentaries. The volume conveys a vast quantity of information in an readable and illuminating narrative.❞

—William Savitt
EXECUTIVE DIRECTOR
INTERFAITH HUNGER APPEAL

❝I found this book to be an excellent introduction to the topic of 'aid' in international relations. The material does not assume that students have much background in the field but does not talk down to students either. It is basic in the sense of fundamental and foundational without being simplistic. Therefore, it will be of great value to me in teaching introductory level students. The book will be especially helpful for students learning all the terminology and acronyms associated with international aid. Kudos to the author.❞

—Dr. Deborah P. Bhattacharyya
ASSOCIATE PROFESSOR AND CHAIR, DEPARTMENT OF SOCIOLOGY
WITTENBERG UNIVERSITY

❝On the eve of a new century, as humanitarian crises escalate and international assistance declines, Hoy has produced an indispensable manual for teachers and students of global development. Undergraduates and educators alike will find *Players and Issues in International Aid* a clear and compelling guide through an otherwise impenetrable thicket of foreign aid institutions and policy perspectives.❞

—Sarah L. White
CHAIR, INSTITUTE ON EDUCATION AND SOCIAL JUSTICE

D1302197

"This is no ordinary introduction to players and issues; this is a primer that provides a critical reading of the state of international aid as we face the twenty-first century. In examining the present system, Hoy provides all the basics for a solid grounding in the 'who' as well as the 'what,' the good as well as the bad, the dominant as well as the alternative frameworks for giving assistance. She offers a hopeful, imaginative vision and some particulars on how to work toward creating that better system. The reader will find detailed information on the well-known as well as lesser-known actors who play key roles in the system, along with a helpful glossary and a useful listing of key institutional players. The crucial need for an informed citizenry is well met by this hard-hitting but fair appraisal of the current international aid system."

—*Kathleen Maas Weigert, Ph.D.*
ASSOCIATE DIRECTOR FOR ACADEMIC AFFAIRS AND RESEARCH
CENTER FOR SOCIAL CONCERNS; UNIVERSITY OF NOTRE DAME

"What is critically needed at this time is a general introduction to all aspects of international aid, and Paula Hoy effectively provides that introduction. Hoy has written an interesting and informative discussion of the intricacies of international aid that will be an excellent addition to the syllabus of undergraduate and graduate courses that address global problems."

—*Andrew Larkin*
PROFESSOR OF ECONOMICS
ST. CLOUD STATE UNIVERSITY

"*Players and Issues in International Aid* provides an excellent overview of the primary institutions involved in international aid distribution. The book is a useful primer for acquainting students with major actors and the objectives, dilemmas, and consequences of international assistance. The author raises important questions regarding the social, political, and human costs of development choices. A must for concerned citizens!"

—*Debra Sabia*
ASSOCIATE PROFESSOR, DEPARTMENT OF POLITICAL SCIENCE
GEORGIA SOUTHERN UNIVERSITY

*Players and Issues
in International Aid*

Books of related interest from Kumarian Press

NONGOVERNMENTS
NGOs and the Political
Development of the Third World
Julie Fisher

ACHIEVING BROAD-BASED
SUSTAINABLE DEVELOPMENT
Governance, Environment and
Growth With Equity
*James H. Weaver, Michael T.
Rock, Kenneth Kusterer*

BEYOND THE MAGIC
BULLET
NGO Performance and
Accountability in the Post–Cold
War World
Michael Edwards, David Hulme

GOVERNANCE, ADMINISTRA-
TION AND DEVELOPMENT
Making the State Work
Mark Turner, David Hulme

MANAGEMENT DIMENSIONS
OF DEVELOPMENT
Perspectives and Strategies
Milton J. Esman

PROMISES NOT KEPT
The Betrayal of Social Change
in the Third World,
Fourth Edition
John Isbister

Players and Issues
in International Aid

PAULA HOY

Kumarian Press

Players and Issues in International Aid.

Published 1998 in the United States of America by Kumarian Press, Inc.,
14 Oakwood Avenue, West Hartford, Connecticut 06119-2127 USA.

Production supervised by Jenna Dixon
Copyedited by Linda Lotz   Typeset by CompuDesign
Text design by Jenna Dixon   Proofread by Beth Richards
Index by Mary G. Neumann

The text of this book is set in 10.5/13 Monotype Sabon.

Printed in the United States of America on acid-free paper by
BookCrafters. Text printed with vegetable oil-based ink.
∞ The paper used in this publication meets the minimum requirements of the
American National Standard for Information Sciences—Permanence of
Paper for Printed Library Materials, ANSI Z39.48-1984.

Library of Congress Cataloging-in-Publication Data
Hoy, Paula, 1969–   .
    Players & issues in international aid / Paula Hoy.
        p.   cm. — (Kumarian Press books on international development)
    Includes bibliographical references and index.
    ISBN 1-56549-072-X (cloth : alk. paper) — ISBN 1-56549-073-8 (paper : alk.
paper)
    1. Economic assistance. 2. Economic assistance—American. 3. International
agencies. I. Title. II. Series.
HC60.H69   1998
338.91—dc21   97-35131

02 01 00 99 98   10 9 8 7 6 5 4 3 2 1   1st Printing 1998

Contents

Illustrations

Acknowledgments

*T*here are a number of people who were instrumental in helping me write this book. I am extremely grateful to Dee Rubin for her careful reading and insightful suggestions, and for the framework of the table in the introduction. This is a much better book for her participation. Trish Reynolds, my editor at Kumarian Press, was supportive from the beginning, and her interest and patience throughout made the process more pleasant and productive. I would also like to thank my exceptional colleagues at Interfaith Hunger Appeal. Francesca Crispino provided critical assistance and calm during the final stages of the project, and I am extremely grateful to our executive director, Bill Savitt, for his guidance and encouragement throughout the years, and, most recently, with this project. And finally I would like to thank my husband Bobby for inspiring, sustaining, and loving me throughout this entire process, and every day.

Introduction

*F*OREIGN AID HAS NEVER been popular, but never before has it been the politically contentious issue that it is today. Elected officials describe international assistance with the most disparaging remarks. The agency charged with administering U.S. foreign aid is struggling to avoid dissolution by a hostile Congress and an apathetic public. And in wealthy countries throughout the world, governments are dropping their levels of aid contributions dramatically, following the example of the United States. What has prompted this antiaid atmosphere? The need in the developing world for international assistance has certainly not abated; thirty-five thousand children die every day from malnutrition and related diseases, and fifty million people live in extreme poverty. And notwithstanding the economic difficulties of the 1980s, it is not a question of donor nations being unable to afford foreign aid; foreign aid budgets rarely constitute more than 3 percent of donor nations' federal budgets—in the United States, the international affairs budget is a mere 1 percent. The fact that international assistance has never precluded or even detracted from domestic assistance is often overlooked in the argument. In the United States, over 20 percent of federal spending in 1996 went to social security, and over 15 percent went to defense. But the 1 percent spent on international affairs is referred to so often that the American public's gross overestimation of international affairs spending is hardly surprising.[1]

It is not economics or a question of unmet needs in the global South that fuels the current attack on international assistance. Typically, it is the often heard exhortation that the United States should concentrate on its own problems before looking overseas to solve foreign problems. However, the weakness of this isolationist argument is exposed when these so-called foreign problems that supposedly do not merit our attention or resources are looked at more closely. In this time of revolutionary globalization and unprecedented interdependence, the so-called third world can no longer be perceived as a distant reality beset with problems that have little or no bearing on our comfortable lives here in the first world.[2] Advances in technology as well as the meteoric growth in private capital flows and international trade have challenged the notion of distance, bringing cultures and currencies from distant lands into our living rooms and bank accounts within minutes. The dangers of underdevelopment a continent away are similarly knocking on our door. The effects of environmental destruction do not stay neatly within national borders; air and water pollution are clearly global problems that threaten every citizen's future. Infectious diseases affect the immune systems of wealthy and poor alike and spread with ease across geographic and demographic borders. Disparities of wealth, underscored globally by the fact that 358 billionaires control more assets than the combined annual incomes of countries where 45 percent of the world's people live, spark unrest and upheaval that reverberate around the globe as international peacekeepers are called to intervene, and global security is jeopardized. Refugees fleeing starvation or violence pour into foreign lands, becoming living illustrations of the fluidity between foreign and domestic problems. In short, the ravages of underdevelopment extend beyond its primary victims to citizens of wealthier countries whose opportunities for investment, health, and continued prosperity are undermined by uneven development in the South. It is in every citizen's interest to promote and support development—and to support an international aid program that works toward that end.

Whether there exists an international aid program that effectively and honestly supports development is a question that is raised throughout this book, and seeking the answer is the challenge presented to readers. This book does not answer that question—it promises only to introduce the key players and issues in the aid business, to provide readers with the apolitical facts that are vital to any informed debate. Focusing primarily on U.S. foreign aid to developing countries and the various channels through which that aid is provided, the present volume supplies the tools required to think critically about foreign aid and the role it plays in the sustainable human development of our world. Chapter 1 examines U.S. bilateral aid and the agency responsible for distributing that aid, the U.S. Agency for International Development (USAID). Chapter 2 explores the World Bank and explains the controversial policy of structural adjustment that dominated aid policy during the 1980s. The International Monetary Fund and the agencies of the United Nations are examined in Chapters 3 and 4, respectively, including analysis of the debt crisis and the recent challenges facing the United Nations. Chapter 5 focuses on Northern-based nongovernmental organizations as conduits of aid, and Chapter 6 looks at the growing role of organizations based in the South in providing aid and stimulating their own sustainable development. Chapter 7 provides a synopsis of the divergent viewpoints on foreign aid that fuel the current debate, as well as an essay by David C. Korten that places the entire discussion in critical perspective.

What Is Foreign Aid?

The term *international assistance* connotes a benevolent donation given to poor countries by generous, rich nations so that the former can meet the primary needs of their citizens. Unfortunately, this is highly simplistic and inaccurate. As upcoming chapters will show, aid does not necessarily go to the poorest countries, it often does not go toward meeting crucial development needs, and it is never a cash donation given with no strings attached —more often, it is a loan provided by a government or international agency that the recipient must pay back within a specified period. There are various categories or types of aid that vary in popularity among donors, but none of them can be considered an outright gift.

Project aid is assistance provided for the creation of a specific outcome— the building of a dam or a road, for example. Despite its lack of an integrated and long-term approach to development, this type of aid has been popular among donors and recipients alike. Donor countries often want to see concrete evidence of their aid monies, and recipient governments welcome the political mileage such construction projects tend to bestow. Program aid is a more general form of aid. It is not tied to specific projects but has an imposing list of terms and conditions that recipient governments must agree to before any assistance is authorized. This form of aid became the preferred package during the debt crisis (as detailed in Chapters 2 and 3). Technical assistance is another category of aid and consists of the provision of equipment or "experts" and advisers who are sent to developing countries to train local populations in development strategies and techniques. Although technical assistance has made significant contributions in such sectors as agriculture and health, there have been questions about who the real beneficiaries of this type of aid are. The fact that 90 percent of the $12 billion spent on technical assistance each year goes to foreign expertise,[3] despite the availability of national experts who need jobs, provides a disturbing answer to the question. Another equally controversial type of assistance is food aid, which consists primarily of cereals, dairy products, fats, and cooking oils that are sold or, in emergencies, given to developing countries. Food aid is a vital source of support and survival for countries facing natural and man-made emergencies, such as famine. Nonemergency food aid, however, is a far more complicated and contentious issue and is discussed further in Chapter 1. Emergency or humanitarian assistance is probably the least controversial form of foreign aid, as there is little to dispute about the provision of food or grants in response to life-threatening disasters. A less benign form of assistance is military aid, designed to strengthen the military establishments of developing countries. Because this form of aid contributes nothing to the economic development of recipient nations (and many argue that it contributes to their economic decline), few donors consider it to be official development assistance. Table I.1 lists the various forms of foreign assistance.

Although each donor nation defines international aid slightly differently, all have three main vehicles through which they provide assistance. Aid that consists of a direct transfer from a donor government to a recipient government is called bilateral aid. Donors also contribute collectively to international organizations (such as the World Bank or United Nations) that exist for the purpose of distributing this multilateral aid. The third channel for aid is nongovernmental organizations (NGOs), private agencies that work in varying capacities in developing countries toward the alleviation of hunger and poverty. Although NGOs, especially the largest ones, are generously supported by both donor governments and multilateral institutions, they strive to maintain their independent, nongovernmental status—a challenge that promises to become more difficult as more and more government funds are directed their way.[4]

The Organization for Economic Cooperation and Development (OECD), sometimes referred to as a "rich men's club" because its membership includes most industrialized countries in the world, defines official development assistance (ODA) as those flows to developing countries and multilateral institutions provided by official agencies that meet the following test: "it is administered with the promotion of economic development and welfare of developing countries as its main objective; and it is concessional (i.e., low interest rates and/or longer payback period) in character and contains a grant element of at least 25%."[5] Inherent in this definition, as sociologist Gunnar Myrdal points out, is the assumption that any resources flowing from the North to the South must be good for the South and conducive to development, a supposition that many so-called beneficiaries in the South would certainly dispute. The OECD definition dates back to 1969, and although its interpretation has broadened over the years, it is important to bear in mind that it is a definition drafted by donors, not recipients.

In the federal budget, Congress classifies foreign aid as funds allocated to bilateral and multilateral programs, international security assistance and military aid, and refugee and Peace Corps programs. Helping victims of natural disasters rebuild homes and feeding refugees of violent wars are the images that are most frequently associated with foreign aid, but emergency relief is only one type of aid, albeit one that has grown tremendously in recent years—in 1995, 10 percent of ODA was emergency funds. Unlike emergency or humanitarian aid, which is motivated by an effort to make a short-term impact to alleviate suffering regardless of political identification and how it might affect the power or wealth of the donor, nearly all other categories of aid are not motivated by such philanthropic impulses.

Table I.1   Forms of foreign assistance

Type of Aid	Description/Purpose	Donor Agency	Example
Project aid	A grant or loan provided to a government agency or NGO, designated for a specific project or outcome	Bilateral and multilateral donors, NGOs	A grant from the Japanese government for the construction of a hospital
Program aid	A policy-based loan given to a recipient government to create certain economic conditions in that country, or to support balance of payments	Bilateral and multilateral donors	A structural adjustment loan provided by the World Bank
Technical assistance	Provides equipment and/or experts for a specific sector or outcome	Bilateral and multilateral donors, NGOs	A team of UN engineers sent to a developing country to set up a water supply project
Humanitarian assistance	Provides grants, materials, food supplies to meet the immediate demands of victims of disasters	Bilateral and multilateral donors, NGOs	Surplus U.S. agricultural commodities (e.g., beans, corn) sent to an NGO's feeding center at a refugee camp
Military aid	To strengthen the military of the recipient government	Bilateral donors	A Military Assistance Program (MAP) grant of U.S. military equipment sold at concessional rates

Why Do Donors Give Aid?

The United States is clear about its motivations for providing aid—the primary objective of U.S. foreign aid is to preserve its own territorial and political security. Foreign aid is also provided to ensure the political security and cooperation of the United States' strategically important allies. And, as the OECD stipulates, aid is given to promote economic growth in developing countries, which serves to open new markets for U.S. goods and provides investment opportunities. USAID, the agency responsible for distributing most U.S. foreign aid, points out that trade generated from aid has more than offset initial costs; between 1990 and 1995, exports to developing countries increased by $98.7 billion, which supported roughly 1.9 million jobs in the United States. Humanitarian concerns also figure in the argument in support of foreign aid, voiced by the moral principle that wealthy governments have an obligation to assist those in need, including those beyond national borders.[6]

The United States is not unique in making national interest the foundation of its aid rationale.[7] There is not a donor country in the world that would deny the impact of interdependence and the importance of creating an orderly world in which international trade can flourish. As a recent *Economist* article pointed out, "if governments want something in return for foreign aid, other than the increase in the welfare of countries receiving it, that something should be the long-term development of secure and prosperous trading partners."[8] Ten percent, or $700 billion, of the U.S. gross national product (GNP) is in the export sector, and developing countries are vital consumers, purchasing nearly 40 percent of total U.S. exports.[9] But international trade is not the only manifestation of our interdependent world, nor the only rationale behind foreign aid budgets. Environmental degradation, contagious diseases, political instability, and population growth are concerns that affect all our lives, and aid is also motivated by these international interests. Aid advocates argue persuasively that it is much cheaper to spend money to prevent disasters than to react to them. When Robert McNamara was secretary of defense under John Kennedy, he argued a point that has been validated over time: the "foreign aid program is the best weapon we have to insure that our own men in uniform need not go into combat."[10]

Foreign aid also has more tangible, direct benefits to donors than the creation of a more stable global order, and despite lofty rhetoric about global harmony, it is these benefits that provide policy makers with the most compelling rationale for supporting foreign aid. Actual foreign aid expenses often come straight back to the donor country in revenues. On average, a quarter of all aid is tied to the recipient country's purchase of the donor country's goods or services. The United States ties more of its aid to the acquisition of its own good and services than does any other OECD country.[11] By law, nearly all U.S. aid must be spent on U.S.-produced items. Approximately 90 percent of military aid in the early 1990s was used to purchase U.S. military equipment and training, and in 1993, foreign aid programs accounted for more than $10 billion in purchased U.S. goods and services. For the developing country receiving such aid, this often means that it has to pay an estimated 15 percent more than prevailing prices. Other kinds of aid, although not explicitly tied, are given in the sure knowledge that the money will be spent in the donor country.

Clearly foreign aid cannot be defined as a philanthropic force for global development, but its self-interested motivations do not necessarily discount the successes it has achieved. Largely due to foreign aid provisions, food production has outpaced population growth in the global South for the past four decades. India's food production, for example, has almost doubled since the 1960s. Seven times more people are literate in the developing world than in 1950. Infant mortality has dropped by more than half, from

180 deaths per 1,000 births to 69 deaths.[12] Increased family planning has been one of aid's most notable successes. The most striking example is in Bangladesh, where in 1970 only 3 percent of women were using contraceptives, and in 1990, 40 percent were. Other significant advances have been made in health, such as the eradication of smallpox in 1977 and the widespread immunization of children for common childhood diseases. International aid also played an important role in supporting democratic reforms in countries such as South Africa, Namibia, Cambodia, Panama, and Haiti. In Africa, where droughts have taken the lives of hundreds of thousands, aid has provided early warning systems that have reduced the large-scale fatalities. Aid's contribution to the building of infrastructure and communications in developing countries is its most visible and controversial success. Thousands of roads, telephone lines, and hospitals now exist in countries where there was no access to markets and no communication or medical facilities, but many of these mega-projects have had disruptive and harmful effects on local populations, who were perhaps considered less important than the shining monuments of Northern aid.[13]

Where Does Aid Go?

Aid has derisively been summed up as people in rich countries helping rich people in poor countries. Regrettably, there is some truth to that summation. The ten countries that are home to two-thirds of the world's poorest people receive only one-third of all aid; in other words, the richest 40 percent of developing countries receive twice as much aid as the poorest 40 percent (Figure I.1). Egypt and Israel, whose economies are far stronger than those of almost every country in Africa, receive nearly a quarter of all U.S. foreign aid, most of which is military or "strategic" assistance. For the most part, aid policies are focused on specific countries rather than on broad objectives such as alleviating poverty. The fact that India, which is home to 27 percent of the world's absolute poor, receives a mere $7 per person in ODA while Egypt receives $280 per person underscores this reality.[14] Further detracting from funds that might otherwise be allocated to the poorest nations are the nations of the former Soviet Union. These new aid recipients in Eastern Europe have received nearly $40 billion from wealthy governments since 1989.[15]

The gulf separating the poorest countries from those considered middle income is widening, not only because the more affluent developing countries receive more aid but also because that aid tends to be more effective in spurring economic growth, due to the presence of the conditions necessary for sustainable growth—political stability and the general absence of conflict.

Figure I.1   Distribution of aid

Those with higher incomes receive the most

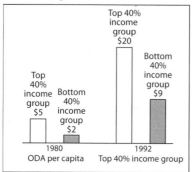

The top 40% income group now gets twice the assistance given to the poorest. In 1980, the ratio was 2.5 to one.

The poorest receive the least

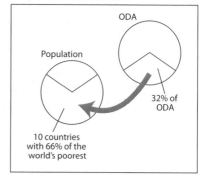

Two-thirds of the world's 1.3 billion poor live in ten countries that together receive less than a third of ODA.

Source: From *Human Development Report 1994* by United Nations Development Programme. Copyright © 1994 by United Nations Development Programme. Used by permission of Oxford University Press, Inc.

So although the success of aid in the top tier of developing countries bodes well for a future of economic ascension, it also widens the gap between rich and poor and adds to the economic polarization of the developing world. Unfortunately, there are few indications that foreign aid will play any part in shrinking this gap. According to Steven Hook, "this problem will only be resolved after the incentives for collaboration have improved or the costs of ignoring transnational problems become prohibitive."[16] With the repeated flare-up of conflicts in the poorest regions of the world, often provoked by the unequal and unjust distribution of resources further diverting funds to emergency relief at the expense of long-term development, one could argue that the cost of ignoring these problems is already too high.

The majority of aid not only fails to reach the countries most in need but also fails to support the sectors most critical to the poorest populations in the world. Despite the fact that the livelihoods of the majority of people in developing countries depend on agriculture, today less than one-sixth of all aid resources supports agriculture. Instead, international aid tends to favor the urban sector, where the poorest do *not* live. Aid is more likely to go toward the construction of an urban hospital than a rural clinic or to be allocated toward higher education rather than primary education. Only about a tenth of all international aid goes to social development sectors such as education, primary health care, and reproductive health, and in the U.S. aid budget, only 0.1 percent goes to basic education and a mere 0.3 percent to basic health care.[17] Social development sectors are often further neglected by the governments of developing countries. In many countries in the global South, the military is better funded than all other organizations, including the government. Global military spending peaked in 1987, and although it has decreased since then, it remains extremely high, especially in developing countries, where, on average, there are about twenty soldiers for every physician.[18] In sub-Saharan Africa, the proportion of gross domestic product (GDP) devoted to military spending increased from 0.7 percent in 1960 to 3 percent in 1991. This practice of diverting resources away from social sectors that promote human development is obscenely rewarded by donors that repeatedly provide the most aid to countries that spend the most on military expenses. In 1992, high military spenders received two and half times more aid per capita than low military spenders.

When developing countries spend more money to arm their militaries than to feed their citizens, it should not be surprising when violent conflicts erupt. Of the increasing number of emergencies that urgently and effectively appeal for aid, a growing number of them are far from natural disasters. And so emergency relief budgets grow, diverting funds from investment in long-term, sustainable development—development that could prevent these conflicts from ever occurring. At a time of decreasing overall aid, only emergency aid is on the rise. Emergency assistance now accounts for 50 percent of all United Nations aid. Emergency aid allocations in the U.S. budget rose from $786 million in 1989 to $2.2 billion in 1993, representing 23 percent of all aid resources and necessitating cuts in child survival activities and sustainable development projects. European donors follow the same trend—in 1991, the European Union's funding of NGO emergency and refugee programs exceeded development grants by 290 percent.[19] So despite the fact that emergency aid does nothing to promote long-term solutions, it promises to continue to be the only category of aid untouched by budget cuts.

Public Opinion

With the exception of aid to victims of disasters, U.S. international aid is under attack from all sides. A cursory review of sound bites and headlines published over the past year reveals the hostile arena in which aid is debated. In the most quoted statement of the year related to aid, Jesse Helms, chairman of the Senate Foreign Relations Committee, declared that international aid is "money down foreign rat holes." And he is not alone in his campaign to damn aid. The public has been bombarded with statements arguing that aid does not work, that it props up corrupt third world governments, or that it spends too much of the federal budget at a time of growing unmet needs at home.

In such an environment, it comes as no surprise to learn that public opinion polls consistently show that Americans think the government gives too much foreign aid—an opinion grounded in the misperception of how much aid is actually provided. In a recent poll conducted by the University of Maryland, people were asked to estimate how much of the federal budget goes to foreign aid. The median estimate was 15 percent, which is fifteen times the actual amount: approximately 1 percent. When asked how much (as a percentage of the federal budget) would be appropriate to spend on foreign aid, the response was 5 percent—five times what is currently spent. Furthermore, the poll revealed that popular opinion of the merits and importance of foreign aid does not reflect the negative opinions of Washington politicians. Sixty-three percent of respondents agreed that "the world economy is so interconnected today that, in the long run, helping Third World countries to develop is in the economic interest of the U.S. Many of these countries will become trading partners for our exports, so in the long run, our aid will pay off economically."[20] Another survey conducted by Harvard researchers found that one in four people questioned assumed that foreign aid was the largest item on the budget. These poll results clearly indicate that politicians do not have the mandate they claim for slashing aid. And yet, because the public is so misinformed about the financial costs of foreign aid, the lack of enthusiasm for aid programs continues.

It is important to distinguish between the antiaid arguments of conservative U.S. politicians and the arguments against aid that have been voiced by left-leaning development scholars, economists, and analysts who find fault with the "aid regime." The Institute for Food and Development Policy (Food First), a nonprofit research and educational center that addresses the root causes of hunger and poverty, conducted an in-depth assessment of aid in 1980. Among its conclusions was that aid reinforces power relationships both within the third world, by benefiting the wealthy elite who are usually in repressive positions of power in their own countries, and between the North and the South. Other critics fault aid for promoting a type of growth and development that is inappropriate and sometimes outright damaging to the poor in developing countries. The Development Group for Alternative Policies, a well-known resource and advocacy group, argues for a complete rehauling of the current aid structure, separating politically motivated aid from development aid, which is the only type of aid that has any meaningful significance for the majority of people in the third world. Aid has also been sharply criticized by "insiders"—people who spent much of their careers working within the aid "industry" and have come away from the experience with damning conclusions about the effectiveness and purpose of foreign aid. Graham Hancock, a British ex–development practitioner, wrote his 1989 book

Lords of Poverty as "an attack on a group of rich and powerful bureaucracies that have hijacked our kindness . . . those that administer the West's aid." Arguing that all too often aid creates monstrous projects that devastate the environment and ruin lives while rewarding corrupt Southern governments and denying the poor their potential, Hancock summarizes aid as a "patronizing insult to [the poor's] unique, unrecognized abilities."[21] More recently, Michael Maren, a journalist whose development career included jobs with the Peace Corps, Catholic Relief Services and USAID, echoed similar arguments about the corruptive and corrosive nature of aid, especially within the context of Somalia, in his 1997 book *The Road to Hell: The Ravaging Effects of Foreign Aid and International Charity.*

Conservative development economists such as Peter Bauer and Basil Yamey argue that aid is detrimental to economic development because it inhibits entrepreneurial skills and motivation and instead fosters dependence. Other economists who share this view argue that aid tends to compensate for failure rather than reward success, becoming in essence a subsidy to bad economic policies and a bloated public sector. Buoyed by income from aid donors, governments with detrimental economic policies are able to mask their mistakes and stay in power, at least for a time, prolonging the damage to economic growth. According to aid critics such as Doug Bandow, developing countries are poor not because they lack capital but because they lack economic freedom; thus, providing capital in the form of aid cannot be considered a solution but is actually an impediment to growth and freedom.[22]

The environmental costs of aid have inspired criticism from Left and Right alike, most of the complaints disturbingly accurate and valid. Capital-intensive projects favored by large aid donors all too often benefit engineering firms in Europe or the United States, at the expense of local communities and ecosystems. Besides the fact that aid fails to reach those who need it most, it also, argue many environmentalists, has had disastrous effects on the environment. Some environmentalists argue that aid is always bad for the environment, because it involves importing foreign technologies and changing traditional lifestyles based on respect for and living in harmony with the environment. In response to heated protests in both the North and the South, many aid providers have recently stepped up their efforts to fund environmental projects and appear more "green." USAID was one of the first agencies to carry out routine environmental assessments on its projects.

Proponents of the market, the most famous being Milton Friedman, argue that the free market is the best vehicle for spurring economic development, and thus aid ought to be restricted entirely to achieving political purposes. Others within this camp, such as the Heritage Foundation, call for "trade, not aid," in the belief that private investment flows will do more than aid to reduce poverty. This argument conveniently ignores the fact that trade barriers imposed by industrialized countries cost developing countries approximately $100 billion a year, which is nearly double what they receive in aid. And although U.S. trade with developing countries is substantial, most of that trade is with higher-income countries within the third world. The lower-income countries supplied a mere 8 percent of U.S. imports and bought just 5 percent of exports in 1991–92.[23] Even those countries with higher levels of private investment do not see a corresponding rise in human development because private resources rarely flow into sectors that address persistent poverty. During the early 1990s, when it was reported in banner headlines that foreign investment in developing countries was reaching new heights, a less reported fact was that just eight countries received two-thirds of that investment—and not one of those countries was in sub-Saharan Africa.

The Decline of International Aid

Despite the fact the public opinion polls reveal that foreign aid has more popular support than policy makers profess, international aid budgets are shrinking in every donor nation of the world. Leading the way in slashing aid is the United States. Once the world leader in aid to developing countries, the United States is now fourth in the world in the amount of money it spends on aid and an embarrassing twenty-first among twenty-one donor countries in the percentage of economic output devoted to foreign aid. In 1995, President Bill Clinton signed legislation that reduced bilateral aid by 22 percent and cut U.S. aid to multilateral institutions by 33 percent. Governments of rich countries now designate an average of just 0.27 percent of their national output to aid, the lowest proportion in twenty years. Indifference and neglect seem to have replaced the "hegemonic meddling" that dominated the major powers' foreign policy during the cold war.[24]

Shrinking budgets are not the only threat to the future of international aid. There is certainly some truth to the critiques that have been presented by intellectuals and politicians alike, and there is ample room for improvement in the ways that aid is budgeted, allocated, and distributed, as upcoming chapters reveal. However, this is hardly cause for abandoning the aid enterprise; it is instead an opportunity for improvement. A decade ago, the chairman of the Development Assistance Committee of the OECD exhorted donors to rethink how they distribute aid: "too much aid is provided in the form of unconnected projects rather than in support of set policies . . . too often requests and responses tend to favor expensive and even unsustainable capital-intensive efforts likely to benefit the higher income brackets in society."[25] The need for an objectives-oriented aid program, especially one focused on capacity building in the South, is greater today than ever before, and the potential for foreign aid to make a sustainable difference in the world we live in has never been greater.

Indeed, the cold war and the threat it represented have been replaced by the threat of cumulative development crises. Today there are more opportunities, and reasons, to promote sustainable development than ever before. The new threats to U.S. security are far more real than the threats of the cold war ever were. It is estimated that the population of Africa will more than double from its current 650 million to 1.6 billion by 2025, raising questions of how the corresponding increases in fuel consumption, wildlife and habitat destruction, and pollution can be held in check.[26] The debt crisis continues in much of the third world, albeit with far less international attention. One in five countries faces a banking crisis, spurring mass emigration from the poorest parts of the world into overcrowded cities and hostile industrialized nations. Environmental degradation threatens the air we breathe and the water we drink; an area of rain forest the size of a football field is destroyed every second. (It is important to look not just to the South when contemplating environmental protection—the United States is the world's greatest consumer of fossil fuels, the primary source of water and air pollution.)

The need for international assistance is not enough to warrant its existence, however. Throwing money at problems does not necessarily solve them, as aid donors and recipients have learned. International aid is at a critical juncture. The new development challenges it confronts demand new and improved strategies, and given the erosion of public support, the margin for error has never been so narrow.

The volume of aid and the sectors to which it is directed correlate in great measure to the political and cultural climate of the donor country. The level of awareness and education among a donor country's population affects the level and allocation of aid it supports. Thus it is hardly surprising that in the United States, where there are widespread misperceptions about the cost of foreign aid, Congress managed to cut the aid budget to the lowest of all industrialized nations, in terms of percentage of national output. The urgent need for an informed citizenry is clear and is the principal motivation behind the writing of this book.

Notes

1. See the Program on International Policy Attitudes' 1995 study "Americans and Foreign Aid: A Study of American Public Attitudes."
2. The term *third world* has its origins in political cold war categorization, with Western democracies constituting the first world, Eastern bloc socialist states making up the second world, and the nonaligned remainder constituting the third world. Because the term implies a hierarchical global structure, with the bottom reserved for the poorest nations, it is generally out of favor today. I prefer to use the term *global South*, but I do refer to the third world throughout the book—the term's accessibility and recognition remain its chief advantages.
3. United Nations Development Programme (UNDP), *Human Development Report 1994* (New York: Oxford University Press, 1994), 76.
4. Chapter 6 discusses in greater detail the implications of government funding for NGOs.
5. OECD, *Development Assistance Committee 1993 Report* (Paris: OECD, 1993), 11.
6. Robert F. Zimmerman, *Dollars, Diplomacy and Dependency: Dilemmas of U.S. Economic Aid* (Boulder, Colo.: Lynne Rienner, 1993), 62.
7. Steven W. Hook has done an in-depth study on how the foreign policies of nations have historically been informed by widely shared perceptions of national interest, how this national interest varies among countries, and how the interests of nation-states can be identified by evaluating their foreign policy record. *National Interest and Foreign Aid* (Boulder, Colo.: Lynne Rienner, 1995).
8. "The Kindness of Strangers," *Economist*, May 7, 1994, 11.
9. USAID web page.
10. Walden Bello, *Dark Victory: The United States, Structural Adjustment, and Global Poverty* (Oakland, Calif.: Institute for Food and Development Policy, 1994), 12.
11. Hook, *National Interest and Foreign Aid*, 133.
12. USAID, *Developments* 2, no. 2 (winter 1996): 1.
13. UNDP, *Human Development Report 1994*, 71.
14. Ibid., 73.
15. Janine R. Wedel, "Aid and Reform in the Former Second World" in *Foreign Aid toward the Millennium*, ed. Steven W. Hook (Boulder, Colo.: Lynne Rienner, 1996), 143.
16. Steven W. Hook, "Foreign Aid: The Illogic of Collective Action," in *Foreign Aid toward the Millennium*, 233–4.
17. "The Kindness of Strangers."
18. UNDP, *Human Development Report 1994*, 50.
19. Marc Cohen, "But the Cupboard Is Bare: The Crisis of Aid," in *Hunger 1996* (Silver Spring, Md.: Bread for the World Institute, 1995), 65–6.
20. Program on International Policy Attitudes, "Americans and Foreign Aid."
21. Graham Hancock, *Lords of Poverty: The Power, Prestige, and Corruption of the International Aid Business* (New York: Atlantic Monthly Press, 1989), 183.
22. For more on this argument, see Doug Bandow and Ian Vasquez, eds., *Perpetuating Poverty: The World Bank, the IMF, and the Developing World* (Washington, D.C.: Cato Institute, 1994).

23. Marc Cohen and Don Reeves, "Development Aid and International Institutions," in *Hunger 1997* (Silver Spring, Md.: Bread for the World Institute, 1996), 86.
24. Hook, *Foreign Aid toward the Millennium*, 227.
25. UNICEF, *State of the World's Children 1990* (New York: Oxford University Press, 1990), 59.
26. Hook, *Foreign Aid toward the Millennium*, 234.

1

U.S. Government Assistance

SINCE ITS INCEPTION, U.S. international aid has been an important foreign policy tool, and as such, it has been motivated by a variety of seemingly contradictory objectives, from strengthening foreign militaries to facilitating reconciliation efforts. Despite the charitable connotations usually associated with any mention of aid, U.S. foreign policy has consistently acknowledged that the primary responsibility of any international assistance program is to preserve the security of the United States. Over the past half century, the United States has spent $233 billion in foreign economic assistance.[1] That aid has gone to Western Europe to help nations there repair the damage wrought by World War II; it has provided more than fifty million couples worldwide with family planning services; and it has secured the support of strategic allies, including countries with horrifying human rights records. U.S. international assistance has also initiated HIV/AIDS prevention programs in thirty-two countries, it has encouraged a sustained dialogue between Israel and Egypt, and it has given away or sold at reduced prices more than 650 billion pounds of agricultural commodities to help feed starving people throughout the world while also subsidizing U.S. farmers. Although the disparate goals, shining achievements, and harmful misdeeds make it nearly impossible to neatly evaluate U.S. international aid, understanding its contradictions and complexities is an important first step.

The History of U.S. International Aid

The European Recovery Program, popularly known as the Marshall Plan, was the first and largest government-sponsored approach to foreign assistance. Initiated in 1948 by the United States, it dispensed over $13 billion toward the reconstruction of Europe in only four years. Motivated by a combination of humanitarian concern, a strategic effort to curtail Soviet influence in Eastern Europe, and the need to restore European markets for U.S. goods, the Truman administration contributed 2.5 percent of its

GNP—a percentage never to be matched again. More than 90 percent was distributed in the form of grants (rather than low-interest loans, as is the norm today), and two-thirds was designated for economic purposes (unlike U.S. aid today, which is designated primarily for military and strategic purposes). The Marshall Plan was heralded as such a success that it became a blueprint for early aid programs in developing countries. When these first aid programs failed to stimulate the same dizzying growth experienced in Europe, the underdeveloped nations of the South were easy scapegoats. It took a few years before donors came to recognize that a huge infusion of capital was bound to have far different results in a developed country in need of mere physical reconstruction than in a country lacking effective political and economic systems.

In 1950, President Truman reiterated the moral imperative for aid when he announced his Four-Point Plan to abolish humanity's "ancient enemies—hunger, misery and despair." As part of Truman's internationalist vision, the Technical Cooperation Administration (TCA) was created with the mandate to "aid the efforts of the peoples of economically underdeveloped areas." The TCA recognized developing countries' need for technical assistance in addition to capital, but little consideration was given to the appropriateness of the technologies and advice transferred.[2] The Marshall Plan came to an end with the creation of its replacement, the Mutual Security Administration (MSA), which provided primarily military aid and defense support and secondarily, economic and food aid. Communist threats, real and imagined, led to the growing importance of military aid during this period. The MSA's economic development component was designed to utilize large sums of money to build economic structures and political allegiances deemed necessary to fight communism. By the mid-1950s, the United States had transferred about 50 percent more foreign assistance than it had during the Marshall Plan, much of it directed to strategic allies in the third world such as India, Pakistan, and other countries in the Far East.[3]

President Kennedy sought to extend the scope of international aid beyond strategic goals to include development goals. He made clear the connection between U.S. security and political interests and foreign assistance, urging "those who want to do something for the United States . . . to channel their energies behind the new foreign-aid program to help prevent the social injustices and economic chaos upon which subversion and revolt feeds."[4] The 1961 Foreign Assistance Act established the Peace Corps and implemented the Alliance for Progress, both of which were aimed at promoting political and socioeconomic development in developing countries, especially in Latin America. Furthering this sense of global community, which for the first time openly included the global South, the United Nations declared the 1960s the First Development Decade and set goals for annual economic growth in the developing world at 5 percent—a goal that the South far surpassed.

Among the outcomes of the 1961 Foreign Assistance Act was the creation of the U.S. Agency for International Development (USAID), which was designed to "promote the foreign, security and general welfare of the United States by assisting peoples of the world in their efforts toward economic development and internal and external security."[5] In 1964, the Office of Disaster Relief was created as part of USAID to be the focal point for U.S. efforts in natural disasters.

As its mandate in the Foreign Assistance Act articulated, USAID's motives for assisting developing countries have always been clear: its primary goal is to further the foreign policy goals of the United States, and those goals include first and foremost to ensure the security of the United States. Aid provided through USAID falls into one of three categories: Economic Support Funds, Development Assistance, and Food for Peace. Additional resources go to the Peace Corps and multilateral institutions such as the World Bank and United Nations.

Arguably, the most important of these categories is the Economic Support Funds (ESFs), which make up more than half of all U.S. economic assistance. ESFs are designed to assist politically important countries experiencing balance-of-payments difficulties through direct cash transfers, commodity import programs, or specific development projects. ESF resources, more than any other type of U.S. aid, are directly aimed at advancing U.S. political and security objectives, and because they are often allocated to countries that allow the United States to maintain military bases on their soil, they are sometimes referred to as thinly disguised rent for access to strategic facilities.[6] The diplomatic importance of ESF resources is evidenced by the fact that the State Department, not USAID, plays the primary role in allocating them, and they are listed in the foreign aid appropriations bill as security assistance. Although Congress mandates that ESFs be used as development assistance "to the maximum extent feasible," that maximum extent rarely exceeds one dollar for every three spent on security expenses. ESFs became an increasingly important foreign policy tool during the Reagan administration, when the number of countries receiving ESFs went from twenty-one in 1981 to thirty-nine in 1985.[7] Today, the majority of ESF resources is allocated to Israel and Egypt; they received 85 percent of the ESF budget in 1994.[8] Although ESFs are restricted from being used for military purposes, they often end up doing just that. Because most of the funds are distributed through unrestricted grants, somewhat like a blank check, they free up funds that allow a recipient country to increase its military spending.

The second category of U.S. foreign aid, Development Assistance (DA), provides grants to support social and economic development programs, usually multiyear projects. Congress allocates the DA budget to specific sectors, such as health, population, education, agriculture, and rural development, allocating approximately $2.3 billion in 1997. Since the 1980s, DA has been cut by roughly 25 percent, making it the most severely cut portion of the international budget. The Development Fund for Africa was established in 1987 as a special type of DA to be appropriated by Congress without earmarks to functional accounts. However, in 1996, Congress eliminated the fund as a separate account within the foreign aid budget. The U.S. government also supports development assistance through a number of other programs outside of USAID, the most recognized being the Peace Corps. Another non-USAID program, the Inter-American Foundation (IAF), is perhaps less well known among the general public, but among aid scholars, it is often lauded as the brightest hope for sustainable development. IAF channels funds directly to the nongovernmental sector in Latin America and the Caribbean, awarding grants to groups that promote entrepreneurship, innovation, and self-reliance. Between 1972 and 1996, IAF approved more than four thousand grants totaling $450 million to support thirty-five hundred organizations.[9] Similarly, the African Development Foundation, established by Congress in 1980, provides development grants to indigenous African groups, associations, and institutions that demonstrate the capacity to serve the needs of their communities.

Food aid is the third category of U.S. foreign assistance and has been a major component of the U.S. aid program since the early 1950s, currently constituting 11 percent of the aid budget. During the 1940s, U.S. grain production grew by almost 50 percent, while domestic consumption lagged far behind. Enormous surpluses (created by the combination of more fertilizers, pesticides, and improved seed varieties) were costing $1 million a day just for storage. In response, the American Farm Bureau proposed that the surplus be offered to food-deficient countries. These developing nations would pay for the food in their own currencies rather than in dollars, to avoid interference with the commercial dollar price demanded from wealthier countries. The foreign currencies generated from food sales would, in theory, be effective catalysts to encourage economic development and promote international trade. Unsurprisingly, the proposal was well received by farmers and politicians alike, and Public Law (PL) 480, also called the Food for Peace Act, was passed in 1954. As stated in its preamble, PL 480 was created to meet three distinct goals: to expand national trade (Title I), to use surplus agricultural commodities to combat global hunger and encourage economic growth in developing countries (Title II), and to develop and expand export markets for U.S. agricultural commodities (Title III).

Although it certainly appeared to be a win-win program, the negative consequences of the Food for Peace program quickly became evident.

Selling food at low prices proved to be a disincentive for local production, as it dampened demand for local products and undercut the prices farmers received for crops. In response to this issue, Congress added the Bellmon determination in 1977, which prohibited shipments of U.S. agricultural commodities unless it was determined that they would "not result in a substantial disincentive to or interference with domestic production or marketing in that country."[10] However, this was hardly enough to allay the criticism that surrounded the program. Critics charged that food aid shifted consumption patterns away from traditional local staples, creating a demand for foreign commodities that were rarely more nutritious and always more expensive. Arguing that PL 480 was nothing more than its original title—"surplus disposal program"—suggested, the Institute for Food Policy charged that at no time was food aid's primary purpose to feed the hungry; instead, it was a way to rid U.S. markets of price-depressing domestic surpluses, open new markets for commercial sales of U.S. farm products, provide support for U.S. military intervention, and extend the reach of U.S. agribusiness into new economies.[11] The result of this drive to open new markets has been disastrous for certain food aid recipients. Food aid to Somalia, for example, was subjected to an investigation by auditors to explore whether PL 480 was discouraging local production. Among their findings: warehouses full of rotting, unsold commodities, as well as the arrival of new commodities coinciding and thus competing with local harvests.[12] A 1985 evaluation of PL 480 found that its four objectives—expanding exports of U.S. agricultural commodities, combating hunger and malnutrition, encouraging economic development, and promoting U.S. foreign policy interests—were, for the most part, incompatible. Owen Cylke, a retired acting director of the Food for Peace program, described it as a "slush fund of the State Department to meet political requirements around the world."[13] The evaluation uncovered example after example of food aid being provided to politically important countries rather than to those most in need—despite the fact that Title III mandates that food be allocated to countries with annual per capita levels at or below the poverty level as defined by the World Bank. In 1989, over one-third of U.S. food aid continued to go to countries that did not have food shortages. For example, Morocco and Egypt, both of which had per capita calorie rates among the highest in the world, received more than $70 million and $171 million, respectively.[14]

Despite certain undeniable failures of food aid, the program plays an important role in the provision of food during emergency situations. And there are some promising indications that lessons have been learned. It is now understood that food aid can occur without upsetting incentives, provided that the food goes to the poorest who could not have entered the market for food anyway or that market-clearing arrangements have been made so as to maintain demand.[15] In 1993, the total PL 480 program was estimated at $1.7 billion, representing more than 10 percent of the U.S. aid budget. NGOs also have an important stake in the PL 480 program. Under Title II's grant program, food is channeled through private organizations and the United Nations World Food Program. In 1992, the United States provided an estimated $710 million worth of food under Title II, including $320 million for emergencies. Title III provides commodity grants to governments that are experiencing food shortfalls. Recipient governments can use the commodities in feeding programs or as reserves, or they can sell it, provided the proceeds are used in a way that benefits the poor and at least 10 percent is directed to indigenous NGOs.

There is a fourth element to the U.S. foreign aid program, and although it is not managed by USAID or directed toward development goals, it consumes a large portion of the aid budget (27.8 percent in 1996) and should not be overlooked—military assistance (Figure 1.1). Military aid is designed to stabilize allied governments facing insurgencies and enhance the military power of friendly states. During the 1980s, the Military Assistance Program (MAP) was the fastest growing aid program. Providing grants of military equipment to U.S. allies, it increased by nearly 600 percent between 1980 and 1986.[16] Other security assistance programs include the Foreign Military Sales (FMS) program, which finances credit sales of U.S. military equipment through the U.S. government or commercial channels. Focused primarily on wealthier countries, mostly in the Middle East, the FMS program is now declining, with just a few recipients, but it remains the most important source of low-cost weaponry for developing countries. The International Military Education and Training (IMET) program is another grant program designed to train foreign military personnel and officers. In 1995, Congress authorized an allocation of $26.4 million for IMET, an increase of 10 percent from the year before, primarily to support the training of European militaries. Although military assistance has been sharply reduced since the heady days of the cold war—from roughly 60 percent of the foreign aid budget in 1988 to 28 percent in 1996—it continues to reflect the U.S. government's preference for security over development. The 1997 military aid budget was $3.3 billion, with nearly 90 percent of it going to Egypt and Israel.[17]

Cold war imperatives guided the direction of aid throughout the 1960s. By the end of the decade, nearly half of all U.S. aid was going to Vietnam, most of it as military assistance. At the same time, foreign aid was under sharp opposition both in the Senate and among the general public. This widespread and vocal discontent led to a repackaging of the aid approach, embodied by the Foreign Assistance Act of 1973, or "New Directions," as it was optimistically labeled. The act was mandated to "give the highest priority to undertakings . . . which directly improve the lives of the poorest of

Figure 1.1   Program composition of U.S. foreign aid, FY 1986, FY 1991, and FY 1996

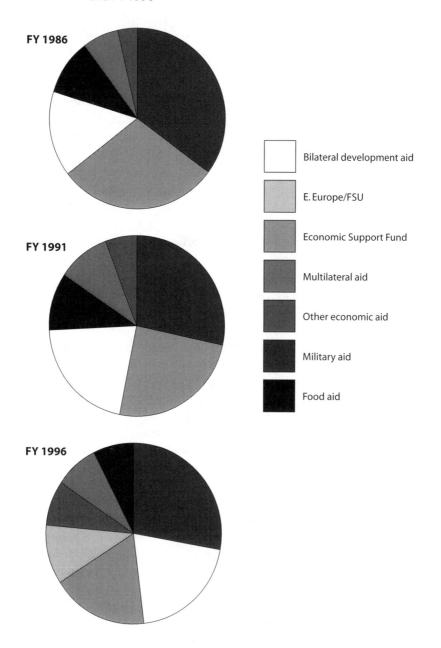

Note: FSU = former Soviet Union

Source: Larry Q. Nowells and Curt Tarnoff, "Foreign Assistance as an Instrument of U.S. Leadership Abroad," National Policy Association Report no. 285 (Washington, D.C.: NPA, 1997), 8. Based on USAID data.

people and their capacity to participate in the development of their countries."[18] Four goals were identified as the new guiding objectives for U.S. bilateral assistance:

1. Alleviation of the worst physical manifestations of poverty among the world's poor,
2. Promotion of conditions enabling developing countries to achieve self-sustaining economic growth with an equitable distribution of benefits,
3. Encouragement of development processes that respect and enhance human and civil rights, and
4. Integration of developing countries into an open and equitable international system.[19]

The act was peppered with references to "supporting self-help efforts" and "democratic participation," and it proposed renewed focus on rural development, small-scale farming, nutrition, education, and population planning. It was hailed as a "significant departure" from the policies of the 1960s that stressed economic indicators of growth. In other words, the New Directions legislation held out promises that it would change foreign aid substantially and benefit developing countries enormously. Unfortunately, the mandate turned out to be more rhetoric than deeds. Little actually changed, and some critics argue that it had an adverse effect. For example, international agencies, in a burst of enthusiasm for community development projects, began redirecting community life without stopping to consider the advice or invite the participation of their intended beneficiaries.[20]

Another component of the 1973 legislation was the Percy Amendment, passed a year later, which represented Congress's efforts to integrate women in development. Until this point, little attention had been paid to the role of women in developing countries—the disproportionate burdens that underdevelopment inflicted on them, as well as their critical role in spurring sustainable development. Scholarship during the 1970s began to analyze women's work, previously dismissed as "invisible" because it was in the informal economy, for the first time and found that women account for 40 to 80 percent of all agricultural production in the South. The Percy Amendment signaled an awakening to the importance of women in development and stipulated in its Section 113 that USAID policies "shall be administered so as to give particular interest to those programs, projects, and activities which tend to integrate women into the national economies of foreign countries, thus improving their status and assisting the total development effort."[21]

The Percy Amendment served as the rationale for the creation within USAID of the Office for Women in Development, a coordination center for technical assistance and research, as well as for future women-focused policies and studies. In December 1993, the General Accounting Office (GAO) was requested by Congress to evaluate how well the Department of State had fulfilled the mandate of the Percy Amendment. The GAO found that progress had been slow and that USAID "has not adequately monitored the implication of its policies and strategies or routinely evaluated the impact of its programs and activities on women."[22] Furthermore, U.S. representatives, who were directed by the amendment to promote women's economic and policy-making participation when they voted in international forums, were found to have failed to adequately do so. Over the past two decades, the women in development (WID) focus has sometimes been accompanied by inadequate "add-women-and-stir" type of solutions. Responding to these inadequacies, development policy and scholarship shifted to a focus on gender. Gender analysis goes beyond the singular examination of women to include analysis of the relationships in society between women and men and the engendered and asymmetrical power relations that play a critical role in any country's development. Reflecting this new focus, on March 12, 1996, USAID instituted a new agency-wide Gender Plan of Action to "ensure the integration of gender considerations into its programs and to continue to foster the institutional changes needed to support women in development."[23]

Two years after the New Directions legislation, two more amendments were added to the foreign aid bill. The first mandated that 75 percent of PL 480 loans go to countries where the annual per capita GNP was less than $300, and the second amendment stipulated that food aid cannot be given to governments that "consistently violate recognized human rights" of its citizens. The food aid law was further amended two years later when "food for development" was added, which forgave the repayment of food aid loans as long as the recipient government used the proceeds from the sale of the food to undertake development programs in agriculture, nutrition, health services, and population planning. Unfortunately, once again well-meaning rhetoric was laden with practical miscalculations. Human rights violators continued to have access to food aid by simply signing a clause stating that the aid would help the needy. Or if not willing to make an empty promise, repressive governments could be exempt from the human rights review altogether by agreeing to channel the aid through NGOs— even government-created NGOs![24] Although these well-sounding acts and amendments had little real impact in correcting bad aid policies and practices, the legislation did bring about structural changes within USAID. By 1978, the agency was far more decentralized, with an increase in the number of people in the field and regional bureaus holding more authority than ever before.

The Recent Past: Carter, Reagan, and Bush

The direction, allocation, and importance of U.S. international aid have risen, fallen, and moved in different directions, depending on the man residing in the White House and the political party controlling Congress. Thus, it is useful to review the recent history of U.S. foreign aid and USAID within the context of the governing administrations.

President Carter was a strong proponent of international aid, motivated by a combination of humanitarian impulses and strategic reasoning. He increased the foreign aid budget substantially, committing U.S. taxpayers to more aid than ever before. Over $8 billion was budgeted to USAID, the World Bank, food aid programs, and other multilateral agencies in 1980.[25] Meeting basic human needs was the focus of much of the aid program, and Carter also sought, albeit with little success, to distance development assistance programs from the chain of command within the State Department by forming the International Development Coordinating Agency (IDCA), an umbrella organization designed to coordinate the multifaceted U.S. aid program. Unfortunately, the legislation that created IDCA failed to delineate the internal structuring required and provided neither USAID nor IDCA with the autonomy it required and, as a result, was ineffective. Carter also revealed his concern for development issues by commissioning two major studies of world poverty, the Presidential Commission on World Hunger and Global 2000. Altruism did not govern the aid agenda, however; security issues continued to take precedence in terms of budget allocations, and the Middle East became the geographic focus. From 1977 to 1989, Israel and Egypt received 47 percent of total economic aid (most of it strategic assistance, not development aid), and as part of the 1979 Camp David accords, Carter promised an annual U.S. commitment of $5 billion to the two countries. Since Camp David, the Middle East has continued to receive on average 51 percent of all U.S. bilateral assistance.[26]

When Ronald Reagan entered the White House in 1981, the vision of aid as a foreign policy tool assumed new significance. Military aid increased from 25 percent of total aid in 1978 to 37 percent in 1988. Meanwhile, development assistance aid decreased from 33 percent to 26 percent over the same period.[27] Carter's emphasis on basic human needs was replaced by an emphasis on strategic support for key allies. Instead of objectives such as the alleviation of human suffering, aid during the Reagan years was more likely to be directed toward influencing the foreign policy behavior of recipients and ensuring that so-called friendly foreign governments stayed in power. ESFs took on unprecedented importance during these years, preferred over other forms of aid because of their fewer restrictions and the speed with which they could be administered. And ESFs accomplished many of the administration's political and security objectives, including promoting peace in the Middle East and, to an arguably lesser extent, promoting economic stabilization through balance of payment and budget support. They also, in the words of a State Department official, helped "allies in dealing with threats to their security and independence"[28]—even if those threats were coming from their own citizens protesting a repressive form of governance. Some of the largest ESF recipients during these years were also the world's most notorious human rights violators: Marcos in the Philippines, Doe in Liberia, and Mobutu in Zaire.

The first Reagan administration was highly skeptical of multilateral assistance and cut funds to all multilateral aid institutions except the International Development Association (IDA), the soft-loan window of the World Bank. Testifying before Congress, Deputy Secretary of State Clifton Wharton rationalized these cuts by complaining that "multilateral agencies do not necessarily reflect U.S. foreign policy in their programs and activities."[29] Central America was the focus of the aid program during the Reagan years, with aid to that region multiplying seven-fold from 1980 to 1987, reaching $1.3 billion in 1989. It was in this region that Reagan's manipulation of the aid budget to address perceived cold war threats was most clear: El Salvador, despite human rights atrocities, continued to receive increasing levels of aid—during the eight-year Reagan administration, it received $3.3 billion, more than $1 million a day.[30] And Nicaragua was the site of a major political scandal when it was revealed that U.S. funding for the antigovernment rebels had continued, despite Congress's prohibition, and that profits from the secret sale of weapons had gone to Iran in exchange for the release of U.S. hostages.

The Caribbean was another area of great interest to the Reagan administration. The Caribbean Basin Initiative (CBI) injected $350 million in economic aid to the region in 1982, removed trade barriers, and provided tax incentives for U.S. business to invest there. The goal was ostensibly to boost the export industry of the Caribbean, but three years after CBI's launching, Caribbean exports to the United States were earning even less than before. Meanwhile, Africa, a continent with little strategic value, received a consistent package of roughly $500 million until the early 1990s, when it increased to $800 million.

Reagan's second term was marked by an increased sense of international cooperation, inspired in large part by the emerging debt crisis and the need for multilateral cooperation to cope with it. The World Bank, once an object of U.S. suspicion, quickly became a principal focus of the foreign aid program. At the 1985 International Monetary Fund (IMF)–World

Bank meeting in Seoul, U.S. Secretary of the Treasury James Baker announced the U.S. proposal for easing the debt crisis, the centerpiece of which was structural adjustment. The stated goal of the Baker Plan was to reduce the net outflow from debtor countries in order to spur growth in their economies. Rather than debt reduction, Baker called on banks to lend an additional $20 billion over three years, through country-to-country negotiations. These new loans never materialized, however, and the plan was abandoned, but not before providing useful precepts for future arrangements, including the handling of debt on a country-by-country basis and the linking of any easing of debt terms with economic reforms under the supervision of the World Bank and the IMF. By 1988, Northern banks had received most of the interest due on old debt and had managed to raise new capital; thus the "banking crisis"—the concern that they might face insolvency—was lifted. This allowed them, for the first time, to focus on the economic crisis of debtor nations, and as a result, in 1989, Treasury Secretary Nicholas Brady announced his plan for debt reduction. The Brady Plan was built on market solutions and called for creditor banks to agree voluntarily to reduce the value of their claims in return for guarantees on the remaining portion of the debt.[31] To qualify for debt reduction, countries had to prove that they would undergo sound economic reforms aimed at encouraging domestic savings and foreign investment. Notwithstanding the new ground that the Brady Plan promised to break in the area of debt reduction, the U.S. aid budget began to shrink. The United States had entered the growing ranks of debtor nations and was burdened with unprecedented trade deficits.

The emphasis on military aid and the promotion of private enterprise as the engine of growth continued into and throughout the Bush presidency, with new attention also focused on growing environmental and population concerns. *Sustainable development* suddenly became part of the White House vocabulary, although it translated into few, if any, changes in policy. When the Berlin Wall crumbled and the cold war was declared over, there were high hopes in the development community that the expected reduction in military budgets would allow for increased funding for development-oriented aid. Instead, the newly independent states of the former Soviet Union were added to the list of aid recipients, pushing the less strategically important nations of the impoverished South further down on the priority list. And strategic interests continued to play a principal role in the setting of the aid agenda, as evidenced by the forgiveness of nearly $7 billion in debt in exchange for Egypt's participation in the Persian Gulf War.

Even before Bush took office, USAID's reputation and record were approaching an all-time low, with both Congress and the general public growing increasingly skeptical of the aid program. The agency had just spent the past six years focusing on large-scale private-sector initiatives and had been assessed as being more responsive to the needs of U.S. foreign policy than to the needs of developing countries.[32] A 1989 study conducted by USAID to review the impact of foreign assistance concluded that "all too often, dependency seems to have won over development."[33]

An International Comparison of Aid

The United States' overseas development assistance is monitored and reported on by the Development Assistance Committee (DAC), a coordinating agency of the Organization for Economic Cooperation and Development (OECD). DAC was established in 1961 to foster coordinated, integrated, and effective international efforts in support of sustainable economic and social development. The United States is one of twenty-two members, with the IMF, United Nations Development Programme (UNDP), and World Bank participating as permanent observers. DAC is the closest thing to a central treaty or organizational structure within the development aid regime,[34] and as such, it provides authoritative policy guidance for members in formulating their aid programs, conducts periodic critical reviews of members' programs, provides a forum for dialogue and the building of international consensus on policy and management issues, and publishes statistics on aid and other resource flows. Although it is often more successful in targeting norms than in eliciting compliance, DAC provides an undeniable service in defining globally recognized parameters of aid, identifying qualitative standards, and establishing guidelines for the reporting and monitoring of aid flows. The most well-known, though often ignored, standard that DAC has established is the target allocation of a minimum of 0.7 percent of a nation's GNP to official development assistance. For our purposes, DAC's annual reviews of donor policies and transfers provide a critical lens through which to evaluate U.S. foreign aid in comparison to that of other OECD members.

According to DAC, financial flows to the global South can be considered official development assistance (ODA) only if they are concessional and have a grant element of at least 25 percent. In other words, the terms of ODA must always be more favorable than the terms recipients would be able to get in commercial capital markets. Additionally, all donors agree that ODA should be provided only when private capital is unavailable. ODA also includes the explicit requirement that funds be used for the purpose of economic development, defined by the World Bank as "sustainable increase in living standards that encompass material consumption, education, health, and environmental protection."[35] This requirement naturally precludes military and security assistance from being included, although it is often included in a country's own calculations of international aid, distorting common perceptions of levels of aid. DAC recently expanded the definition of ODA to include aid that never even leaves the donor nation, such as support for refugees hosted by donor countries, further distorting the analysis of how much development assistance actually reaches developing countries.

Between 1970 and 1990, the volume of global ODA transfers to developing countries more than doubled. Aid flows increased steadily throughout the 1980s, peaking at $60.9 billion in 1992, then declining to $59.2 billion in 1994.[36] Whereas the early 1990s witnessed a decrease in bilateral flows, multilateral aid increased to a record $16.8 billion in 1992. When private financial flows (including investments and commercial loans) are added to the mix, the total resource flow from North to South amounted to nearly $200 billion in 1992.[37] However, when the volume of ODA is considered, it is important that it be kept in perspective. ODA represents a tiny share of resources available to most donor countries—for most countries, far less than the target 0.7 percent of their GNP. The Persian Gulf War provides an acute illustration of resource distribution: the first *three days* of the war in 1991 cost the United States more than one and a half times its total ODA for a full year.[38]

Membership in DAC is constantly growing, with Ireland, Spain, and Portugal the most recent members. In terms of percentage of national wealth, however, Denmark is the most generous donor in DAC. In 1995, it committed just under 1 percent of its GNP to international aid, which is higher than the DAC standard. Its Scandinavian neighbors, as well as the Netherlands and France, also consistently provide aid at higher than average levels. Whereas approximately $34 of an American family's annual taxes goes toward official aid, in Denmark, roughly $900 per family is added to the aid budget. In addition, although Western European and Scandinavian countries provide smaller net volumes of aid, their aid is often more developmentally oriented, and proportionally more of it is allocated to least developed countries. For instance, Denmark directs as much as 25 percent of its aid to basic education and primary health and nutrition services, compared with Germany, which allocated a mere 2 percent to these sectors in 1993.[39] Most other donor nations, however, tend to favor infrastructure and production projects over development ones. Japan, for example, has regularly directed over a third of its aid to large construction and production projects (Table 1.1).

Although the levels and allocations of ODA vary from donor to donor, a common characteristic of all donors' aid is its attachment to various terms and conditions, making it "tied aid." All donors tie a large percentage

Table 1.1   Major purposes of economic aid, 1993 (commitments as a percent of total bilateral aid)

Country	Infrastructure/ Production[1]	Social Programs[2]	Program/ Budget Asst.	Food	Emergency Aid	Debt Relief	Other[3]
Canada	24.0%	9.5%	4.0%	4.4%	4.2%	11.2%	42.2%
France	23.4	38.1	15.0	0.4	2.3	1.9	19.1
Germany	33.5	25.3	2.2	2.1	9.2	10.3	17.4
Italy	17.6	14.9	1.4	5.5	20.3	30.6	8.7
Japan	34.7	22.6	4.4	0.3	0.2	16.9	7.8
United Kingdom	32.0	30.8	9.3	3.0	11.9	3.2	9.6
United States	11.1	23.1	27.3	9.4	8.6	7.0	10.6
OECD Average	31.4	25.1	9.7	2.8	6.1	10.2	14.7

[1] Transport and communication, energy, agricultural production, industry, mining and construction, trade, banking, and tourism.
[2] Education, health and population, and planning and public administration.
[3] Multisector programs, administration, and unspecified.

Source: Larry Q. Nowels and Curt Tarnoff, "Foreign Assistance as an Instrument of U.S. Leadership Abroad," National Policy Association Report no. 285 (Washington, D.C.: NPA, 1997), 13. Based on data from OECD, *Development Cooperation 1995 Report.*

(the average is about 25 percent) of their aid to various ends. Donors can demand that their aid be used for specific projects or programs or for the purchase of certain commodities or services. Frequently aid is tied to the requirement that the recipient purchase goods or services from the donor, even if those goods could be purchased less expensively elsewhere and regardless of whether those goods are even needed by the recipient. Recipients of military aid are almost always required to purchase equipment and arms, albeit at reduced rates, from donors' defense departments or contracted companies, thus boosting revenues back home. This goes far to explain the interest, especially in the United States, in maintaining high levels of security and military assistance. Tied aid is just one of the many contradictions inherent in the international aid system—it is clearly driven by the needs of the supplier (usually the donor), often at the expense of the country it claims to be assisting. It is broadly recognized that the tying of aid increases costs to the recipient by as much as 20 to 30 percent. And despite the fact that the level of exports generated by tied aid is so small that the macroeconomic benefit to the donor is negligible, it continues to constitute up to half of some donors' total bilateral assistance.[40]

From the early days of the Marshall Plan, the United States was the leading donor of official aid and seemed to take great pride in being the world leader in assisting the poor. In 1989, Japan replaced the United States as the largest donor in terms of absolute amount of funds transferred. According to OECD figures, Japan provided $15.5 billion in development aid in 1995, compared with $7.3 billion that the United States provided. Japanese aid has been subjected to many of the same criticisms lodged against U.S. aid in its early years—a large percentage of its aid (roughly 40 percent) is provided as loans rather than grants, and it is very tightly tied to the purchase of Japanese goods and services. Japanese aid also tends to favor large infrastructure projects instead of institution-building projects, which are currently the vogue among Western donors. Unlike U.S. aid, the Japanese foreign aid program places far fewer professionals in the field, and also unlike U.S. aid, it is received with widespread support by the citizens at home.[41]

Not only has the United States lost its number-one ranking in terms of dollars spent on ODA, it has also dropped in rank in terms of percentage of economic output devoted to foreign aid (Figure 1.2). The United States gives 0.1 percent of its GNP, the lowest percentage of all twenty-one members of DAC, including the smallest and newest members, Ireland and Portugal. Officials at OECD worry that the United States' cutback in foreign aid will have a domino effect in other donor countries; just as the United States launched an impressive international effort to provide aid after World War II, the fear is that it will now lead in the opposite direction.

Nordic Aid as a Model

The Nordic countries—Sweden, Finland, Norway, and Denmark—are commonly perceived as having the most pro-development, altruistic, and progressive aid programs. With a combined population of just 3.2 percent of the total population of OECD countries, the Nordic share of ODA in 1990 was 7.9 percent. Sweden, Norway, and Denmark have consistently surpassed the target of 0.7 percent of GNP as ODA and in some cases have exceeded a full 1 percent in aid allocations. Nordic support for international aid is most apparent in its per capita disbursement, which measures the degree to which aid imposes burdens on and is accepted by the overall population. The DAC average in 1990 was $67 per capita, the Finnish average was $143 per capita, and Norway provided $232 of aid per Norwegian. The United States' contribution of $38 per citizen in 1993 pales in comparison.

However, quantity does not guarantee or even suggest quality, and in this area too the Nordic countries provide an impressive example. Nordic countries have consistently supported many development priorities in their aid programs: environmental protection, public health and education, and promotion of human rights and democracy. Their bilateral aid flows are directed to varying sectors, depending on the expertise and interest of the donor state: Danish aid projects tend to emphasize rural development and increased food production; Finland emphasizes forestry, fisheries, and social development; Norway strongly supports family planning and children's rights; and although Sweden's sectoral priorities are more ambiguous, health care and small-scale rural industry have received special attention in recent years.

Since its earliest aid programs, Nordic aid has been provided with the understanding that representatives of developing countries will be directly involved in decision making and implementation of any aid-supported project. Subsequent development legislation has codified this approach. Aid recipients are viewed as partners, and typically just a handful are

The OECD's concerns are proving to be well founded. Governments of rich countries now designate an average of only 0.04 percent of their national GDP to poor countries, the lowest proportion in twenty years. Between 1994 and 1995, the drop was 9.3 percent in real terms, and it was expected to drop even more in 1997.[42] Disaster relief, which soared from 2 percent of total ODA in 1989 to 7 percent in 1994, is leaving development-oriented programs severely underfunded. DAC continues to reinforce selected. Tanzania was a primary recipient through the 1980s and 1990s, and India, Bangladesh, and Mozambique have all received consistent support over the years.

Although the bilateral programs of the Nordic countries were strengthened by the end of the 1970s, multilateral agencies continue to receive strong support, especially United Nations agencies. A case in point is UNICEF, which received roughly 40 percent of its budget from Nordic countries in 1990. The DAC average for multilateral support is 24 percent, which is far surpassed by the Nordic average of 30 percent. Similarly, NGOs receive strong support, receiving 5 percent of Denmark's official aid budget in 1992 and more than 10 percent of Norway's.

Nordic countries have served as compelling role models in terms of both the quantity and the quality of their aid packages. Lately, however, as globalization sweeps the world, some have begun to question whether commercial interests are now threatening the "purity" of Nordic aid. Economic growth has certainly received greater attention and emphasis in recent years, while the social aspects of development have been pushed somewhat to the back burner. As Nordic aid becomes more business oriented and less distinguishable from that of other DAC donors, many are bemoaning the "the death of the Nordic model." Further challenging Nordic aid is the split within these countries over membership in the European Union (EU). With Sweden and Finland now members of the EU and Norway's firm vote against joining, the common Nordic platform will surely become less cohesive and may even cease to exist. On the other hand, as members of the EU, Nordic states can influence that community and introduce their vision of development there. This small block of countries has always been influential beyond their size, and there is reason to be hopeful that notwithstanding new economic challenges, they will continue to serve as a model of international aid.

the argument that the cycle of underdevelopment can be broken only through integrated economic and development strategies that address the root causes of potential conflict and include the enhanced participation of all people and sustainable environmental practices. Wise words, but few seem to be listening.

It is important to note that the predominantly Western donors that make up DAC do not constitute the entire international donor community.

Figure 1.2 Foreign aid burden sharing, 1962–95

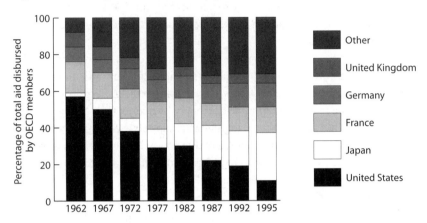

Source: Curt Tarnoff and Larry Q. Nowells, "Foreign Assistance as an Instrument of U.S. Leadership Abroad," National Policy Association Report no. 285 (Washington, D.C.: NPA, 1997), 10. Based on OECD data.

Although non-DAC donors, often categorized as OPEC countries (members of the Organization of Petroleum Exporting Countries), are relatively new donors, the growth of their aid has been swift. In 1970, the total ODA from OPEC donors was a mere $40 million; by 1990, they provided over $9.5 billion in aid. This increase in aid coincided with the rise in oil prices during the 1980s, and the recent decline in oil prices and the consequences of the Gulf War have impacted aid levels in the opposite way. Like DAC donors, OPEC nations use aid as a means to promote trade and strengthen their political ties; Saudi Arabian aid has typically concentrated on relatively few recipient countries, with the majority going to Egypt and Turkey. In 1994, Kuwait overtook Saudi Arabia as the largest non-DAC donor, providing over $550 million. Overall, however, non-DAC aid plummeted in 1994 to just $1.4 billion, less than half the 1991 volume.[43]

USAID and the Clinton Administration

In 1992, Senator Patrick Leahy, a Democrat from Vermont and chairman of the Foreign Operations Subcommittee of the Senate Committee on Appropriations, declared that "our international assistance program is exhausted, intellectually, conceptually, and politically," and called for "a total reexamination of foreign aid."[44] To its credit, USAID rose to the challenge of reexamining its mandate and restoring its reputation. USAID administrator Brian Atwood proposed to redirect the aid program in the name of "preventive diplomacy." The end of the cold war deprived many aid programs of their stated rationales, namely, the containment of communism, and seemed to raise questions about the need for a foreign aid program. USAID was quick to point out that new threats that require aid-related solutions had replaced the old: population growth, degradation of the global environment, political repression of many developing countries' governments, and continuing obstacles to economic growth.

Atwood oversaw the streamlining of USAID's stated goals from thirty-three to five:

1. Provision of humanitarian relief
2. Stabilization of population growth
3. Promotion of democracy
4. Environmental protection
5. Broad-based economic growth

All these goals, promised USAID, would "aim at building indigenous capacity, enhancing participation and encouraging accountability, transparency, decentralization, and the empowerment of communities and individuals."[45] In the face of mounting criticism and even threats by Congress of dissolution, USAID has been forced to mount a public-relations campaign to remind the American public of its significant success in meeting its goals. Among its accomplishments, USAID eagerly points out its newly formed Disaster Assistance Response Teams (DARTs), which provided effective humanitarian relief in countries such as Rwanda and Bosnia. In family assistance, historically one of the agency's strong points, USAID (and its predecessor organization) takes credit for financing the basic research leading to oral rehydration solution, generally considered one of the most important medical breakthroughs of the twentieth century. Additionally, over fifty million couples have been introduced to family planning, and USAID has become the recognized technical leader in HIV/AIDS prevention programs in the developing world, with programs in thirty-two countries. USAID also points to its success in assisting thirty-six of the fifty-seven nations that made the transition to democracy during the past fifteen years, providing programs that support voter education, election monitoring, party building, and public information campaigns. And last, USAID's environmental programs focus on reducing the long-term threats to the global environment, particularly loss of biodiversity and climate change.

In the past two years, USAID has undergone broad reorganization and "rightsizing" to streamline the agency. Admittedly, many of the changes are the direct result of unprecedented pressure by a Republican Congress,

---

USAID and Microenterprise

Microenterprise development provides credit and economic opportunity to the disenfranchised poor to help ensure that the benefits of economic growth are available to all. USAID's Microenterprise Initiative was launched in 1994, and $120 million a year for 1996 and 1997 were allocated for microenterprise projects.

USAID-supported microenterprise projects have had tremendous success throughout the world:

- Technical assistance of $15 million from USAID to Bank Rakyat in Indonesia (BRI) in the early 1980s led to the development of a profitable state-owned bank that serves the poor. BRI currently attracts savings from thirteen million Indonesians and lends to more than two million entrepreneurs.
- USAID contributed $5.9 million for the start-up investment in BancoSol in Bolivia. Today the bank reaches over 60,000 clients and has no need for further subsidy.
- USAID microenterprise funding of $6 million in Ecuador supports programs that will reach 138,000 clients between 1996 and 1999.
- In cooperation with government and private institutions, USAID's work in Uganda increased financial services to rural businesses and will reach over 10,000 people.
- In Nicaragua, USAID support for ACCION, Catholic Relief Services, Opportunity International, FINCA, and Pro Mujer will result in the provision of financial services for over 50,000 clients, 80 percent of whom are women.

USAID press release, January 27, 1997.

---

but the results have been significant: twenty-four overseas missions have been closed, seventy senior staff positions have been eliminated, total staff has been reduced by over 1,750, project design time has been reduced by 75 percent, and regulations have been cut by 55 percent. Yet despite these reforms, the agency continues to come under fierce attack by certain members of Congress who succeed in misrepresenting the levels of foreign aid spending and the size of USAID's budget. Comments such as those of Senator Jesse Helms, who declared in 1994 that "the foreign aid program has spent an estimated $2 trillion of the American taxpayers' money" (an outrageously inflated estimate by any standard), only exacerbate misperceptions.[46] Despite assumptions to the contrary, the U.S. foreign aid budget is a mere 0.117 percent of its GNP, the lowest percentage in the world. The USAID budget represents less than one-half of 1 percent of the federal budget. Even in real dollar terms, aid programs are at their lowest level in fifty years.[47]

U.S. international aid has focused on a different continent practically every decade: Western Europe in the late 1940s, Asia in the 1950s, Latin America in the first part of the 1960s, and Indochina in the latter half of the 1960s and into the 1970s. The Middle East was the focus during the 1980s, and there were hopes that with the end of the cold war the so-called peace dividend would provide more aid for the poorest countries in the South, regardless of their political leanings. Instead, the focus has shifted back to Europe—to the former Soviet Union and Eastern Europe, where the perceived need to consolidate the political gains there have become a priority (Table 1.2).[48] In 1996, aid to the former Soviet republics constituted almost 17 percent of the bilateral aid budget, while the entire continent of Africa received just under 12 percent. Assistance programs are overseen by two legislatively mandated State Department coordinators, one for the newly independent states (NIS) under the Freedom Support Act, and the other for Central Europe under the Support for East European Democracy (SEED) Act. Although these are not developing countries, they are, in the words of USAID, "misdeveloped and . . . out of sync with international market forces."[49] U.S. trade with the region has more than doubled in the last decade, and private investment, previously virtually nonexistent, is now well over $10 billion. Bolstered by the fact that aid has already played a significant role in assisting the private sector in the NIS to dominate economic activity, Congress recently allocated close to $1.3 billion of the 1997 aid budget to the region.

When Bill Clinton was elected to office in 1992, the development community took great comfort in his speeches promising to restore aid's role in promoting sustainable development and democracy around the world. One of Clinton's first actions was to oversee the redirection of USAID. The creation in 1993 of the President's Council on Sustainable Development only raised development-oriented expectations. The council was mandated to advise the president on sustainable development issues such as population and consumption and natural resource management and to recommend appropriate action strategy. It certainly sounded like the dawning of a new day for U.S. international assistance.

But then came the 1994 congressional elections, and the new Republican majority quickly silenced Clinton's idealistic notions for foreign aid. The chairman of the Senate Foreign Relations Committee immediately caught the nation's attention by holding hostage much of U.S. foreign policy, including nearly four hundred foreign service nominations, to

Table 1.2   Leading recipients of U.S. aid, FY 1991 and FY 1996
(country obligations, mill. $)[a]

Country	FY 1991	FY 1996
Israel	$3,650[b]	$3,000
Egypt	2,300	2,118
Turkey	804	355
Bosnia	0	246
Greece	351	224
Russia	0	179
India	134	158
Jordan	92	123
Rwanda	41	121
Ukraine	0	119
South Africa	50	117
Philippines	561	43
El Salvador	295	57
Nicaragua	219	27
Peru	199	85
Bolivia	191	75
Honduras	157	26
Portugal	144	1

a The first 11 countries listed were the leading recipients in 1996; the other 7 were among the top 11 in 1991.
b This number includes a one-time $650 million supplemental cost related to Persian Gulf War costs.

Source: Larry Q. Nowels and Curt Tarnoff, "Foreign Assistance as an Instrument of U.S. Leadership Abroad," National Policy Association Report no. 285 (Washington, D.C.: NPA, 1997), 6. Based on USAID data.

press his own demands for major changes in U.S. foreign policy, including the elimination of USAID. Stating that "our foreign policy institutions are a complete mess," Jesse Helms proposed that USAID be replaced by a foundation that would channel aid for education, health, and agriculture through grants to companies and nonprofits. Although USAID quickly mounted a successful campaign for its survival, its budget was cut drastically. Meanwhile, as the federal officials feuded among themselves about foreign policy, civil strife had erupted in Rwanda, with thousands of innocent civilians caught in the bloody crossfire. The U.S. president who had charmed the development community just a year before blocked the dispatch of fifty-five hundred peacekeeping troops as requested by the United Nations, arguably contributing to the deaths of thousands of Rwandans.[50]

In the current antiaid climate, USAID has been put on the defensive: every aid dollar is justified by showing how it benefits or returns directly to U.S. citizens. Aid is no longer evaluated in terms of the benefits to developing

Reforming Aid Programs

In 1996, Senator Jesse Helms, chairman of the Senate Foreign Relations Committee, insisted that it was no longer necessary to retain all existing U.S. government foreign affairs agencies. He suggested merging USAID, the U.S. Information Agency (USIA), and/or the Arms Control and Disarmament Agency (ACDA) into the State Department. In doing so, Mr. Helms hoped to save the taxpayer half a billion dollars a year and improve the efficiency of U.S. foreign policy at the same time.

The debate over consolidation has been around for a number of years, and it is now time to get down to action. A sound plan for restructuring U.S. foreign affairs machinery should pay heed to the following facts and principles:

- The potential for budget savings is limited. Senator Helms's estimates of savings, which came originally from the administration, are unrealistically high for agencies whose aggregate operating expenses are only $3 billion a year. A recent Brookings/Council on Foreign Relations task force estimated that cuts of $100 million to $200 million in annual spending were more attainable.
- The different agencies at issue often do very different types of work. Many USAID employees are technical specialists in one field or another. The majority of USIA staff, like other journalists, are dedicated to the open sharing of information and to keeping a critical eye on governments. Diplomats, by contrast, specialize in quietly resolving differences between countries and in studying politics rather than agronomy or sanitation.
- Although some budget hawks insist on consolidation, others are wary. In congressional testimony, for example, former Republican Representative Mickey Edwards argued against it on the grounds that the State Department has significant management problems that make it ill-suited to absorb other agencies and that this country benefits from a strong bilateral aid agency.

It is time to change the debate from whether we should reform U.S. foreign policy machinery to how we should do so. Then we should get on with it— and provide enough for aid, diplomacy, and other international activities as well. Turning points in history are terrible things to waste bickering over bureaucracies.

Excerpted from Michael E. O'Hanlon," Reforming Aid Programs," *Washington Times*, April 4, 1997. Reprinted with permission of *The Washington Times*.

country recipients, but rather in terms of how it helps the United States' own self-interests—as suggested in a USAID newsletter entitled "Foreign Aid: What's in It for You?" USAID notes that 70 percent of the money appropriated for bilateral aid is spent in the United States, and half of U.S. multilateral aid is spent on U.S. goods.[51] Replacing the cold war rationale for aid as a means to contain communism is today's rallying call for international aid to help the United States compete successfully in the global marketplace. Aid is now motivated by domestic economic interests that demand the opening of new markets for U.S. products; the fact that U.S. exports to developing countries rose by 11 percent in 1995 (and totaled a record $215 billion in 1994), which translates into over four million jobs for Americans, is one of USAID's favorite statistics in its campaign to popularize aid. Economic development is encouraged primarily so that third-world citizens can become consumers of U.S. goods. And the promotion of democracy throughout the world, another goal of USAID, is presented as a vital precondition to secure U.S. investment overseas.

Since 1995, the United States, the wealthiest nation in the world, has ranked dead last in the list of industrialized donors in terms of percentage of GNP allocated to foreign aid. Japan, France, and Germany all provide more aid in dollar volume than the United States. The 1995 international aid budget cut bilateral aid by 22 percent and multilateral aid by 30 percent; of the $12.3 billion budget, roughly half was allocated to security programs, most of that going to Israel and Egypt. Meanwhile, funds for development and humanitarian assistance were cut from $8.4 billion in 1995 to $7 billion in 1996, and development aid to Africa was cut by 22 percent. Although Congress argued that it simply could not afford to increase the aid budget, it voted to spend $11 billion more on defense than the administration even requested.[52] As David Lumsdaine points out, the United States could double its foreign aid expenditures by reducing military spending by just 3 percent.[53] Even food aid, once a stable, politically popular component of the aid program, has been cut. At the 1995 Food Aid Convention, the Clinton administration announced that the United States will reduce its aid levels to 2.5 metric tons from 4.4 metric tons.

Throughout its history, foreign aid has never been popular. Even the greatest foreign aid success, the Marshall Plan, was deeply criticized and sharply opposed by the American public at the time. And the public often has good reason to be critical. Foreign aid, although representing less than 1 percent of the federal budget, still has the potential to do serious harm. U.S. aid to dictators such as Marcos in the Philippines and Mobutu in the former Zaire (now called the Democratic Republic of Congo) not only insulated them from popular upheaval and, in effect, silenced the voice of the people but also added to those regions' instability and tainted the

United States by tying Washington to illegitimate autocrats.[54] But aid can, and does, do enormous good as well. The elimination of smallpox, the increase in child survival rates, the thousands of schools and clinics that have been built, the monitored elections that bring people to a voting box for the first time in their lives—all are inspiring testaments to U.S. international assistance. Undeniably, U.S. aid is laden with contradictions and competing priorities that must be weighed and somehow balanced. U.S. aid is charged with a very tall order—relieving human suffering, promoting economic growth, and stabilizing volatile governments, while advancing U.S. strategic and commercial interests. Is it possible, or even conceivable, that it can do it all? The United States is now the world's only superpower, a role that demands leadership. President Clinton subtitled his recently released 1998 international affairs budget "Supporting America's Global Leadership." If the United States is to be a global leader, foreign aid will undoubtedly play a crucial role.

Notes

1. Robert F. Zimmerman, *Dollars, Diplomacy and Dependency: Dilemmas of U.S. Economic Aid* (Boulder, Colo.: Lynne Rienner, 1993), 3.
2. Jan Knippers Black, *Development in Theory and Practice: Bridging the Gap* (Boulder, Colo.: Westview Press, 1991), 49.
3. Steven W. Hook, ed., *Foreign Aid toward the Millennium* (Boulder, Colo.: Lynne Rienner, 1996), 122.
4. Zimmerman, *Dollars, Diplomacy and Dependency*, 10.
5. Sue Ellen M. Charlton, *Women in Third World Development* (Boulder, Colo.: Westview Press, 1984), 200.
6. Stephen Hellinger, Douglas Hellinger, and Fred M. O'Regan, *Aid for Just Development: Report on the Future of Foreign Assistance* (Boulder, Colo.: Lynne Rienner, 1988), 28.
7. John W. Sewell and Christine E. Contee, "U.S. Foreign Aid in the 1980s: Reordering Priorities," *U.S. Foreign Policy and the Third World: Agenda 1985–86,* ed. John Sewell, Richard Feinberg, and Valeriana Kallab (New Brunswick, N.J.: Transaction Publishers, 1985), 100.
8. Curt Tarnoff and Larry Q. Nowels, "U.S. Foreign Assistance: The Rationale, the Record, and the Challenges in the Post-Cold War Era," National Planning Association Report no. 275 (Washington, D.C.: NPA, 1994), 8.
9. Inter-American Foundation information brochure.
10. Zimmerman, *Dollars, Diplomacy and Dependency,* 18.
11. Frances Moore Lappé, Joseph Collins, and David Kinley, *Aid as Obstacle: Twenty Questions about Our Foreign Aid and the Hungry* (San Francisco: Institute for Food and Development Policy, 1980), 93.
12. Graham Hancock, *Lords of Poverty: The Power, Prestige, and Corruption of the International Aid Business* (New York: Atlantic Monthly Press, 1989), 170.

13. Zimmerman, *Dollars, Diplomacy and Dependency*, 179.
14. Ibid., 180.
15. Robert Cassen and associates, *Does Aid Work? Report to an Intergovermental Task Force*, 2nd ed. (New York: Oxford University Press, 1994), 139.
16. Elizabeth Morrison and Randall Purcell, eds., *Players and Issues in U.S. Foreign Aid: Essential Information for Educators* (West Hartford, Conn.: Kumarian Press, 1988), 9.
17. Michael O'Hanlon and Carol Graham, *A Half Penny on the Federal Dollar: The Future of Development Aid* (Washington, D.C.: Brookings Institution Press, 1997), 22.
18. Steven W. Hook, *National Interest and Foreign Aid* (Boulder, Colo.: Lynne Rienner, 1995), 122.
19. Sewell and Contee, "U.S. Foreign Aid in the 1980s," 104.
20. Hellinger, Hellinger, and O'Regan, *Aid for Just Development*, 22.
21. Charlton, *Women in Third World Development*, 202.
22. International Center for Research on Women (ICRW) information pamphlet.
23. *Gender Action, A Newsletter of the USAID Office of Women in Development* 1, no. 3 (1997): 4.
24. Mark F. McGuire and Vernon Ruttan, "Lost Directions: U.S. Foreign Assistance Policy since New Directions," *Journal of Developing Areas* 24 (1993): 154.
25. Lappé, Collins, and Kinley, *Aid as Obstacle*, 9.
26. Tarnoff and Nowels, "U.S. Foreign Assistance," 6.
27. Zimmerman, *Dollars, Diplomacy and Dependency*, 4.
28. Ibid., 126.
29. Hook, *National Interest and Foreign Aid*, 134.
30. Tarnoff and Nowels, "U.S. Foreign Assistance," 6.
31. Jeffrey Sachs, "Making the Brady Plan Work," *Foreign Affairs* (Summer 1989): 87.
32. McGuire and Ruttan, "Lost Directions," 154.
33. Zimmerman, *Dollars, Diplomacy and Dependency*, 3.
34. Robert E. Wood, "Rethinking Foreign Aid," in *Foreign Aid toward the Millennium*, ed. Steven W. Hook (Boulder, Colo.: Lynne Rienner, 1996), 25.
35. Hook, *National Interest and Foreign Aid*, 19–20.
36. OECD, *Development Assistance Committee 1996 Report* (Paris: OECD, 1996), 89.
37. Ibid., 20.
38. Olav Stokke, ed., *Foreign Aid toward the Year 2000: Experiences and Challenges* (Portland, Oreg.: Frank Cass, 1996), 70.
39. UNDP, *Human Development Report 1994* (New York: Oxford University Press, 1994), 74.
40. Catrinus Jepma, *The Tying of Aid* (Paris: OECD, 1991), 13.
41. Black, *Development in Theory and Practice*, 69.
42. "Aid: Falling Fast," *Economist*, June 22, 1996, 43–4.
43. OECD, *Development Assistance Committee 1995 Report* (Paris: OECD, 1995), 115.
44. Zimmerman, *Dollars, Diplomacy and Dependency*, xii.
45. USAID press release, 1994.
46. Quoted in Program on International Policy Attitudes, "Americans and Foreign Aid: A Study of American Attitudes," March 1, 1995.
47. USAID, *Developments* (winter 1997): 1.
48. Wood, "Rethinking Foreign Aid," 23.
49. USAID congressional presentation, FY 1997.

50. According to Human Rights Watch/Africa Watch.

51. Doug Bandow, "Economic and Military Aid," in *Intervention in the 1980s: U.S. Foreign Policy in the Third World*, ed. Peter J. Schraeder (Boulder, Colo.: Lynne Rienner, 1989).

52. Thomas Lippman, "U.S. Loses Rank in Global Giving," *Washington Post*, June 18, 1996, A10.

53. David Halloran Lumsdaine, *Moral Vision in International Politics: The Foreign Aid Regime, 1949–1989* (Princeton, N.J.: Princeton University Press, 1993).

54. Doug Bandow, "Economic and Military Aid."

2

World Bank and Regional Development Banks

ALL DONORS CHANNEL A PORTION of their official assistance through intermediary international agencies that allocate this collective aid to needy countries. This is multilateral aid, and the largest player in this system is the World Bank. The specialized agencies of the United Nations also play a significant role in the distribution of multilateral assistance.

By the end of the 1960s, there was increasing pressure on Northern countries to distribute their aid multilaterally rather than bilaterally. At the beginning of the decade, only 10 percent of all official development assistance (ODA) was allocated to multilateral institutions; by 1985, multilateral aid constituted roughly 30 percent of all international aid.[1] The argument in favor of multilateral aid was, and continues to be, a strong one. Critics of bilateral aid claim that duplication and confusion are virtually inevitable when, for example, fifteen donor countries send separate aid packages with varying demands and objectives to a single recipient government. The result tends to be scenarios such as occurred in Kenya, where aid workers from various bilateral programs, eager to assist with water supply difficulties, ended up providing the country with eighteen different makes of water pumps.[2] It is also argued that because multilateral aid is allegedly not controlled by a single government's interests, it is less political than bilateral aid. Indeed, the World Bank stresses that its lending decisions are based solely on economic considerations and are not influenced by the politics of either recipient or donor countries. Reflecting on the Reagan administration's initial dislike of institutions such as the World Bank for the very reason that they did not sufficiently reflect U.S. foreign policy interests, it is easy to give credence to this argument. Even today, Congress tends to oppose allocations for multilateral institutions because it believes that they make funds too readily available to countries that actively oppose the United States or that have socialist, state-controlled economic systems. The United States channels far less than the average 30 percent to multilateral institutions; in 1996, just 8 percent of its international aid was multilateral.[3] Notwithstanding Congress' position, there are many World Bank members (and bank loan recipients) who strongly contend that since its inception, the World Bank has been under the thumb of its largest shareholder—the United States.

From the perspective of recipient countries, the unified front embodied by such large institutions as the World Bank can be somewhat overwhelming and often leaves developing countries with little, if any, leverage. In addition, a review of the World Bank's country loan allocations shows that the World Bank is "no more impartial to the resource, investment and security interests of multinational corporations and the governments they strongly influence than are the US bilateral programs"[4] During the 1980s, multilateral institutions came under unprecedented and often valid attack from NGOs in both the North and the South that pointed to numerous environmentally, socially, and economically detrimental projects funded by the World Bank at the expense of the poorest populations.

The World Bank

Components

In 1944, leading economists from Europe and the United States gathered in Bretton Woods, New Hampshire, to propose a new international economic order, given Europe's dire need for reconstruction and economic rehabilitation in the aftermath of World War II. These meetings have been called the most ambitious economic negotiations the world has ever seen, and they produced the World Bank, the International Monetary Fund (IMF), and the General Agreement on Tariffs and Trade (GATT). These Bretton Woods institutions were designed to facilitate the reconstruction and rehabilitation of Europe by providing credit, regulating international monetary exchange, and liberalizing trade. Although the goals of the Bretton Woods institutions have expanded and changed over the years, the initial program that focused on Europe was an enormous success—in the two decades after 1945, the ruined economies of Europe and Japan grew faster than ever before, or since.[5]

The World Bank is officially composed of four distinct institutions: the International Bank for Reconstruction and Development (IBRD), commonly referred to as the World Bank (the two titles are used interchangeably here); the International Development Association (IDA); the International Finance Corporation (IFC); and the Multilateral Investment Guarantee Agency (MIGA). Although all four institutions have the common objective of raising the standards of living in developing countries, IFC and MIGA are not considered aid institutions.

IBRD's founding purpose was to facilitate private capital transfers to help rebuild Western Europe after the war. Today its goal is to make loans and provide economic development and reconstruction assistance for developing countries. For the first twenty years, World Bank loans went to support, for the most part, large infrastructure projects—favorites were electric power plants, highways, and cash crop agriculture. The terms of bank loans are slightly better than average market rates and only slightly concessional; thus they are not considered ODA by the OECD. The majority of IBRD's funds are raised by borrowing in the international capital markets. The bank issues bonds, which have the highest rating (triple A), making them one of the safest investments available to individuals and private institutions in more than a hundred countries. Additional capital is derived from member countries' subscriptions in capital shares. In many ways, the World Bank is similar to a joint stock company in which the shareholders are the member governments.[6] IBRD is governed by a board of governors, comprising representatives from each member country.

Voting rights are dictated by member's subscriptions, with the largest contributors enjoying a comfortable majority of votes. The United States, Japan, and the European Union together control 55 percent of all votes. The Netherlands, one of the smallest countries in Europe, controls roughly the same percentage of votes as China, the world's most heavily populated country (1992 figures). The board of governors consists of one representative per member state, but all decisions are made by the board of executive directors, which is controlled by the five largest shareholders. One director is elected for every group of fifteen countries (excluding the five largest shareholders), and this director votes for the entire bloc, irrespective of dissent within the group. As Kunibert Raffer, an expert in development assistance, points out, this voting arrangement is "not only highly undemocratic but it would also be considered highly unorthodox in any private joint stock company."[7] The president of the bank is elected by the executive directors. Indicative of the North's hegemony in the leading international financial institutions, the World Bank president has always been an American, and the head of the IMF has always been a European.

IDA was established in 1960 to provide an alternative for the poorest developing countries, which could not afford the bank's "hard loans." IDA loans, which are considered ODA, are interest free and do not require the repayment of principal to begin until ten years after the signing of the loan agreement. There is a 0.75 percent annual charge on IDA loans, and maturities are thirty-five to forty years. Only countries with a per capita income below a certain standard are eligible for IDA funds, and this is usually the only source of external funds available to these countries, which are considered too large a risk for any other lenders. IDA financing is different from that of IBRD—it has to be replenished with hard funds by

donor nations every three years, thus subjecting it to greater financial inse-
curity. In recent years, the United States has added greatly to that insecu-
rity by threatening to cut in half its commitment of $1.3 billion to IDA.
(After months of negotiating, in March 1996, donors of IDA, including
the United States, agreed to contribute $11 billion over the next three
years.)[8] IDA is administered by the same staff as IBRD, and voting power is
also similar—based on countries' subscriptions and provision of supplementary resources. World Bank loans and IDA loans are almost identical
in everything except their financial terms, and one country can receive
both types of loans, leading to a very real and common paradox whereby
new aid becomes the method of financing old aid.

Although IFC is not an aid institution, it merits mention here for its
increasingly important role in promoting private investment in developing
countries. Established in 1956 "to promote growth in the private sector of
[developing countries'] economies and help to mobilize domestic and foreign capital for this purpose,"[9] IFC is the only branch of the World Bank
allowed to invest in or extend credit to private companies in the South. In
keeping with its much quoted pledge "to go where others will not go, and
do what others will not do," it has been one of the only financial institutions, public or private, to invest in Africa. With investments in thirty-
three countries worth $911 million, IFC has earned higher returns on its
mining investments in Africa than anywhere else in the world.[10] In addition to
providing loans and making investments, IFC also advises on privatization
and helps countries set up or improve their stock markets. Unfortunately, little collaboration occurs between IFC and the World Bank. Experts contend that this lack of communication only weakens the bank, which is in
dire need of information and know-how about the private sector—
arguably the most important sector in development today. Although its
relationship with the World Bank may be less than ideal, IFC receives
strong support from most member countries, which generally applaud its
free-market ideology.

History

In many ways, the World Bank is an evolving institution. It has tackled its
mandate to promote economic development in many different ways
throughout its fifty-year history and, it is hoped, learned much in the
process. During the 1960s, the bank's activities centered on development
planning. In the following decade, it espoused a basic needs doctrine, in
which social needs figured prominently. This changed again radically during the 1980s, the decade of structural adjustment (described below),
when all eyes were on the market and macroeconomic reforms. "Good

governance" seems to be the catchphrase of the 1990s, and human development is once again a focal point. Much of the current shift in emphasis is a result of strong protest, from North and South, against structural adjustment, as well as heightened concern for human rights, gender issues, and environmental protection.

The World Bank became the largest source of international development assistance during the tenure of Robert McNamara, who headed the institution from 1968 to 1980. In 1968 the World Bank was lending about $1 billion a year for 62 new projects; by 1980, this figure rose to $12 billion a year for 266 projects.[11] Strong emphasis was placed on funding projects that would meet basic human needs, and the agricultural sector was a favorite recipient. McNamara brought a moral tone to the World Bank's perspective on aid, declaring in 1973 that "the fundamental case for development assistance is a moral one."[12] However, despite his uplifting promise to reach those in absolute poverty, evidence suggests that his agricultural strategy accelerated a process of agricultural modernization and integration into global markets that increased inequality and displaced rural people living in traditional subsistence farming communities.[13]

During the 1970s, and in great part due to the persistence of its president, the World Bank expanded its definition of development to include an evaluation of basic needs and investment in human resource development, in addition to its favorite indicator—economic growth. However, in the surge of lending, little attention was focused on where the funds ended up. By the late 1970s, five of the top eight recipients were authoritarian or repressive regimes, such as Brazil, the Philippines, and Indonesia. As Raffer and Singer aptly point out, "human rights records of right-wing dictators certainly never blocked projects."[14] Echoing this concern was a U.S. senator from South Dakota who in 1977 rose on the Senate floor to protest the fact that the World Bank intended to increase loans to four newly repressive governments twice as fast as to all others. These governments—Chile, Uruguay, Argentina, and the Philippines—all received major new loans after the onset of torture and repression.[15] Although the bank stressed that its lending decisions were based exclusively on apolitical economic considerations, there were numerous examples of "strategic nonlending" that revealed a political bias. Chile is an apt example: during Allende's presidency (a socialist government), the country was deemed too great a risk and received no loans, but following Pinochet's coup, brought about with the help of the United States, the country suddenly became creditworthy.[16] The tremendous growth in World Bank lending during McNamara's tenure led many critics to complain that the bank cared more about pushing out new loans than about how the money was spent. Since then, the bank has made an effort to improve the quality of lending and now directs its funds toward more small-scale development projects. However, there remains a disturbing shortage of local participation in project planning and design.

In one of his many speeches, McNamara declared that "the rich countries have a responsibility to assist the less developed nations. It is not a sentimental question of philanthropy. It is straightforward issue of social justice."[17] Noble words perhaps, but they also reveal McNamara's naive (or presumptuous) view that strengthening economies is a neutral act. As those directly affected by bank programs know all too well, "no development is neutral; the expansion of one sector is almost always at the expense of another."[18] Perhaps the most glaring examples of the bank's attempt to strengthen one sector at the expense of another are its projects to strengthen infrastructure without regard to the environmental and human costs.

One of the most famous examples of irreparable harm inflicted by the World Bank in the name of development is the Polonoroeste project, a road-building and agricultural colonization scheme in Brazil. In 1985, the bank had raised more than $400 million to construct a national highway that connected the populous south-central region to the rain-forest region in the north. Thirty-nine rural settlement centers were built to attract landless people to the northwestern province of Rodonia, where free land was promised amidst the dense rain forests. Over ten thousand Amerindians belonging to over forty tribal groups were said to be living in the rain-forest region at the time.[19] The results, even by World Bank standards, were disastrous. By 1987, almost all the jungle had been slashed and burned by landclearers, whose crops had scarcely a chance of producing anything amidst the ash and burned soil. Satellite photographs taken that year showed six thousand forest fires burning across the entire Amazon basin—the single largest human-caused change on earth readily visible from space.[20] The incidence of malaria approached 100 percent in some areas, sending failed settlers back to their urban centers carrying a highly resistant and lethal form of the disease. The original inhabitants, the tribal groups, fared even worse; many of them were menaced with physical extermination by measles and flu epidemics. Even the bank admitted that the project was a "an ecological, human and economic disaster of tremendous dimensions."[21] Unfortunately, the World Bank's history, especially during the 1980s, is littered with examples of mega-projects that caused either environmental harm or the displacement of indigenous populations.[22]

Structural Adjustment

During the 1980s, developing countries faced the worst economic recession in fifty years. An intolerable debt burden combined with forbidding terms of trade resulted in a stagnation of world trade. Prices of developing countries' exports fell drastically—prices of primary commodities fell by over 30 percent from 1980 to 1985, and aid flows were less in 1985 than they had been five years before. High interest rates associated with the global recession only exacerbated the pressures of the debt burden. By the end of 1985, the accumulated debt of the third world as a whole had grown to $888 billion, and in many countries, the debt-service payments (payments owed on past borrowing) represented between a quarter and a half of their export earnings. Not surprisingly, incomes were also at an all-time low, falling 0.6 percent in developing countries as a whole.[23]

The World Bank issued its first structural adjustment loans in 1980 to five countries. Totaling over $500 million, they represented about 5 percent of total loan commitments and marked a new direction in bank lending, from specific project lending to sectoral or macroeconomic lending (called program lending). The loans were disbursed quickly, with the goal of relieving a country's balance-of-payments deficit or repaying interest due to private banks. In order to receive a loan, the recipient government had to undergo a program of thorough structural adjustment designed to make its economy more efficient and capable of sustained growth.[24]

Components of structural adjustment reform fall into four categories: trade policy, resource mobilization, efficient use of resources, and institutional reforms.[25] Or as Robert Wood describes them, the four Ds: devalue, decontrol, deflate, and denationalize.[26] In the black-and-white text of a loan agreement, these categories may seem somewhat benign, but how they translated into policy and touched the lives of the poor was far from mild.

Luring foreign investment and promoting international trade were the motivations behind the trade policy component, and the most common method used to achieve this was a currency devaluation. Despite its merited unpopularity, most economists agree that devaluation is often a necessary adjustment for countries with deteriorating economies, because it brings the currency in line with a market-indicated level, thus averting even more drastic price inflation. A devaluation of the local currency makes exports cheaper and imports prohibitively more expensive. This obviously has a far more detrimental effect on countries whose main staple foods are imported—the exchange-rate devaluation results in food prices rising far beyond the reach of most of its citizens.

To further attract foreign investment and trade, governments were also required to put a hold on wages. If wages were not cut, as was often the case, they were prevented from rising in order to reduce inflation and make exports more competitive. In Mexico, real wages fell by 30 percent between 1981 and 1984, and in Peru, they fell by 13 percent.[27] International trade was further promoted by cutting tariffs and improving export incentives.

Resource mobilization typically translated into massive budget cuts.

Structural adjustment loans nearly always demanded a radical reduction in government spending in order to control inflation and reduce the demand for capital inflows from abroad. Not surprisingly, the first and most drastic cuts were made in the social service sectors such as health, education, and welfare. Between 1979 and 1983, per capita expenditures on health decreased in nearly half the African countries for which data exist and in more than half the countries in Latin America. Real per capita expenditures on health services fell by 80 percent in Ghana from 1974 to 1982 and by 78 percent in Bolivia from 1980 to 1982.[28] Cuts in food subsidies were equally common and caused violent protests in countries such as Algeria, Sudan, and Venezuela. Although hardly exculpating the World Bank's disregard for the impact of its mandates on the poor, it is important to point out that recipient governments sometimes ignored viable options to mobilize funds other than these drastic cuts. For instance, to the delight of its international travelers, many state airlines in Africa continued to be subsidized, while subsidized health care was the first to be cut.[29] Even more egregious was the fact that military spending continued to rise in most loan-receiving countries. In the nations of sub-Saharan Africa, the poorest countries in the world, military spending rose from 0.7 percent of GNP in 1960 to 3 percent of GNP in 1990.[30]

The third component of structural adjustment loans, the promotion of efficient use of resources, brought about revisions in prices, deregulation, and frequently the privatization of state-owned companies. Mexico underwent one of the greatest sweeps, privatizing everything from banks and television stations to plantations. Within a few years, the government privatized hundreds of state enterprises and sold roughly a thousand properties. Even though foreign investment flowed in—from $2.6 billion in 1990 to $4.7 billion in 1991[31]—it served primarily to make the rich even richer. As a record number of Mexican names appeared on the Forbes 400 list, hundreds of thousands of less visible Mexicans lost their jobs in the name of increased efficiency. The revision in energy prices was one area that generally had little adverse effect on the poor, as they consume little purchased energy anyway, and these price revisions constituted a significant savings for developing countries, many of which spend roughly as much on energy subsidies as they receive in aid.[32]

The goal behind the final component—institutional reform—was the strengthening of those institutions deemed important or associated with the quest for markets and investment. Over 80 percent of structural adjustment loans given from 1980 to 1986 called for the strengthening of public investment programs. Marketing support for agriculture and support for industry, including price controls, were also typical adjustment requirements.[33]

Inherent in all structural adjustment programs was an enormous

International Labor Organization Claims Privatization in Africa Can Have Positive Impact on Employment

In sub-Saharan Africa, the World Bank and the IMF identified the dominant role of state enterprises as a key factor in poor economic performance. Some 67 percent of World Bank–IMF lending to African countries in 1989–91 involved public enterprise reform, and a high proportion focused on selling off state-owned enterprises. Privatization is usually associated with its negative impacts—it often causes hiring freezes, layoffs, or early retirements. Additionally, this policy reform has often created a new set of problems for governments, which must struggle to pay termination benefits and address the broader social consequences of job losses.

Privatization of state enterprises has certainly had a negative short-term impact on employment, says the International Labor Organization (ILO) *World Labour Report 1995*. But in the long term, the report says, the impact is more likely to be positive, as privatized companies may be better managed, with larger capital, and may actually create jobs.

The pace of privatization in Africa has actually been relatively slow. Six countries—Benin, Ghana, Guinea, Mozambique, Nigeria, and Senegal—accounted for two-thirds of the divestitures from the late 1980s to the early 1990s, which for the most part have been small in scale, according to the ILO. Of those countries grappling with privatization, there has been a range of government responses. At one end of the spectrum is Togo, where job losses have occurred with no compensation or alternative employment opportunities being provided. On the other end is Guinea, where an elaborate compensation program was worked out.

Some thirty-two thousand workers were removed from public-sector payrolls between 1985 and 1989 through a combination of early retirement and voluntary departure with sizable benefits packages. Of those retrenched before 1990, some 36 percent had not obtained another job by 1992. The 64 percent who found new employment were on average better off, with real earnings double their public-sector level.

Excerpted from *Africa Recovery* 9, no. 2 (August 1995).

measure of conditionality—a country would receive a loan only if it agreed to the prescribed reforms. Ironically, conditionality was never envisaged in the World Bank's constitution, and in large part, it was reflective of the growing skepticism about the nature and role of governments in the South. In fact, the demand that the state be rolled back from economic life reflected the bank's belief that domestic failure was to blame for the high levels of debt. Raffer contends that the strict conditionality of structural adjustment was "based on a firm confidence that they [the World Bank] know what is best for recipient countries, that they have got hold of the sacred truth."[34] In turn, mounting debt pressured Southern governments to acquiesce to conditions that they would not have usually accepted. Conditionality continues to be a dominant feature of World Bank loans today, although the emphasis on economic reform has recently been replaced with a focus on good governance.

The early 1990s revealed that many of the World Bank's most "adjusted" customers experienced an increase in production and exports yet failed to achieve sustained economic growth. Rather than the flow of new investment that was expected in these newly reformed nations, in many cases, just the opposite—disinvestment—took place. The bank was forced to look beyond economic reform and consider other key ingredients for successful economic development. Recognizing that many developing countries lacked the administrative and governmental framework vital for attracting investment and sustaining economic growth, the bank instituted a new focus on governance. It defined governance as "the manner in which power is exercised in the management of a country's economic and social resources for development,"[35] and attached to its loans good governance conditions aimed at addressing a number of key problems in the exercise of power. Economic liberalization conditions have been replaced with new conditions of governmental accountability, transparency, and predictability on the part of politicians and bureaucrats in the absence of the rule of law. Put in less polite terms, the new conditions are aimed at reducing the level of corruption that seemed rampant in many developing countries.[36] This sudden interest in encouraging democracy has struck many observers as hypocritical and even dubious, given the bank's and other bilateral donors' history of supporting dictatorships in strategically important countries throughout the world. In defense, the bank's position is that the end of the cold war has changed the rules of the game, rendering strategic support to repressive dictators obsolete and opening the door for aid to deserving, well-governed recipients. Although critics continue to argue that the practice of conditionality represents an intrusion on recipients' sovereignty, the interdependent, globalized nature of the current world order questions the principle that political management is strictly the responsibility of individual governments.

Evaluation of Structural Adjustment

In the early 1980s, field staff of the United Nations Children's Fund (UNICEF) in Latin America and Africa began reporting increasing cases of malnutrition among women and children. In 1982, they undertook a

study of the impact of the world recession on children and the international response to it. The study revealed that "a very real deterioration was taking place in the lives of children around the world" and urged immediate action.[37] UNICEF argued that structural adjustment policies were weakening the health and educational standards of children, which, in effect, was undermining developing countries' most valuable resources —human resources—and thereby weakening their future. For the first time, widespread international attention focused on the negative consequences of structural adjustment, and within months, the World Bank was facing loud demands to place a human face on its structural adjustment programs.

Further research by UNICEF as well as NGOs in the field revealed increasing cases of malnutrition in many countries. After years of decline, infant mortality was on the rise in countries such as Ghana and Brazil, and the rate of low-birth-weight babies increased in at least ten countries from 1979 to 1982. Diseases once thought to have been eliminated reappeared, such as yellow fever in Ghana and malaria in Peru. And these were only the documented cases—for most countries, information was not available because of weak or nonexistent health statistics. Education was also adversely affected; primary school attendance fell, and dropout rates increased in Chile, Ghana, and Bolivia.[38] Data also showed that low-income households in the informal sector and those on minimum wage in the formal sector suffered the most by adjustment policies. In short, the net results of structural adjustment policies were reduced employment, higher prices for basic commodities, and a drastic cut in basic services, especially health, education, and sanitation. Tanzanian president Julius Nyerere articulated the Southern reaction to structural adjustment when he poignantly asked, "must we starve our children to pay our debts?"

After a decade of structural adjustment, the number of people living in poverty in Latin America rose from 130 million in 1980 to 180 million at the beginning of the 1990s.[39] Frances Stewart, a well-known development specialist, found that the adjustment policies that were widely adopted in Africa did not succeed in restoring growth in most countries.[40] In fact, they were often accompanied by continued economic deterioration. An additional negative effect, in many cases, was that they weakened a comparative advantage that many African countries had in nontraditional agriculture and industry. Most of the reforms required by structural adjustment were geared toward the ultimate goal of export-led growth— an objective that in most cases was never achieved. A World Bank study of adjustment loans in seven countries showed that only two were able to increase their export earnings substantially.[41] The environmental costs of structural adjustment were often just as high as the human cost. The rise in unemployment and fall in wages led to accelerated migration to areas

with marginal land and a fragile environment, and cuts in government spending included the few programs focused on environmental protection. It is important to note, however, that cuts in government spending sometimes helped the environment too by eliminating common environmentally harmful subsidies such as pesticides.

MIT economist Lance Taylor argues that the World Bank and the IMF misdiagnosed the problem when they prescribed structural adjustment. It was not the faulty economic structures within developing countries that caused the economic crisis in the South, but the two macroeconomic shocks of the drastic oil price rise and the ensuing debt crisis. This external instability cut off flows of capital that had been pouring into developing countries and caused a massive outflow of developing countries' resources that could have gone to domestic investment.[42] Although the World Bank never went so far as to abandon its justification for pushing structural adjustment, one of its chief economists conceded that "we did not think that the human costs of these programs could be so great, and the economic gains so slow in coming."[43]

In 1989, two very different assessments of structural adjustment in Africa were released. The first, issued by the World Bank and UNDP, was entitled *Africa's Adjustment and Growth in the 1980s* and suggested that there was evidence that adjusting countries had achieved a slightly higher economic growth rate. Gross domestic product per person grew in Ghana and Uganda each year between 1988 and 1993, and although hardly an indication of success, there is evidence that the alternatives to structural adjustment were no more successful. Among the countries that rejected structural adjustment loans, none experienced economic growth, and most were worse off.[44] The bank more recently argued that structural adjustment's role in reducing the deadweight of government regulation allowed farmers to plant more, yielding food surpluses in countries such as Tanzania and Nigeria. In addition, government belt-tightening eliminated swaths of subsidized social programs, along with thousands of bogus names from civil service payrolls. Notwithstanding the few statistics that could be spun into success stories, the bank was forced to concede that "current growth rates among the best African performers are still too low to reduce poverty much."[45]

The second report, *African Alternative Framework to Structural Adjustment Programmes*, issued by the United Nations Economic Commission for Africa (ECA), reached different conclusions. Arguing that the World Bank's analysis was based on faulty use of data and only limited consideration of all available evidence,[46] ECA proposed an alternative to structural adjustment: structural transformation, which would rely heavily on a human-centered strategy of economic recovery. In response, the World Bank published another report, *From Crisis to Sustainable*

The Most Structurally Adjusted Country in Africa: Ghana

In 1983, Ghana's economy was on the brink of collapse. Long-term economic decline, triple-digit inflation, deteriorating terms of trade, drought, and political instability convinced the military government to accept World Bank and IMF conditions for financial assistance. The two financial institutions designed a structural adjustment program that was to bring Ghana back into the global economy. Ghana went along with the structural adjustment plans and prescriptions, reforming its economy and earning the reputation as the World Bank's star pupil. Governmental price and distribution controls were removed. The currency was devalued, and state enterprises were privatized. In turn, inflation stabilized as government spending decreased. Economic growth rates rebounded from a –1.3 percent annual average during 1973–83 to 5 percent a year since 1983. Exports increased, and foreign aid flowed in. Ghana, the most structurally adjusted country in Africa, was touted as a shining example of the benefits of structural adjustment.

However, despite impressive increases in economic growth, the lives of the majority of Ghanaians did not improve. Population increases diluted the effect of a strengthened economy. Inflation, though down significantly, averaged close to 40 percent for much of the 1980s. Interest rates remained prohibitively high, and, most critically, investment failed to occur. On the contrary, private investment declined for much of the 1990s. There is reason to believe that the adjustment process itself, and the factors that arose from it, was the greatest constraint to investment. The attempt to limit inflation caused credit ceilings and sky-high interest rates, making business expansion

---

Development, which emphasized the need for African development and adjustment to be guided by a long-term perspective and priorities of human development, structural change, and accelerated growth.[47]

Back in 1982, UNICEF had argued that "no adjustment programme is acceptable which allows children to be sacrificed for the sake of financial stability."[48] Yet this happened, and it did not need to. UNICEF repeatedly urged the international donor community to consider alternatives—namely, adjustment with a human face. Few could deny the need for structural changes in many developing countries, but these changes could have been accompanied by an explicit government commitment to protect vulnerable groups during the adjustment process. UNICEF's proposal also envisioned a broader definition of adjustment that would give greater priority to achieving sustainable economic growth in the medium term, which, it warned the bank, might require more external finance and less emphasis on achieving short-term stabilization.[49]

virtually impossible. Additionally, as Ghana won international accolades for its market liberalization and decrease in government spending, the cost of education and health services suddenly rose beyond the reach of the average Ghanaian. In 1989–94, there was only one physician for every twenty-three thousand Ghanaians, as compared with one for every fifteen thousand in 1980–85.

In the absence of investment, foreign aid became all the more important and available, as donors were happy to reward Ghana's adjustment record. Development assistance accounted for 11 percent of Ghana's national income in 1994, almost double the figure for 1984–87. Much of the aid has gone into export activities such as gold mining, a non-renewable resource; timber, an environmentally damaging industry; and cocoa, which is subject to great volatility in the world market. The "gift" of foreign aid has also, for the most part, come in the form of low-interest loans, causing Ghana's external debt to nearly quadruple since 1980.

Even the World Bank now acknowledges that Ghana should not be oversold as a success story, given the challenges that still lie ahead, including the large agenda of reform that remains unfinished. In a recent Oxfam poverty report, the bank conceded that Ghana will need another two decades at current growth rates before it joins the ranks of middle-income countries, and another fifty years before the average Ghanaian crosses the poverty line.

From Anna Rich, "Structural Adjustment in Ghana," in *Hunger 1997* (Silver Spring, Md.: Bread for the World Institute, 1997). Reprinted with permission.

Prior to 1985, the World Bank and the IMF had never regarded the poverty implications of their adjustment programs.[50] In the latter part of the decade, and in great part as a result of the UNICEF and ECA studies, they underwent a radical change in attitude.[51] In the late 1980s, the World Bank and the IMF launched efforts to buffer and in some cases compensate some of the groups that had been most adversely affected by structural adjustment programs. Confirming the indisputable fact that the bank had failed the poor in the most fundamental ways was a never published but widely publicized internal evaluation written by former World Bank vice president Willi Wapenhans in 1992. The Wapenhans report provided evidence that the number and proportion of faulty loans, characterized by "poor design, poor management and poor implementation," had increased since policy lending was introduced, and it described the "culture of containment" prevalent at the bank, whereby staff were judged more by the number of new projects that had funds committed than by the projects' success rates.[52] The Wapenhans report revealed that notwithstanding the bank's somber acquiescence in responsibility for the failings of structural adjustment and policy lending in general, there was still much room for improvement. Renewed rhetoric regarding the need to integrate poverty concerns into country and sector analysis is meaningless if unaccompanied by important and necessary changes to the basic design of policies.

The World Bank Today

The World Bank is no longer the singular and dominant development institution it was twenty years ago. Today it operates in a global environment where private capital dominates the financial flows to developing countries. When James Wolfensohn became president of the World Bank in June 1995, his first priority seemed to be to transform the institution to adapt to the realities of the new economic world order. The changes he has proposed in many ways mirror the recent changes undergone at USAID as part of its "reinvention" process: streamlining the loan approval process, improving evaluation, and increasing the budget for staff training. Wolfensohn appears to be truly dedicated to reshaping the World Bank in the context of new global realities, but as a recent *Economist* article pointed out, the World Bank's "history is peppered with radical, and badly executed overhauls. The most recent, and most damaging, took place in 1987 when the entire staff was sacked and then hired again from the top down."[53] It remains to be seen whether this will merely be another failed attempt.

At the 1996 annual meeting of the World Bank and the IMF, Wolfensohn distinguished himself from his predecessors by leading a campaign to relieve the debts of the world's poorest countries. His proposed initiative would relieve the debts of up to forty-one of the most indebted nations in the third world. The plan is likely to cost between $5.6 billion and $7.7 billion over the next decade, $2 billion of which the bank would contribute.[54] Another break from the past was evidenced in the World Bank's recent proposal to lead a drive to raise more than $200 million from international donors to provide small loans for the poor to start their own businesses. Loans would be provided to local banks that specialize in training and advice, which would then issue small loans of roughly $100 to be repaid with modest interest. The bank estimates that this effort could finance credit for a million prospective entrepreneurs a year.[55]

Although Wolfensohn has hardly shied away from cooperation with the nongovernmental community, the bank's history of collaboration with NGOs predates his tenure, going back to the late 1980s. Before 1989, NGOs were involved in about fifteen World Bank–financed projects a year, but in 1989 alone, the number of projects involving NGOs rose to about

fifty. The bank seldom makes grants directly to NGOs, but prefers to provide funding to the recipient government, which then passes funds on to
NGOs. The few exceptions to this rule are World Bank grants to the
International Planned Parenthood Federation for its work on population in
Africa and occasional grants to NGOs involved in working with women,
through the bank's Women in Development Division. The establishment of
the NGO-Bank Committee, a forum for the exchange of views between
NGOs and World Bank managers, is another indication of the bank's
efforts to improve relations with the nongovernmental community.[56]

In turn, NGOs (as Chapter 5 describes) have taken advantage of their
access to the World Bank to voice their critiques and protests, often in
response to the bank's disastrous record on the environment. As Polonoroeste showed, bank projects all too often proved to be ecological disasters.
In recognition of its failings, the bank set up the Global Environment
Facility (GEF) in 1991 to fund projects designed to bring about global
environment gains. Jointly administered by the World Bank, the UNDP,
and the United Nations Environment Programme (UNEP), each agency
shares responsibility according to its expertise. UNDP identifies projects,
carries out preinvestment studies, and provides technical cooperation;
UNEP provides environmental expertise through a scientific and technical
advisory panel that formulates guidelines for project selection; and the
World Bank administers the facility and is responsible for investment projects. GEF's core purpose is to help developing countries explore ways to
help the global environment. Focusing on four priority areas—global
warming, destruction of biological diversity, pollution of international
waters, and depletion of the ozone layer—GEF has established trust funds
that assure countries of long-term income for environmental protection.
Despite the fact that the facility is one of the few mechanisms that exist
for funding environmental projects, it is not without its critics. Bruce Rich,
a well-known environmentalist who wrote a comprehensive review of the
bank's impact on the environment, claims that GEF, like the bank itself, is
reflective of industrialized countries' view that "the global environmental
crisis [is only] a matter of more money for foreign assistance projects, this
time ones with a green hue."[57]

Recently the World Bank has redirected many of its programs toward
the goal of creating conditions in developing countries for a healthy and
thriving private sector.

The Role of Private Capital

In 1995, World Bank lending to developing countries was $21 billion; that
same year, $170 billion of private money flowed to developing countries.[58]

Figure 2.1 Recent capital flows to developing countries from all sources

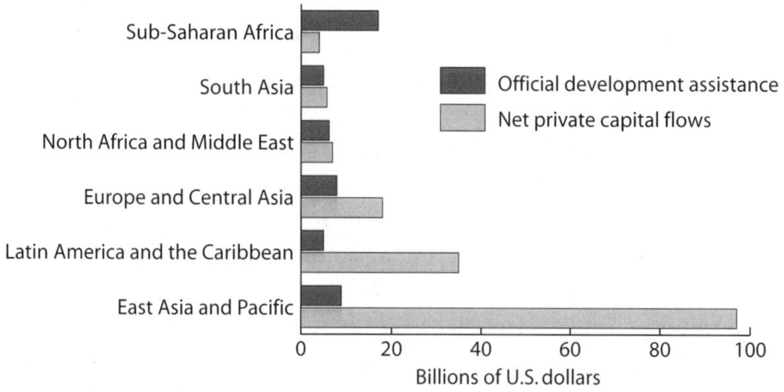

Note: Aid figures are annual averages for the two-year period 1993–94, the most recent for which data are available; private flows are for 1995.

Sources: Michael O'Hanlon and Carol Graham, *A Half Penny on the Federal Dollar: The Future of Development Aid* (Washington, D.C.: Brookings Institution Press), 35. Based on data from Organization for Economic Cooperation and Development, *Development Cooperation 1995* (Paris: OECD, 1996), A67, A96; World Bank, *World Debt Tables,* vol. 1 (Washington, D.C. World Bank, 1996), 11.

The role of private bank lending to developing countries has been expanding widely since the 1970s and early 1980s, when, for the first time, leaders of developing countries had an alternative to World Bank loans. And unsurprisingly, private loans were often preferred—World Bank loans and bilateral loans from donor governments were, for the most part, tied to either strict policy adjustments or, in the case of bilateral aid, to imports from donors or to externally managed technical assistance projects.[59] Private capital has only become more important in recent years, when aid flows from OECD donors have been at their lowest level in two decades. Donors appear more than ready to pull back their aid budgets and allow private capital to step in, arguing that aid is "less important than healthy access to markets, capital and technology."[60] From 1992 to 1994, private capital flows from the United States increased by more than 150 percent in current dollars.[61] Market-based transfers, which include direct investments, commercial bank lending, and bond lending, totaled $110 billion in 1994 and represented more than 60 percent of all capital flows from industrialized to developing countries (Figure 2.1).[62]

The fact that the World Bank's traditional project-financing role is gradually being replaced by capital markets places the institution at a crossroads. It can either try to compete with the private sector or take advantage of the flexibility provided by the availability of private funds to pursue social and sustainable development projects. The bank's recent focus on nonincome aspects of development has moved its lending into new areas such as the environment, social welfare systems, education, and primary health care. At the same time, the bank is working hard to bring the private sector into the center of its strategies and operations. It has created a visible, aggressive private-sector staff function that has helped raise awareness of the World Bank in the private sector and has also launched a major program of second-generation policy reforms aimed at legal and other institution building, as well as regulatory reforms—all of which are deemed vital prerequisites of private investment.

At a time when developing countries are suddenly called "emerging markets," it is easy to lose sight of those countries whose markets are hardly emerging and are consequently of little interest to the international financial community. The staggering figures of private capital flows are limited primarily to newly industrialized countries and not to those countries that need it most. Investors want to put their money in countries with established records of industrialization and political stability. So as the middle-income countries become flooded with private capital, the poorest countries get left further behind as the chasm between rich and poor grows wider. Of the total private capital flows from 1989 to 1992, 72 percent went to just ten countries, including Mexico, China, Brazil, Nigeria, and the Republic of Korea. Meanwhile, all the countries in sub-Saharan Africa combined received just 6 percent of foreign direct investment in the late 1980s.[63] And in 1995, the entire sub-Saharan region, excluding South Africa, received less than the sum invested in Chile alone.

For all their talk about market solutions, industrialized nations often fail to practice what they preach. While exhorting, and even forcing, developing nations to remove trade restrictions and protectionist policies, industrialized countries favor free trade only when it benefits them—for instance, insisting on the removal of tariffs on the labor-intensive goods in which developing countries are most competitive, while leaving intact most of the protection for industry and agriculture in their own countries. Trade barriers in developing countries are estimated to cost developing countries $500 billion, almost ten times what they receive in aid.[64] At a time when free trade is viewed as the miraculous solution to economic ills, it is ironic that twenty-four industrialized countries are more protectionist than they were ten years ago (1992 figures).[65]

Regional Development Banks

Modeled on the World Bank, regional development banks were created to provide capital, primarily to governments, to spur economic growth in the regions they represent: Africa, Asia, Latin America, and the Caribbean.

The World Bank and Early Childhood Development

The concessional-loan component of the World Bank, the International Development Association (IDA), lends funds to the seventy-nine countries with annual per capita incomes below $865. One billion children live in these countries, most of which are in Africa. An African child's odds of dying before the age of five are more than one in three.

Recognizing that investments in education, health care, family planning, and nutrition generate strong and interrelated benefits, IDA has dramatically increased its support for these basic social services in recent years. IDA lending for education, health, and nutrition was over 33 percent of all IDA investment lending during 1994–95, compared with 19 percent in the late 1980s. IDA is playing a central role in supporting a number of new early childhood development projects that provide a full range of health and education benefits to children. Some examples are:

- Bolivia's Integrated Child Care Development Project: By the end of 1999, this project will have installed about 9,000 day-care centers to provide nonformal, home-based, integrated child development services to over 200,000 children aged six months to six years. Roughly 16 percent of all children living in urban areas will be covered by the project.

- Nigeria's Development Communications Project: Piloting the use of mass media to promote healthier early childhood development, this project provides educational television programs for children aged three to six years. For children without access to television in their homes, it supports the installation of televisions in child-care centers in fifteen local government authorities.

- India's First and Second Integrated Child Development Projects: These two projects are expected to reach about seventeen million preschool children in addition to about seven million pregnant and nursing women in four Indian states. One of the core goals is to provide a range of basic services, including nonformal preschool education, supplementary feeding, health and nutrition education, parenting education, and maternal and child health referrals.

Public Information Center, External Affairs Department, World Bank , "IDA—Saving and Improving Children's Lives," September 25, 1995.

Like the World Bank, they raise funds through members' contributions and by borrowing on international capital markets, and each has a soft-loan window similar to the World Bank's IDA. In today's global climate of free-flowing capital, questions have been raised whether regional development banks should be closed down and turned into purely aid-giving institutions through their soft-loan windows. Although this will surely be debated with varying intensity, depending on the bank in question, it is important to recognize that these banks are vital sources of funds for middle-tier countries for which access to private markets is precarious at best and that are not eligible for concessional loans. Regional development banks also fill an important role in providing policy and technical advice, and unlike the World Bank, they are allowed to lend to the private sector without government guarantee.

Inter-American Development Bank

The Washington-based Inter-American Development Bank (IDB) is the oldest of the regional banks, founded in 1959 by the United States and nineteen Latin American countries. The main function of IDB is to promote the investment of public and private capital in the region, using the region's own capital and mobilizing additional funds for economic and social projects. The bank also works to foster foreign trade and offers technical assistance in designing and implementing development plans. IDB now lends more to Latin America than does the World Bank. Unlike the voting structure of the World Bank, developing members of IDB hold the majority of votes, and there are specific constraints on the distribution of votes to ensure that the voting power of regional developing members is never reduced below 53.3 percent.[66] IDB identifies five critical areas as its priorities for the 1990s: social reform, productive and technical modernization, strengthening of the private sector, restructuring of the state, and support for greater involvement of all members in decision making. At the end of 1993, IDB's cumulative lending and technical cooperation was $65 billion, 38 percent of which was allocated for physical infrastructure, such as energy, transportation, and communication.[67]

African Development Bank

The African Development Bank (AfDB) is the most beleaguered of the regional banks. In 1995, it became the first multilateral development bank to lose its coveted triple-A rating, and its ongoing record of bad debt threatens future operations.[68] Founded in 1966 with the mandate to promote development projects for the economic and social advancement of its member states, AfDB currently directs the lowest percentage of aid (a mere 4 percent) to human development—a paltry amount, especially since the bank serves the world's poorest region.[69] In 1973, the African Development Fund (ADF) was established as AfDB's concessional arm, offering soft loans to its neediest members. However, years of poor management and politicization prompted many donor countries to withhold funds from ADF. By the end of 1994, AfDB's arrears were almost four times the 1990 level, with Zaire and Liberia holding 80 percent of the bank's delinquent loans. After a two-and-a-half-year delay, at its 1996 annual meeting, donor country members finally committed to three-year replenishments for ADF totaling $2.6 billion. The bank spent the early 1990s concentrating its efforts on reorganizing management, firing 70 percent of its management staff, and improving its lending portfolio. The ADF replenishment, although a mark of approval for these reform efforts, still fell $400 million short of the bank's initial request.

Asian Development Bank

Do developing countries that are able to attract more than $100 billion in private capital still need a government-run bank that makes annual commitments of about $5 billion? This question was raised at the 1996 annual meeting of the Asian Development Bank (ADB).[70] Twenty-nine years after its establishment, the ADB continues to provide technical assistance and lend funds to promote the economic and social progress of its members in the Asian and Pacific region. Although the region has witnessed a boom in economic progress, with sharp increases in growth rates, per capita income, and life expectancy, it continues to be the home of approximately three-quarters of the world's one billion poor people. Membership in the bank has grown to fifty-six members; forty are from the Asia-Pacific region, four of which are recent graduates from the ranks of borrowing countries: Hong Kong, Taiwan, China, and Korea. However, voting power continues to be dominated by developed countries, which hold 55 percent of the voting rights. The ADB's soft-loan arm, the Asian Development Fund, is intended to help the poorest countries in the region with forty-year interest-free loans. Unfortunately, the fund was in danger of running out of money in 1997, partly because the United States was in serious arrears on its contribution. In such a context, political arguments regarding contribution assessments are more frequent than loan disbursement decisions. Non-Asian members argue that the newly rich Asian countries, the "tigers," ought to increase their contributions; by the end of 1995, East Asian countries, with the exception of Japan, had contributed less than

0.3 percent of the resources for the fund. Meanwhile, other members argue that funds from the bank's ordinary lending program, which has been very successful, with some countries even repaying loans early, could be used to augment the fund.[71] In 1994, the ADB instituted a new policy that ensures that 40 percent of total loan volume and 50 percent of all projects focus on social and environmental sectors.[72]

Caribbean Development Bank

The Caribbean Development Bank (CDB) is the newest of the regional banks, established in 1970 to promote its members' economic cooperation and integration, with particular attention to the needs of the lesser-developed members. Membership consists of all eighteen of the Commonwealth Caribbean countries, plus Britain and Canada. The bank helps finance specific projects in the fields of agriculture, fisheries, livestock, tourism, mining, and others, with priority given to regional projects. A third of all CDB loans are concessional, offered through a variety of special funds.

Notes

1. Kunnibert Raffer and H. W. Singer, *The Foreign Aid Business: Economic Assistance and Development Co-operation* (Brookfield, Vt.: Edward Elgar Publishing, 1996), 40.
2. Ibid., 15.
3. Curt Tarnoff and Larry Q. Nowels, "U.S. Foreign Assistance: The Rationale, the Record, and the Challenges in the Post–Cold War Era," National Planning Association Report no. 275 (Washington, D.C.: NPA, 1994), 9.
4. Frances Moore Lappé, Joseph Collins, and David Kinley, *Aid as Obstacle: Twenty Questions about Our Foreign Aid and the Hungry* (San Francisco: Institute for Food and Development Policy, 1980), 29.
5. "Bretton Woods Revisited," *Economist*, July 9, 1994, 69–75.
6. Raffer and Singer, *Foreign Aid Business*, 48.
7. Ibid., 50.
8. "Beyond Band-Aids," *Economist*, March 23, 1996, 15.
9. World Bank Annual Report, 1994.
10. "Investment in Africa," *Economist*, November 9, 1996, 95.
11. William Savitt and Paula Bottorf, *Global Development: A Reference Handbook* (Denver: ABC-CLIO, 1995), 128.
12. Bruce Rich, *Mortgaging the Earth: The World Bank, Environmental Impoverishment, and the Crisis of Development* (Boston: Beacon Press, 1994), 83.
13. Ibid., 91.
14. Raffer and Singer, *Foreign Aid Business*, 47.
15. Rich, *Mortgaging the Earth*, 99.

16. Raffer and Singer, *Foreign Aid Business*, 47.

17. Nicholas Eberstadt, *American Foreign Aid and American Purpose* (Washington, D.C.: American Enterprise Institute for Public Policy Research, 1988), 42.

18. Lappé, Collins, and Kinley, *Aid as Obstacle*, 46.

19. Rich, *Mortgaging the Earth*, 27.

20. Ibid., 28.

21. Graham Hancock, *Lords of Poverty: The Power, Prestige, and Corruption of the International Aid Business* (New York: Atlantic Monthly Press, 1989), 131.

22. Another example of the bank's disastrous impact on the environment is a coal mining and power plant scheme in Singrauli, India, that is one of the largest single sources of carbon emissions on earth. See Rich's *Mortgaging the Earth* for additional examples.

23. UNICEF, "Adjustment with a Human Face," in *State of the World's Children 1987* (New York: Oxford University Press, 1987), 91.

24. Walden Bello, *Dark Victory: The United States, Structural Development, and Global Poverty* (Oakland, Calif.: Institute for Food and Development Policy, 1994), 26.

25. John Clark, *Democratizing Development: The Role of Voluntary Organizations* (West Hartford, Conn.: Kumarian Press, 1991), 178.

26. Robert E. Wood, "Rethinking Economic Aid," in *Foreign Aid toward the Millennium*, ed. Steven W. Hook (Boulder, Colo.: Lynne Rienner, 1996).

27. UNICEF, *State of the World's Children 1987*, 94.

28. Ibid., 93.

29. Clark, *Democratizing Development*, 179.

30. UNDP, *Human Development Report 1994* (New York: Oxford University Press, 1994), 75.

31. Bello, *Dark Victory*, 40.

32. Clark, *Democratizing Development*, 179, 181.

33. Ibid., 178.

34. Raffer and Singer, *Foreign Aid Business*, 155.

35. Quoted in Carol Lancaster "Governance and Development: The Views from Washington," *IDS Bulletin* 24 (January 1993): 9.

36. Ibid.

37. UNICEF, "Adjustment with a Human Face."

38. Ibid., 93.

39. Bello, *Dark Victory*, 52.

40. Frances Stewart, "The Many Faces of Adjustment," *World Development* 19, no. 12 (1991): 1852.

41. Clark, *Democratizing Development*, 184.

42. Bello, *Dark Victory*, 34.

43. Ibid., 55.

44. Jeffrey Sachs, "Growth in Africa," *Economist*, June 29, 1996, 19–21.

45. Quoted in Savitt and Bottorf, *Global Development*, 12.

46. Bill Rau, *From Feast to Famine: Official Cures and Grassroots Remedies to Africa's Food Crisis* (London: Zed Books, 1991), 101.

47. Richard Jolly, "Adjustment with a Human Face," *World Development* 19, no. 12 (1991): 1816.

48. Ibid.

49. UNICEF, *State of the World's Children 1987*, 95–7.

50. As Chapter 3 describes, the IMF and World Bank worked closely throughout the 1980s in designing and implementing their similar and complementary aid packages.

51. Stewart, "Many Faces of Development," 1857.

52. Quoted in Raffer and Singer, *Foreign Aid Business*, 165.
53. "Mr. Wolfensohn's New Clients," *Economist*, April 20, 1996, 63–4.
54. "Mr. Wolfensohn Sets the Score," *Economist*, October 5, 1996, 95.
55. Ibid.
56. World Bank, *How the World Bank Works with Nongovernmental Organizations* (Washington, D.C.: World Bank, 1990), 16.
57. Rich, *Mortgaging the Earth*, 181.
58. "All of a Sudden Every Banker Is a World Banker," *Economist*, July 27, 1996, 61–2.
59. Steven W. Hook, *National Interest and Foreign Aid* (Boulder, Colo.: Lynne Rienner, 1995), 31.
60. Steven W. Hook, ed., *Foreign Aid toward the Millennium* (Boulder, Colo.: Lynne Rienner, 1996), 9.
61. Robert F. Zimmerman and Steven Hook, "The Assault on U.S. Foreign Aid," in *Foreign Aid toward the Millennium*, 61.
62. Hook, *Foreign Aid toward the Millennium*, 3.
63. UNDP, *Human Development Report 1994*, 62.
64. According to UNDP figures. Marc J. Cohen, "The Road Not Taken—The United States Government and Hunger," in *Hunger 1994* (Silver Spring, Md.: Bread for the World Institute, 1993).
65. UNDP, *Human Development Report 1992* (New York: Oxford University Press, 1992), 6.
66. Raffer and Singer, *Foreign Aid Business*, 56.
67. Savitt and Bottorf, *Global Development*, 226.
68. Raffer and Singer, *Foreign Aid Business*, 57.
69. UNDP, *Human Development Report 1994*, 73.
70. "The Asian Development Bank: Help Yourselves," *Economist*, May 4, 1996, 78.
71. Ibid.
72. Overseas Development Institute, "Rethinking the Role of Multilateral Development Bank," ODI briefing paper, November 1996, 5.

3

International Monetary Fund

T HE INTERNATIONAL MONETARY FUND (IMF) is not officially
considered an aid-giving institution. It is neither a bank nor a development agency. However, it merits consideration here because it is a crucial player in the world of finance in the global South, and its programs
have an enormous effect on aid recipients' budgets, balances of payments,
and their domestic and economic policies.

Like the World Bank, the IMF was established at the Bretton Woods
conference in July 1944. In response to the economic turbulence wreaked
by the depression and the war, two economists, Harry Dexter White and
John Maynard Keynes, proposed a system that would provide for the unrestricted conversion of one currency into another, eliminate restrictions and
practices such as competitive devaluations, and establish a clear and
unequivocal value for each currency. They called for the establishment of a
permanent international organization that could promote international
economic cooperation while supervising this system, and in 1945, the
International Monetary Fund came into official existence when twenty-
nine countries signed its Articles of Agreement.

The IMF is governed by a board of governors on which each member
government is represented. However, decision-making power is vested with
the twenty-one members of the executive board, whose voting power is
determined by members' quotas, which reflect their shares in world output, trade, and foreign exchange reserves. Five executive directors are
appointed by the five members with the largest quotas (the United States,
United Kingdom, Germany, France, and Japan), with the United States
holding approximately 21 percent of all voting power.[1] Many Asian countries complain that the economic growth of developing countries, especially those in Asia, has not been adequately reflected in the allocation of
quotas. Using a rough estimate of the defining measures, developing countries should have about 40 percent of the IMF's quota, but the distribution
is widely out of line.[2] Most IMF funds that go toward loans and credits
come from members' quotas or capital subscriptions. All members contribute relative to their own economic size, and the more a member contributes, the more it can borrow in times of need.

Although the fund is most commonly associated with the billions of dollars it pumped into the economic system during the debt crisis, its primary function is one of surveillance and analysis. Its power over developing countries is immense, but it has little more than the power of advice over the economies of industrialized nations. It conducts annual bilateral consultations with individual countries, multilateral surveillance twice a year, and constant program monitoring. The IMF also maintains an extensive program of technical assistance through staff missions to member countries in the areas of central banking, balance-of-payment accounting, taxation, and other financial matters.

When the fund began operations in 1947, one of its primary functions was to monitor and ensure the observance of the exchange rate rules, which at the time were tied to the value of gold. During the 1970s, unstable monetary and financial conditions throughout the world forced the IMF to admit that the system of fixed exchange rates was not working and to move to a system of flexible exchange rates. In 1978, a flexible exchange rate was legalized, and the fund amended its constitution to broaden its functions to include the supervision of economic policies that influence balance of payments in this new economic environment.[3] Today the fund is made up of 179 member countries that have pledged to cooperate to maintain a productive and global economic environment that encourages trade, creates jobs, expands economic activities, and raises living standards throughout the world.

Most relevant to our discussion of international aid is the fund's financial assistance activities, whereby credits and loans are extended to members with balance-of-payments difficulties. As of August 31, 1996, the IMF was disbursing credits to sixty-one countries for an approved amount of $44.5 billion.[4] During the 1980s, following the debt crisis, over half of all developing nations were recipients of IMF loans, all of which required the recipient's agreement to a number of radical reforms—the IMF-prescribed stabilization program.

The Debt Crisis and the IMF's Response

On August 30, 1982, the Mexican government announced that it was unable to meet the payments on the principal of almost $20 billion of its public-sector debt owed to about fourteen hundred foreign banks, effectively setting off the debt crisis. By the end of the year, thirty-five countries were in arrears.[5]

The standard explanation is that the debt crisis was caused by a dangerous combination of unforeseeable events. First, in the mid-1970s, oil prices rose to their highest level, flooding banks with massive deposits from oil-rich nations. Eager to find new customers, banks turned to the global South, where countries were equally eager for an infusion of capital to offset their rising energy costs. For non-OPEC developing countries, debt to private banks rose from 20 percent in 1971 to 46 percent in 1982; for the newly industrializing countries, 67 percent of their total debt was owed to private banks.[6] Then, in 1980–82, interest rates turned sharply higher while commodity export prices tumbled to new lows. In its 1982 annual report, the IMF stated that "non-oil primary commodity prices in mid 1982 were lower than at any other time for more than three decades." Because developing countries were typically dependent on just one or two commodities as a means to gain foreign exchange, this drop in prices left them unable to service their mounting debts. Related to this problem was the decline, in both volume and terms, of international trade. For instance, in 1981, Tanzanians had to produce four times as much cotton or ten times as much tobacco to buy a truck as they did five years earlier.[7]

Corrupt Southern governments only exacerbated the situation. Mercenary leaders in many developing countries continued to borrow and spend as if nothing had changed, while instituting absurd regulatory regimes of permits and licenses that squashed farmers and entrepreneurs while lining the pockets of bureaucrats. One of the most disturbing examples of such corruption was in the former Zaire, where President Mobutu was said to have stashed away in personal foreign accounts assets equal to his country's entire external debt.[8]

Gradually, all sources of new capital dried up, and debt service exceeded revenues to a convoluted extent—in 1987, the IMF received some $8.6 billion more in loan repayments and interest charges than it lent out.[9] Money that might have been used to build health clinics or primary schools went instead to Western banks and multinational institutions, while indebted countries dumped more and more of their resources at reduced rates, thereby depleting nonrenewable resources and further depressing prices. For many countries, there was only one way out: compliance with the rigorous policy reforms demanded by the World Bank and the IMF in exchange for renewed access to international capital. Similar and complementary to the World Bank's structural adjustment policies, the IMF's stabilization programs required a combination (or all) of the following measures: devaluation of currency, reduction in government spending, introduction of wage controls, increase in interest rates, withdrawal of government from regulation and subsidy, privatization, and removal of barriers to foreign investment and trade. In essence, the reforms were driven by the international financial institution's belief that the only way developing countries could emerge from debt would be to "export their way out."[10] However, this was completely contingent upon a growing global economy, which was not the reality at the time. Even the economic superpower the United States had become a debtor nation, with its external debt projected in 1990 to be greater than that of all underdeveloped countries combined.[11] The World Bank acknowledged, in its 1983 annual report, that "the world economy must regain the momentum it achieved in 1976–78, without that, the developing countries' prospects are bleak indeed."[12] Yet despite these concerns, the World Bank and the IMF continued to urge their Southern customers to ride "the world economy roller-coaster"[13]—whatever the costs.

While the IMF rationalized its policies as simply creating a positive business climate, the vicious circle of poverty only accelerated throughout the decade. The human costs—the rising rates of malnutrition and infant mortality—are well documented. Violent deaths were added to the toll as "IMF riots" erupted in countries such as Peru and Zambia when IMF austerity measures were imposed. The environment also suffered the consequences of this new business climate—the drive to increase exports accelerated the exploitation of raw materials and natural resources in countries such as Tanzania and Ghana. In Tanzania, the push for exports led to a 25 percent loss of forest from 1980 to 1993. As the rates of poverty rose, landless families were pushed into environmentally sensitive areas where, in order to survive the day, they were often forced to compromise the future—razing plots in the rain forests, plowing steep slopes, and shortening fallow periods, all of which only perpetuated their poverty.[14] Even the IMF eventually (and quietly) acknowledged that its stabilization programs "pressed for measures that were more severe than necessary."[15]

In addition to the human and environmental costs of IMF policies, leaders of developing countries had to face the political consequences of adjustment. The recent presidential race in Zambia illustrates the political costs of compliance with IMF demands. When Frederick Chiluba was elected president in 1991, becoming the first president to oust his predecessor via the ballot box, the election was lauded as a model of democratic transition. A mere two years later, with IMF funding secured in the interim, Chiluba's party stood to lose power, not to mention public support. What had happened? For the first time in thirty years, state hospitals and clinics were charging fees; there were tariffs for water and electricity; and subsidies for fuel and mealie meal, the staple food, were long gone. With the trade liberalization measures, also prescribed by the stabilization program, Zambia's industries were fighting a losing battle in competition with imports; three-quarters of the textile factories closed in one year, and almost a third of the commercial farmers stopped production, unable to sell their record wheat crop due to a glut of subsidized U.S. flour imported from South Africa. As the headline of an *Economist* article that covered the story suggested, "Blame the IMF."[16]

By 1989, banks and creditor governments alike came to the painful real-ization that debt reduction would have to be considered if recovery was to be achieved. The new U.S. secretary of the treasury, Nicholas Brady, pro-posed a three-year plan, the essence of which was the introduction of offi-cial collateral from the IMF, the World Bank, the Inter-American Bank, and the Japanese government in exchange for a reduction in bank claims. Calling it "voluntary debt reduction," banks were able keep the same expected value of repayment by accepting greater security in exchange for lower claims. By 1994, there had been eighteen Brady deals covering $191 billion in eligible debt, forgiving $61 billion in debt equivalent and requiring less than $25 billion in official agency enhancements.[17] The plan's primary goal—to prevent the collapse of big banks, which undoubtedly would have triggered an international financial crisis—was certainly achieved. The plan also made an important contribution in restoring confidence in Southern economies; private capital inflows resumed, and debtor countries' access to voluntary capital markets was restored.[18] The secondary goal of economic growth in debtor countries was not as successful, although the plan's advo-cates found comfort in their achievement in transforming the conventional model of third-world development from inward-oriented, state-interven-tionist, populist strategies toward trade liberalization, privatization, deregu-lation, and fiscal reform.[19] Reform of developing countries' economies was clearly needed and was not without its accomplishments. However, the pri-ority was always to correct the *banking* crisis, not the crisis of hunger and poverty. So it is not surprising that with such priorities in mind, the medicine often ended up being more painful than the disease.

Thanks to the advocacy work of international organizations such as UNICEF, the world was forced to witness the human face of the debt crisis and the costs of the remedies prescribed to solve it. However, there was another less tangible but equally destructive cost of structural adjustment and stabilization policies, and that was the damage done to the potential for future North-South partnerships in global development. When strong Northern governments and institutions prescribe a cure for an economic crisis that they had a hand in creating, and that cure suggests Southern culpability—and penance—for the crisis, the hope for a future of genuine global partnership does not look promising.[20]

Debt Today

Jubilant declarations in the early 1990s that the debt crisis was over must be understood within the context of how the debt crisis was defined from the outset. As William Savitt points out, the debt crisis was always a crisis of international banking—not a development crisis: "even at its height in the mid-1980s, the crisis that made the headlines was never . . . about global poverty, or hunger, or slashed AIDS education and high bread prices, was never, in fact about the South—the debtors—at all."[21] And so it was the crisis of international banking that was declared over by the beginning of 1990. Of course, how much banks will collect of the outstanding arrears owed by third-world nations, and under what terms, remains an important question for shareholders and executives. But for one-half of the debt equation, for the lenders, the debt crisis is finished, and it has been for some time.[22]

For the other half—for the borrowers, the governments, and, above all, the people of the South—the crisis grinds on. The World Bank and the IMF classify forty poor countries as "heavily indebted," meaning that they have debts of at least twice their annual export revenues. By the end of 1994, these countries owed over $200 billion among them. In even worse shape are those countries classified as "severely indebted low-income countries" (SILICs), which have debt-to-GNP ratios of larger than 80 percent. In 1995, there were thirty-two countries in this category, twenty-five of them in sub-Saharan Africa.[23] However, the community of borrowers is hardly a homogeneous group, and it is increasingly necessary to draw important distinctions. From the banking perspective, the debt crisis was concentrated in Latin America, where governments received the majority of their loans from private banks looking for a profit. However, the region that suffered the most as a result of both crushing debt and structural reforms was, without a doubt, Africa (Figure 3.1). Most of the lending to Africa was not the commercial bank loans that captivated the world but bilateral and nation-to-nation credits due to governments. Multilateral agencies account for about a quarter of the debt, but because law requires that they be the first to get paid, they end up receiving nearly 40 percent of all debt-service payments. So although the crisis may be over in terms of U.S. banks' return to profitability and capital infusions returning to Latin America, Africa remains in crisis—a crisis that is measurable in undelivered social services, endemic food shortages and malnutrition, and rotting infrastructure.[24] Even if the continent grows as the World Bank projects that it will, Africans will likely have to wait another forty years or so before the economy allows their wages to rise to the level they were at in the mid-1970s.[25]

Given the severity of IMF demands and their crushing impact on the most vulnerable citizens of debtor countries, it is not surprising that the Southern perception of the IMF is far from rosy. Proof of this can be found in today's headlines. A January 17, 1997, *New York Times* article reported that protests in Haiti erupted into violence, costing one young man his life as demonstrators took to the streets, burning tires and

Figure 3.1 Rising debt

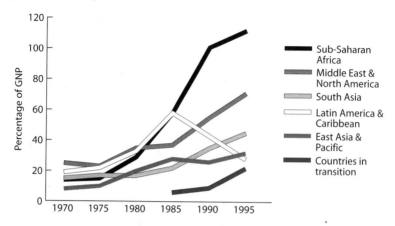

Total debt as a percentage of GNP increased in all regions over the period 1972–93. Latin America's high debt levels of the 1980s have since fallen. Sub-Saharan Africa's debt, which has continued to soar, now surpasses its GNP.

Note: Data for sub-Saharan Africa excludes South Africa.
Source: UNICEF, *The State of the World's Children 1996* (Oxford and New York: Oxford University Press, 1996), 53. Based on data from World Bank, *World Debt Tables 1994–95*, vol. 2 (Washington, D.C.: World Bank, 1994).

demanding that the government suspend negotiations with the IMF. The small country, known for its thriving civil society, is home to the Anti–International Monetary Fund Committee, made up of more than 160 grassroots organizations.[26]

In 1994, even Northern banks and governments were found to be premature in their assessment of the end of the banking crisis when Mexico was once again the scene of what was called "the first big financial crisis in the emerging market era." Vast amounts of short-term dollar debt were falling due, and the country had virtually no reserves. Panic in the financial community spread while private investors jumped out of almost every emerging market, causing a ripple effect of damage to developing economies from Brazil to Thailand. The IMF reacted quickly, committing to lend $17 billion virtually overnight (and without obtaining the necessary approval from the board, as certain disgruntled members would hasten to add). It was the most money the IMF had ever lent, representing almost a fifth of its liquid assets. President Clinton also pushed through a highly controversial bailout package that amounted to a loan of $12.5 billion. Like the crisis before it, this was a banking crisis, and the IMF's and the donor governments' motivation was not to protect the Mexican victims of the crisis but to bail out the short-term bondholders.[27] Michel Camdessus, managing director of the IMF, acknowledged that the fund's failure to anticipate the Mexican crisis exposed "a global problem with the culture of the fund,"[28] and he ordered a reexamination of the institution's short-comings. However, typical of the fund's long-standing tradition of secrecy, the report was never released to the public. By the summer of 1996, this crisis too was declared over. The gloomy predictions of the end of the emerging market phenomenon were not fulfilled, and in early 1997, Mexico announced that it would repay $4.7 billion of the $10.5 billion it still owes the United States ahead of schedule.

With private capital once again pouring into developing countries, it is easy to lose sight of the fact that the wealthier countries are receiving almost all of it. For the majority of countries in sub-Saharan Africa, the end to their debt crisis is far from sight. Instead of flows of capital, they are witnessing shrinking aid allocations, leaving them trapped in a vicious circle whereby their crippling debt prevents them from making vital investments in health and education, and the dearth of private investment only increases their reliance on foreign aid. The argument for debt relief strengthens every day, as the weight of debt becomes more and more unbearable. Approximately forty of the world's poorest countries are classified by the World Bank as having an "unsustainably high" debt burden; their total debt is more than 220 percent of their exports. Granted, some of these countries are mired in governmental corruption that is even more oppressive than their debt, and for them, debt relief would offer little comfort, as it would surely only line the pockets of well-placed polititians.

The IMF and the World Bank have always been wary of the idea of providing debt relief, even to countries that were actively pursuing economic reform. Arguing that it would set a bad example and might harm their own financial health, they stalled on debt-relief propositions for years. Eventually, increasing pressure by NGOs helped them realize that it is counterintuitive to continue to ignore those reforming but struggling countries. A recent debt-reduction plan concedes the writing off of 90 percent of bilateral debt to those countries that still have unsustainable levels of debt after following IMF-prescribed policies for at least three years. If after three years of reform their debt remains above a sustainable level, the IMF will agree to begin to reduce multilateral debt.[29] Debt reduction inched closer to actually providing relief in October 1996, when the World Bank and the IMF announced a new plan called the Heavily Indebted Poor Country (HIPC) Initiative, which aims to cut the debt burdens of up to forty-one countries to sustainable levels over six years (Table 3.1). The key to the plan is the creation of the HIPC fund, to which the World Bank and other multilateral creditors will contribute to build up resources to relieve debt to sustainable levels. The World Bank pledged $500 million to the fund and promised another $2 billion, provided other creditors pay their share.[30] The IMF, meanwhile, has been reluctant to contribute any of

Table 3.1   Highly indebted poor countries in Africa, 1997

Country	Total External Debt ($ mn)	Net Present Value of Debt[a] ($ mn)	Total Debt Service ($ mn)	Exports of Goods and Services ($ mn)	Debt Service/ Exports (%)	Net Present Value of Debt/Exports (%)[b]
Burkina Faso	1,267	646	48	366	13.2	176.5
Côte d'Ivoire	18,952	16,596	1,046	4,527	23.1	366.6
Ethiopia	5,221	3,435	155	1,140	13.6	301.3
Guinea-Bissau	894	582	16	48	33.7	1,212.5
Mali	3,066	1,805	80	656	12.2	275.2
Mozambique	5,781	4,429	173	485	35.7	913.2
São Tomé/Prin.	277	142	2	13	16.2	1,092.3
Uganda	3,564	1,868	137	642	21.3	291.0

[a] The sum of all future debt-service obligations on existing debt, discounted at market interest rates.
[b] Debt is deemed "unsustainable" if this ratio is higher than 250 percent.

Notes: (1) All figures are for 1995. (2) mn = million.
Source: Africa Recovery 10, no. 4 (January–April 1997), 10. Based on data in World Bank, Global Development Finance, 1997.

its own funds, proposing instead to raise money from members to replenish the Enhanced Structural Adjustment Facility.[31] The tough performance criteria in the framework of the new debt relief initiative has led many critics, such as the Economic Commission for Africa (ECA), to accuse the IMF of a minimalist approach that offers "as little debt reduction, for as few countries, as late as possible."[32] ECA also claims that the World Bank and the IMF have structured the package so as to limit the costs to themselves, revealing paralyzing conflict of interest and lack of objectivity. Although it continues to be debated whether the HIPC package would have been better balanced if an independent commission had been in charge of its design, the World Bank and the IMF have inarguably taken an enormous first step in admitting, for the first time, that debts can be canceled. In March 1997, Uganda was selected as the first beneficiary of the new debt-relief plan, and it is expected that over $300 million of the country's $1.9 billion external debt will be cut.

The IMF and the World Bank

The IMF and the World Bank tend to be referred to in one breath. Even their names add to the confusion surrounding what the two agencies do. One of the founders, John Maynard Keynes, admitted that he thought that the World Bank should be called a fund and the IMF should be called a bank. At their founding, they were called the Bretton Woods twins, and in recent years, many have argued that they have become identical twins, bringing into question the necessity of maintaining them both. Before considering whether their similarities have rendered one obsolete, it is necessary to step back and compare them objectively.

Despite profound similarities between the IMF and the World Bank in membership, philosophy, activities, and objectives, the primary goals of the two institutions remain distinct. The bank is primarily a development institution, and the fund seeks to maintain an orderly system of receipts and payments between nations. In many ways, the World Bank is certainly more like a fund. Its goal is to provide loans to encourage economic development, whereas the IMF oversees monetary and exchange rate policies. Although the fund does actually have a fund from which countries can borrow, it is not primarily a lending institution. Whereas the World Bank works somewhat like an investment bank—borrowing from investors to lend to recipients—the IMF works sort of like a credit union whose funds come from membership fees and quota subscriptions and whose members have access to that common pool of resources in times of need.[33] All member nations, rich and poor, have the right to financial assistance from the IMF, unlike the World Bank, which lends only to governments of developing nations. Usually, money received from the fund has to be repaid within three to five years, and in no case more than ten years.[34]

Since the 1970s, collaboration between the bank and the fund has grown closer than ever. The bank realized that economic development works only when sound underlying financial and economic policies are in place, and the fund recognized that short-term adaptations of financial policies do little to correct the long-term inefficient use of resources or the lack of adequate resources.[35] The result of this recognition was the establishment in 1988 of the Structural Adjustment Facility, which was set up to coordinate the two institutions' surveillance and enforcement activities, especially in sub-Saharan Africa (where thirty-six of the region's forty-seven countries have undergone structural adjustment programs administered by the World Bank or the IMF). It was at this point, many argue, that the two institutions became practically indistinguishable, "as both became the enforcers of the North's economic rollback strategy. The unification of the IMF and the World Bank treatments came to be known to its patients as 'shock therapy.'"[36]

The difference between the World Bank's structural adjustment and the IMF's stabilization programs is "one of time horizon and range of instruments."[37] The fund is concerned with financing and correcting balance-of-payments deficits in the short term, whereas structural adjustment policies are intended to encourage a sustainable, long-term balance-of-payments position. IMF conditionality aims at reducing inflationary pressures in the economy by cutting government expenditures; raising taxes; and encouraging saving, monetary discipline, trade liberalization, and stable exchange rates. World Bank conditionality aims to improve the supply efficiency of the economy by such measures as privatization and the promotion of free markets.[38] The distinction between the two policies has become blurred, and based on the IMF's recent funding activities in Mexico, it appears that the fog will only thicken.

A final similarity between the World Bank and the IMF worth noting is their well-established reputations of secrecy. World Bank and IMF activities and evaluations are notoriously private, although the World Bank has recently made significant strides in allowing an outside eye to peek inside. Meanwhile, the IMF still operates behind tightly closed doors. Minutes of meetings are sealed, as are annual reviews of each member country. Jeffrey Sachs, director of Harvard's Institute for International Development, urges the IMF or the public, if necessary, to pull down this protective wall, noting that "the IMF, strangely enough, is without any professional scrutiny in the world. It has the right to be exposed to the glare of bright light."[39]

The shifting world order has opened new opportunities for the two institutions' paths to once again diverge toward distinct and mutually useful goals. As the World Bank begins to focus more closely on the human development needs of the global South, the IMF is taking a leading role in aiding the postcommunist countries of the former Soviet Union and Eastern Europe. The globalization of financial markets now allows for unprecedented levels of capital to travel at the speed of light; private currency traders trade $1.3 trillion a day, an amount that exceeds the total foreign exchange reserves of all governments. Such forces clearly cause a power shift whereby governments increasingly have only the appearance of free choice when setting economic rules. As Jessica Mathews argues in a recent *Foreign Affairs* article, "markets are setting de facto rules enforced by their own power."[40] If, as Mathews argues, a globalized economy signals a loss of autonomy and power for governments, the role of the IMF in guiding and monitoring economic policies will become all the more challenging in the coming millennium.

Notes

1. Frances Moore Lappé, Joseph Collins, and David Kinley, *Aid as Obstacle: Twenty Questions about Our Foreign Aid and the Hungry* (San Francisco: Institute for Food and Development Policy, 1980), 125.
2. Jeffrey Sachs, "Beyond Bretton Woods," *Economist*, October 1, 1994, 26.
3. David D. Driscoll, *The IMF and the World Bank: How Do They Differ?* (Washington, D.C.: International Monetary Fund, 1989), 11.

4. IMF, "IMF at a Glance," information sheet, September 1996.
5. Robert E. Wood, "Rethinking Economic Aid," in *Foreign Aid toward the Millennium*, ed. Steven W. Hook (Boulder, Colo.: Lynne Rienner, 1996), 232.
6. Ibid., 263.
7. Ibid., 267.
8. Ibid., 251.
9. William Savitt and Paula Bottorf, *Global Development: A Reference Handbook* (Denver: ABC-CLIO, 1995), 11.
10. Wood, "Rethinking Economic Aid," 231.
11. Ibid.
12. Quoted in ibid., 321.
13. Ibid.
14. Alan Durning, "Ending Poverty," in *State of the World's Children 1990* (New York: Oxford University Press, 1990), 145.
15. Robert Cassen and associates, *Does Aid Work? Report to an Intergovernmental Task Force,* 2nd edition (New York: Oxford University Press, 1994), 62, 66.
16. "Blame the IMF," *Economist*, November 20, 1993, 47.
17. William Cline, "Managing International Debt," *Economist*, February 18, 1995, 18.
18. Ibid.
19. Ibid.
20. Savitt and Bottorf, *Global Development*, 13.
21. Ibid., 10.
22. Ibid.
23. Overseas Development Institute, "Poor Country Debt: A Never Ending Story," in *ODI briefing paper* (London: ODI, March 1995).
24. Savitt and Bottorf, *Global Development*, 10.
25. Sachs, "Beyond Bretton Woods," 24.
26. "Protests Erupt across Haiti as Leaders Push Austerity," *New York Times*, January 17, 1997, A3.
27. "Hazardous Morals," *Economist*, February 11, 1995, 19.
28. Quoted in Jeff Gerth and Elaine Sciolino, "IMF Head: He Speaks and Money Talks," *New York Times*, April 2, 1996, A10.
29. "Multilateral Debt: Lost Souls," *Economist*, March 23, 1996, 81.
30. "Investment in Africa," *Economist*, November 9, 1996, 95.
31. The Structural Adjustment Facility and Enhanced Structural Adjustment Facility were set up in 1986 and 1987, respectively. With initial resources of about $12 billion, the facilities were designed to lend to low-income countries, establishing a procedure to build consensus on an adjustment program.
32. Quoted in "ECA Analyzes Concerns over HIPC Package," *Africa Recovery* 10, no. 4 (January–April 1997), 12.
33. Driscoll, "IMF and the World Bank," 4.
34. Ibid., 5.
35. Ibid., 13.
36. Quoted in Walden Bello, *Dark Victory: The United States, Structural Adjustment, and Global Poverty* (Oakland, Calif.: Institute for Food and Development Policy, 1994), 30.
37. Cassen, *Does Aid Work?*, 69.
38. Kunnibert Raffer and H. W. Singer, *The Foreign Aid Business: Economic Assistance and Development Co-operation* (Brookfield, Vt.: Edward Edgar Publish-

ing, 1996), 156.

39. Quoted in Gerth and Sciolino, "IMF Head," A10.

40. Jessica Mathews, "Power Shift," *Foreign Affairs* 76, no. 1 (1997): 57.

4

United Nations

THE UNITED NATIONS (UN) came into existence on October 24, 1945, as a joint commitment by the fifty original members to work together to avoid another war on the scale of the one that had just ended. The UN is organized under six main organs, all of which are dedicated to the preservation of, or struggle for, global peace: the General Assembly, the Security Council, the Economic and Social Council (ECOSOC), the Trusteeship Council, the International Court of Justice, and the Secretariat. The UN's funding comes from member governments' contributions and grants, and unlike the Bretton Woods institutions, voting power is not determined by members' contributions or wealth but is instead allocated on a one-country, one-vote basis. The fact that the world's wealthiest nations do not have a monopoly on voting power, as they do in the World Bank and the IMF, arguably frees the UN to design programs that tend to be more responsive to the needs of individual countries rather than driven by profit or commercial and strategic interests. Four-fifths of the UN budget is allocated to economic and social development, and seventeen specialized agencies work on various aspects of the development process, supervised and supposedly coordinated by ECOSOC.

Despite the recent media attention on the United Nations revolving around issues of its leadership, unpaid dues by members, and proposals for reform, the specialized agencies of the UN remain, for most people, somewhat of a mystery. With its greeting cards and celebrity spokespersons, UNICEF is the only UN agency likely to be broadly recognized. The other specialized agencies do, however, tend to receive some international attention for their role in coordinating the well-known UN conferences. Notwithstanding the often ludicrous costs of these conferences, they serve an important function in raising global awareness of key development issues, such as the environment and gender. The 1990 World Summit for Children, organized by UNICEF, was the largest global summit meeting ever held and witnessed the agreement of over 150 world leaders on a series of specific goals for improving the lives of children. The 1993 UN Conference on Human Rights marked the first time that the alleviation of poverty was recognized as a basic human right. And the 1992 Conference on the Human Environment focused international attention on the health of the planet and governments' role in linking development with environmental protection. In short, UN conferences help establish international norms for the way governments treat their citizens and serve to mobilize action to address global problems.

Described below are the UN agencies most directly involved in the provision of assistance, both directly and indirectly, to developing countries.

Food and Agriculture Organization (FAO)

FAO was founded in 1945 and was the first UN specialized agency established after World War II, with the primary goal of achieving global food security. Today, FAO is the largest agency within the UN system, with 174 member nations and an annual budget of roughly $650 million (in 1996–97). The four main tasks of FAO are:

1. To carry out a comprehensive program of technical advice and assistance for the agricultural community;
2. To collect, analyze, and disseminate information;
3. To advise governments on policy and planning; and
4. To provide a neutral forum where governments and experts can discuss food problems.

FAO is also active in the provision of emergency assistance, in collaboration with the World Food Program. Technical assistance is provided through FAO's field projects in developing countries, which are designed to strengthen local institutions, provide training, and develop new techniques to increase crop production. FAO has made significant progress preventing soil erosion, designing pest control programs, and perfecting breeds of local crops. However, it has also been criticized for duplicating the work of other UN agencies—and doing so less efficiently, hampered by the huge bureaucracy at the agency's headquarters in Rome, where more than half of its employees work. One of FAO's unique strengths, however, has been the establishment of a Global Information and Early Warning System, which monitors global food stocks based on nutritional and socioeconomic indicators and issues monthly reports on the world food situation. The reporting of food stocks and production is clearly an important function, and a controversial one. FAO recently published a study on the prospects of food and agriculture that projected continued improvements in per capita food supplies to the year 2010. This drew fire from Worldwatch Institute, a respected global environmental research institute, which accused FAO of "misleading political leaders" by "overestimating food production." FAO insists that there is, and continues to be, an unacceptable imbalance in food production among the different regions in the world, caused by a downward trend of investment in agriculture and the low level of research and transfer of technology in developing countries. The World Food Summit, held in Rome in November 1996, was convened by FAO in large part to address these unacceptable trends. At the summit, the director-general of FAO articulated the warped priorities at play in the world when he reported that the national budget for the UN food agency is "less than what nine developed countries spend on dog and cat food in six days and . . . less than 5 percent of what the inhabitants of one developed country spend each year on slimming products to counter the effect of overeating."[1]

International Fund for Agricultural Development (IFAD)

IFAD was established in 1977 as one of the outcomes of the 1974 World Food Conference. It is the only UN agency with the single mandate to promote progress by and for the rural poor, and toward this end, it mobilizes financial aid in the form of concessionary loans for agricultural programs, helping to finance rural development projects and agricultural production. The bulk of IFAD's resources is available in soft loans to the poorest developing countries. The loans are repayable over fifty years and are designed to diversify and improve food production systems, with priority given to small-scale farming initiatives. IFAD also has a separate special program that supports projects in sub-Saharan African countries suffering from drought and desertification. IFAD is often noted for its success in making multilateral structures more democratic, and active participation by beneficiaries of their programs is sought. In 1994, IFAD's membership consisted of 22 Northern (OECD) countries, 12 oil-exporting (OPEC) countries, and 116 developing countries. Despite the fact that 60 percent of IFAD's funding comes from OECD nations, votes are divided equally among the three groups.[2] During IFAD's first ten years, it funded over two hundred projects in ninety countries.

United Nations Development
Programme (UNDP)

UNDP is the world's largest source of multilateral grant assistance, with an annual budget of roughly $1 billion, providing "a greater variety of services to more people in more countries than any other development institution."[3] UNDP promotes economic growth and higher standards of living by supporting (not implementing) projects in agriculture, health, housing, public administration, industry, trade, and other fields in 175 countries. With field offices in 134 countries, UNDP has unprecedented field presence, and it has an important role in coordinating the activities of a variety of agencies and developing sustainable relationships with local governments and communities. The majority of UNDP staff are locally recruited nationals. UNDP is the largest source of technical assistance to developing countries, allocating more than half of its budget to technical expertise. UNDP uses an internationally recognized formula to allocate its funds; this indicative planning figure projects the amount of aid that will be available to a country over a five-year period based on population, per capita GNP, and other welfare criteria. Such criteria obviously identify the poorest countries as the primary aid recipients—87 percent of UNDP's resources are allocated to the world's poorest nations, but critics complain that such a system fails to consider recipient nations' human rights or governance records. In 1986, UNDP established a Division for Women in Development and a Division for Non-Governmental Organizations. It also administers a number of special-purpose funds, such as UNIFEM, which provides direct financial and technical support to low-income women in developing countries and funds activities that involve women in decision making in their communities and countries.

Critics charge that UNDP tries to do too much and, as a result, spreads itself too thin. Admittedly, the agency lacks a clearly defined mission and focus, and in recent years, it has set out in the ever-popular quest of reinvention. By the end of 1995, UNDP headquarters staff had been reduced by 24 percent and country officers by 8 percent from 1991 levels. Additionally, the agency announced a more streamlined focus on six main themes: poverty elimination and grassroots participation, environmental and natural resource management, management for development, women in development, technology transfer and adaptation, and technical cooperation among developing countries.

Perhaps UNDP's greatest achievement, at least in the North, has been its contribution toward improving the definition of development and how it is measured. Arguing that development cannot be promoted by the single-minded pursuit of economic growth, UNDP contends that there is no automatic link between income growth and economic progress. Sustainable human development is the process of widening people's choices and improving their level of well-being; it is development that not only generates economic growth but also distributes its benefits equitably, that regenerates the environment rather than destroying it, and that empowers people rather than marginalizing them. The Human Development Index, UNDP's development indicator, is unique in that it identifies people, not numbers, as the center of development. It measures human development by ranking countries on the basis of life expectancy, education, and basic purchasing power, while accounting for statistical variations among national data to allow effective cross-national comparisons. The annual *Human Development Reports* provide an updated ranking of countries by health, sanitation, the treatment of women, and other aspects of life that give a more accurate picture of day-to-day existence than economic figures alone ever could. In 1995, the report focused on the disparities between men and women, reporting that 70 percent of the world's poor and 67 percent of the world's illiterate are women. The 1996 report examined the widening gaps between rich and poor within countries and among continents—a problem, argues UNDP, exacerbated by the failure to put people at the center of development in both developing and industrialized nations.

United Nations Environment Programme (UNEP)

UNEP was established as the UN's environmental conscience following the Conference on the Human Environment. The 1972 conference held in Stockholm, Sweden, witnessed the adoption of the Declaration on Human Environment and the Action Plan, offering recommendations for governments and international organizations to protect life, control contamination, and improve settlements. The UN mandated UNEP to coordinate and provide policy guidance for sound environmental action and to promote environmental law and education throughout the world. Its role is a catalytic one, designed to prompt environmental action in other agencies while remaining relatively nonprogrammatic itself. Thus, its entire budget is often smaller than the cost of a single World Bank project; up until 1990, it hardly exceeded $40 million a year.[4] An important contribution that UNEP made in the area of policy guidance was in the crafting of the term *sustainable development*, which envisioned an integrated approach in working on environmental issues. UNEP's main concerns are the sustainable management of natural resources, climate change, desertification

Lessons of UNDP's *Human Development Report:*
Poverty Does Not Mean Only Lack of Income

Pakistan's economic growth is enviable, but 61 percent of the population lacks the health, education, and nourishment needed to climb out of poverty. Argentina's income is among the highest in the developing world, but 20 percent of its rural population lives in financial poverty, and 29 percent lacks access to safe water.

These two examples prove a point: people's lives are not measured by income alone. That idea has been at the heart of all *Human Development Reports* since the first was produced in 1990. We cannot rely on growth trickling down automatically. It takes government policy and action to ensure that income helps citizens expand their choices and gain adequate health, education, and resources for themselves and for their children—in other words, to achieve human development.

The 1996 Human Development Index (HDI) ranks Canada, the United States, Japan, the Netherlands, and Norway as the top five in order of human development, while listing Cyprus, Barbados, Bahamas, the Republic of Korea, and Argentina as the top five among developing countries.

"The fact is that over the last 30 years developing countries have made much more progress in human development than in income growth," says Richard Jolly, chief author of the report." But that progress has been uneven, leaving some regions far behind." Although the proportion of children in primary school rose from 60 percent to 73 percent over the past fifteen years in South Asia, it fell in seventeen sub-Saharan African countries.

Rich or poor, countries can achieve similar human development with widely varying incomes. Thus, Nepal is 151 on the HDI and Senegal 153, with per capita income of $190 and $750, respectively. Just as there are vast differences in human development among countries, so, too, there are often extreme differences within countries, both in wealth and poverty and in human development. There are often substantial differences between rural and urban access to essential health services. In many countries, rural access to potable water, adequate sanitation, and health clinics falls far behind that in urban centers. In Sierra Leone, 90 percent of the urban population has access to health facilities, compared with only 20 percent of the rural population.

UNDP, press release, July 17, 1996.

control, pollution, oceans, human settlements, and renewable sources of energy. UNEP, which is the only UN agency to have its headquarters in a developing country (Kenya), is the international leader in the field of environmental science information, including the coordination of Earthwatch, an international surveillance network composed of the Global Environment Monitoring System (GEMS), the Global Resource Information Database (GRID), and INFOTERRA, a computerized referral service to sources in over 130 countries for environmental information.

UN High Commissioner for Refugees (UNHCR)

In 1951, the UN General Assembly appointed UNHCR to replace the International Refugee Organization, which had settled more than a million displaced persons following World War II. Although UNHCR is often associated with images of workers in refugee camps, prior to the 1980s, it had relatively little involvement in relief and emergency work. Instead, it was founded to promote the international endorsement of standards for the treatment and definition of refugees, and its limited operational work focused primarily on providing legal protection for refugees. UNHCR is not only the principal beneficiary of international refugee law, it is also the trustee of it—one of the high commissioner's most important responsibilities is to ensure that all signatories to conventions comply with provisions. In 1975, the influx of Khmer refugees from Cambodia into Thailand pulled the agency into a more action-oriented role. In 1980, it established an emergency unit, and it has been under consistent pressure from certain members (mainly the United States) to expand its operational capabilities. When operational, UNHCR relies heavily on its relationships with NGOs, especially the International Rescue Committee and the Cooperative for American Relief Everywhere (CARE), with which it has many stand-by agreements that allow for quick deployment of aid. UNHCR field staff tend to be generalists rather than technicians, and once again, NGOs are counted on to provide technical expertise and specialist support. UNHCR's reliance on NGOs has been the source of some heated criticisms, such as Graham Hancock's accusation that UNHCR's slack supervision over the NGOs that it funds has allowed them to commit flagrant abuses.[5] Additionally, UNHCR's resolute self-perception as a coordinator and catalyst for operational activities rather than as an actor has led some critics to charge that it is burdened by bureaucratic procedures and has an overly legalistic approach to protecting refugees.[6] Notwithstanding these complaints, the agency's continued popularity and support seem firmly secured; with twenty-seven million refugees in the world today, UNHCR provided aid and protection to twenty-three million of them in 143 countries in 1994 alone.

United Nations Children's Fund (UNICEF)

UNICEF was founded in 1946 to extend massive relief to Europe and China in the aftermath of World War II. Seven years later, it became a permanent agency, and over the years, its mission has shifted from relief to development. Today, UNICEF's primary goal is to improve the lives of children and youth of the developing world by providing community-based service in primary health care, social services, water supply, formal and nonformal education, nutrition, and emergency operations. The reduction of infant mortality rates has been a consistent objective of UNICEF's work, and one of the agency's most significant successes was the development of an inexpensive solution to combat mortality from childhood diarrhea. In 1968, dehydration caused by diarrhea was killing four to five million children a year; that same year, UNICEF (with financing from the U.S. government) came up with a solution called oral rehydration therapy (ORT). Costing about ten cents a pack, ORT consists of a combination of glucose and salt that allows water to stay in the digestive tract long enough to be absorbed. Today, the number of children dying from dehydration by diarrhea is half of what it was in 1968, and child mortality worldwide has also been halved. Another significant contribution that UNICEF made to the well-being of children everywhere was its role in drafting the Convention of the Rights of the Child, the legal instrument that protects human rights for children. This convention, which is the most quickly and most widely ratified human rights convention in history, effectively transformed children from powerless charges to human beings with rights of their own. Well-known economist Amartya Sen accurately termed the package of rights "a cross-cultural moral minimum," and as of June 1997, all but three countries in the world had ratified it, suggesting that it could become the first universal law in history.[7] UNICEF's advocacy for children has also been evidenced by its successful pressure on poor countries to spend less on building expensive hospitals and more on bringing basic health care to their poorest citizens. But perhaps its greatest advocacy success was in bringing international attention to the human costs of the structural adjustment programs implemented by the World Bank in most developing countries during the 1980s (discussed in Chapter 2).

Like most UN agencies, much of UNICEF's work is done in partnership with other agencies of the UN system. A partnership with the World

Health Organization (WHO) brought about one of this century's landmark successes in health: the eradication of smallpox and the immunization of 80 percent of the world's children against five deadly diseases (polio, tetanus, whooping cough, diphtheria, and tuberculosis). Together, the two agencies' health initiatives are saving some three million lives each year. In recent years, a growing proportion of UNICEF's funds and programs has been directed to emergency situations and the provision of relief aid. In 1995, it spent 25 percent of total program expenditures in twenty-one countries affected by armed conflict and ten countries afflicted by natural disasters, up from 8 percent directed at emergency assistance only five years before. UNICEF's roughly $1 billion annual budget is funded primarily through contributions from its forty-one member governments and intergovernmental organizations, but it also raises money through the sale of greeting cards, making it one of the most well-known and popularly supported UN agencies.

UN Population Fund (UNFPA)

Founded in 1969, UNFPA is the largest internationally funded source of assistance for population programs in developing countries. With a focus on reproductive health care, family planning, and information and education about population issues, it provides support in over 140 countries. Taking its cue from the strategy endorsed by the 1994 International Conference on Population and Development, the fund emphasizes linkages between population and development and focuses on meeting the needs of individual women and men rather than on achieving demographic targets. Recently it provided $500,000 to the Red Cross and Red Crescent Societies to assist their work with refugees in central Africa. UNFPA has always emphasized the need for family planning and reproductive health care services during emergency situations. As a result of its pressure and funding, reproductive health care is now included in the provision of emergency aid at the outset of a crisis, bringing assistance to women with complicated pregnancies, assisting with childbirth, and providing aid to victims of sexual violence, as well as providing family planning. Like many UN agencies, UNFPA relies heavily on its relationships with NGOs, directing roughly 15 percent of its funds to NGO projects. UNFPA is governed by a joint board with UNDP and is funded entirely by voluntary contributions from its eighty-five donors, which in 1995 provided $313 million. U.S. support for UNFPA has been inconsistent at best. In 1985, a provision in the supplemental appropriations bill prohibited any U.S. foreign aid funding that "supports or participates in the management of a program of coerced abortion or involuntary sterilization."[8] At the time, China's one-child-per-couple policy had come to light, and antiabortion groups charged UNFPA with collusion with the Chinese government. Responding to strong lobbying, Presidents Reagan and Bush both determined that UNFPA was disqualified for U.S. funding, despite the fact that a USAID review had found no evidence of UNFPA support of, much less collaboration with, the Chinese government. Nafis Sadik, UNFPA's executive director, consistently stressed that "coercion has no part in population and family planning. It is morally wrong and ultimately it will not be effective. This has always been UNFPA's position and it will never change."[9] Finally, somebody listened. In 1993, President Clinton determined that UNFPA's program in China did not render it ineligible for U.S. assistance and provided the organization with $14.5 million.

World Food Programme (WFP)

WFP is the largest source of food-in-development assistance in the UN system, providing roughly a quarter of the world's food aid. Established in 1963, WFP's main objective is to mobilize and deliver emergency food in times of crisis and to provide food to support development. A decade ago, two out of every three tons of food provided by WFP was used for development. Today, the opposite is true, with 70 percent of 1994 expenditures going to people impacted by man-made disasters. WFP's three main activities are categorized as food for life, which provides emergency food; food for growth, which involves the provision of food to pregnant women and to children; and food for work, which uses food supplies as an incentive to get local communities' participation in development activities such as construction and reforestation. Food for work is targeted at the poorest segments of the population and has been replicated by many NGOs. Save the Children and Oxfam are among the many NGOs that are active in the local distribution of WFP food aid. Unlike UN agencies such as UNDP and UNFPA, which fund other agencies' development programs, WFP is primarily operational. Its field staff assists in preschool and school feeding programs and conducts projects in forestry, soil erosion, and land rehabilitation. As the incidence of violent conflict and civil strife increases throughout the world, WFP has increasingly focused on its most effective role—assisting in the coordination of large-scale relief operations. Sponsored jointly by FAO, WFP's funding comes from donor countries' contributions in both commodities and cash, the Food Aid Convention, and the International Food Reserve.

World Health Organization (WHO)

WHO was established in 1948 with the distinct objective of the attainment of the highest possible level of health for all people. Directing and coordinating the world's health programs, WHO facilitates technical cooperation among nations to promote research and establish standards in various fields. WHO's six regional committees (the Americas, Eastern Mediterranean, Europe, Western Pacific, Southeast Asia, and Africa) concentrate their efforts on the promotion and development of comprehensive health services. Program activities include the improvement of environmental conditions, the control and prevention of disease, the development of health services, biomedical research, and the implementation and planning of health programs. WHO's most well-known and significant success story was the eradication of smallpox (with the help of UNICEF). It is currently on course to eradicate polio by the year 2000, as it strives to fulfill its motto "Health for All by the Year 2000." Recently the agency has concentrated its efforts on spearheading the fight against AIDS.

The UN in Crisis?

Under the terms of its 1945 Charter, the UN is funded by cash assessments from member states, based on their share of the world economy and their ability to pay.[10] As of October 1996, member states owed the UN a total of $2.5 billion, a debt made all the more onerous by the fact that the UN is prohibited by law from borrowing from commercial institutions. The United States' share of the UN regular budget is $321 million a year, which roughly translates to $1.25 per American. However, it has been years since the United States paid its share—the United States currently owes the UN more than $1.5 billion. The unprecedented financial crisis facing the UN—and the lack of member support that it represents—illustrates two conflicting yet valid perspectives regarding the international agency.

The first perspective maintains that the United Nations is a flawed institution. U.S. support for this view, especially emanating from Congress, is clearly evidenced by its blatant refusal to pay dues owed to the agency. Much of the U.S. government's justification for withholding funds from the UN lies in the complaint that the agency is grossly mismanaged and riddled with corruption. In a special report in June 1995, a *New York Times* headline declared, "Mismanagement and Waste Erode UN's Best

Intentions"; the article went on to report alarming scandals and widespread examples of bureaucratic inertia.[11] For instance, $3.9 million disappeared from UN headquarters in Mogadishu, Somalia, during the civil crisis there in 1994, and investigators believed it to be an inside job. Even UNICEF, one of the UN's most respected agencies, disclosed that its Kenya operation had lost as much as $10 million to fraud and mismanagement by employees there. Examples of waste and mismanagement are apparently equally abundant: overuse of consultants for research on obsolete topics or for flagrant self-promotional efforts. The financially strapped Secretariat was reported to have requested that $150,000 in the current budget be allocated to hire consultants to secure public support for activities related to the UN's fiftieth anniversary celebrations.[12]

Mismanagement is able to thrive in an environment where a shortage of auditors results in departments and agencies being audited only once every six years on average. And seemingly nobody could track the staff until the agency's payroll was computerized, barely a year ago. One long-time official described with exasperation and anger the "appalling inefficiencies and backbiting and corruption." The *New York Times* article concluded with the distressing assessment that the UN is afflicted with "tenacious cancers . . . [that] have debilitated the world organization, demoralized its own staff and severely undercut its support in the United States and elsewhere."

With governments around the world cutting back on their aid budgets, it is little wonder that when it comes time for annual contributions to the UN, the institution undergoes close scrutiny. However, even casual perusal of the work of the various specialized agencies reveals alarming similarities: well-intentioned mandates that virtually echo one another; programs of one agency being replicated by another, without collaboration; and overall duplication that seems oddly out of place in this time of emphasis on the efficient use of funds. The fact that there are three separate food agencies based in Rome with a total workforce of nearly ten thousand underscores the impression of inefficiency. Adding fuel to the critics' fire is the disturbing absence of collaboration among the various institutions. Although they are all UN agencies, they are all completely autonomous and in competition for ever scarcer funds. Although successful collaborations, such as UNICEF's and WHO's work on immunization efforts, have reaped much attention and praise, there is still a great need for organized partnerships, especially in emergency situations, where the absence of collaboration at all levels—bilateral, multilateral, and nongovernmental—increases the risks for everyone involved.

In the face of such charges, many of them indisputable, the United Nations confronts its greatest and most introspective challenge. The agency must now take stock of its flaws and, rather than wasting any additional time or resources in defending or disputing allegations, work hard and fast to correct them and chart a new path. After all, equally indisputable is the institution's enormous potential. It remains the only international organization with the potential to provide multilateral solutions to the economic, political, and social problems of our increasingly interdependent world. And, as a cursory look at the various UN agencies mentioned earlier reveals, the organization is certainly not without substantial achievements: UNICEF effectively promoted universal immunization and focused the world's attention on the needs of children, WHO mobilized worldwide action for the eradication of smallpox, FAO created an early warning and monitoring network for food production, UNFPA put the issue of balanced population growth on the world's agenda, and UNDP is a respected and important partner of many developing countries on their path to development.[13]

However, past accomplishments do not guarantee future success, nor do they justify continued investment in an ailing institution. Reform is clearly in order, and fortunately, it is slowly under way. In large part, the institution's current financial crisis is both symbol and cause of its poor performance. Despite evidence of wasted funds, it is also true that the UN is severely underfunded by its members. As a recent *Economist* article argued, "governments instruct the UN to do a certain job, fail to give it the money needed, and yet conclude that it is the UN that is at fault, not themselves."[14] For the past few years, the UN has run out of money two-thirds of the way through the year, forcing it to borrow from peacekeeping funds—money that should go to reimburse countries that provided peacekeeping troops and equipment. Many within the UN argue that there are insufficient funds to carry out comprehensive reform, but under the watchful eye of new Undersecretary General for Administration and Management (in effect, the chief financial officer) Joseph Connor, the UN has begun to cut costs and staff. The bureaucratic hurdles in the way of real reform cannot be overemphasized. Secretary of State Madeline Albright likened the UN to "a business with 185 members of the board; all of them with strong and contradictory opinions . . . and each with a brother-in-law who is unemployed."[15] However, a zero-growth budget remains the goal of those committed to reform. In February 1996, Connor announced that 10 percent of the UN's permanent staff of ten thousand would be laid off, and an additional $14 million in efficiency and staff savings is currently being implemented.

Although Jesse Helms, chairman of the Senate Foreign Relations Committee, may argue that the UN is a "power-hungry and dysfunctional organization" that threatens U.S. national interests and thus is deserving of U.S. withdrawal,[16] it is important to point out that he and even more mainstream members of Congress do not articulate the views of the U.S.

majority. Opinion polls conducted by Times Mirror, the Americans Talk Issues Foundation, the Pew Research Center, and the University of Maryland's Steven Kull revealed that the UN has far more support than politicians' sound bites would suggest. In surveys from mid-1995 and 1996, 76 percent of those polled chose the UN as the best "policeman of the world," and the UN won a favorable rating from 67 percent of Americans.[17] Some poll data even show that the UN has stronger support in the United States than almost any other institution, including the executive and legislative branches of the U.S. government.[18] In fact, foreign policy experts warn that Washington's hostility to the UN is damaging to the national interests of the United States. John Whitehead, a former deputy secretary of state who is now chairman of the Federal Reserve Bank of New York, reported that "there are indications that our country's negative attitude towards the UN, our refusal to pay our dues, our rather brutal discarding of the Secretary General, have all created animosity around the world."[19]

Only time will tell how the UN will fare in facing its newest, most important challenge. The stakes have never been higher. Should the bureaucratic quagmire continue to be the operating environment, it is not difficult to foresee the collapse of this potentially great institution—and every nation in the world would suffer the loss. However, there is reason to be hopeful. A new secretary-general was sworn into office in January 1997: Kofi Annan, the first person from sub-Saharan Africa (Ghana) ever to hold the job. Early indications suggest that reform is at the top of his agenda; he immediately pledged to continue to maintain a zero-growth budget, and in the past year, the headquarters staff in New York, Geneva, and Vienna was cut by one-tenth. The fact that Annan has spent his entire career at the UN and has intimate knowledge of its strengths and weaknesses bodes well for the chances of reform. Plans for the UN's restructuring were expected to be announced in July 1997. Among the proposals was likely to be the merging of at least three departments currently dealing with economic and social affairs.

It would be unrealistic to look upon the new secretary-general as the silver bullet of renewal and repair. In all the attention surrounding UN reform, the role of its member states in achieving this reform is often overlooked. However valid the critiques of duplication and waste among the specialized agencies may be, it is not something that the secretary-general can fix. That is the responsibility of the General Assembly, the collection of all UN members, which is notorious for its inability to reach consensus. For five years, the General Assembly has been working on issues such as Security Council membership and the Agenda for Peace, with little resolution or progress. Although all 185 member nations easily agree that the UN needs improvement, they have been unable to agree on a common and collective vision of a new, improved United Nations.

Notes

1. Celestine Bohlen, "Pope Tells UN Group Population Control Is No Cure for Hunger," *New York Times*, November 14, 1996, A15.
2. Kunnibert Raffer and H. W. Singer, *The Foreign Aid Business: Economic Assistance and Development Co-operation* (Brookfield, Vt.: Edward Elgar Publishing, 1996), 44.
3. UNDP Annual Report, 1995.
4. Bruce Rich, *Mortgaging the Earth: The World Bank, Environmental Impoverishment, and the Crisis of Development* (Boston: Beacon Press, 1994), 243.
5. Graham Hancock, *Lords of Poverty: The Power, Prestige, and Corruption of the International Aid Business* (New York: Atlantic Monthly Press, 1989), 10.
6. Frederick Cuny, "Refugees, Displaced Persons and the UN System," in *U.S. Foreign Policy and the UN System*, ed. Charles William Maynes and Richard Williamson (New York: W. W. Norton, 1996), 187–211.
7. UNICEF Annual Report, 1996.
8. Planned Parenthood Federation of America, "UNFPA and Family Planning Assistance to China," background information, May 1995.
9. Ibid.
10. Member countries also provide voluntary contributions for special programs.
11. Christopher Wren, "Mismanagement and Waste Erode UN's Best Intentions," *New York Times*, June 23, 1995, A12.
12. Ibid.
13. UNDP, *Human Development Report 1994* (New York: Oxford University Press, 1994).
14. "The United Nations Heads for Bankruptcy," *Economist*, February 10, 1996, 41.
15. Wren, "Mismanagement and Waste," A12.
16. "Lexington: Hello World," *Economist*, November 16, 1996, 30.
17. Thomas Omestad, "Foreign Policy and Campaign '96," *Foreign Policy* 105 (winter 1996–97): 54.
18. Barbara Crosette, "Experts' Study Say Attacking the UN Hurts the U.S.," *New York Times*, August 20, 1996.
19. Ibid.

5

Northern NGOs

NORTHERN-BASED NONGOVERNMENTAL organizations (NGOs) are an increasingly significant source of aid to the South, collectively providing more aid to developing countries than the World Bank. The past fifteen years have witnessed an explosion in the number of NGOs in OECD countries, from sixteen hundred in 1980 to twenty-five hundred in 1990 and well over five thousand in 1995.[1] Organizations based in the United States are usually referred to as private voluntary organizations (PVOs), although the two terms are generally used interchangeably. In fact nongovernmental is somewhat of misnomer, as most of these organizations do depend in some measure on government funds. In 1995, some four hundred U.S.-based organizations raised $7 billion for overseas aid, about a third of which came from government sources.[2] But regardless of the level and implications of the government support they receive, NGOs undeniably offer a real alternative in the South to both bilateral and multilateral aid.

What Are NGOs?

NGOs are nearly impossible to define or categorize. There is no such thing as a typical NGO. Their diversity encompasses every feature imaginable: size, operating style, geographic focus, religious background, programmatic orientation and so forth. For almost any aspect of third-world society and economy, there is an NGO working within that sector in some way. Many NGOs are organizational structures created by religious denominations, established to respond to a perceived need, such as Catholic Relief Services (CRS) and Lutheran World Relief (LWR).[3] Other NGOs spring from a single individual's motivation, such TechnoServe, which was created by Edward Bullard in 1968 to "provide business know-how to the rural poor . . . so they can generate surpluses and provide for themselves."[4] NGO size ranges from organizations with multi-million-dollar budgets and staff in the hundreds, such as CRS and World Vision, to tiny organizations dedicated to a single objective, such as Dental Health International.[5] Programmatic focus is another area of enormous diversity within the nongovernmental arena. Organizations such as CARE and CRS work in almost all aspects of economic and social development,[6] whereas other organizations are uniquely specialized. Heifer Project International, for example, concentrates on rural development, providing needy farmers with animals on the condition that recipients provide livestock to others in their community. Operational styles also vary greatly, from a purely funding role for other agencies working in the field (such as the Ford Foundation) to organizations that, although not foundations, work exclusively through Southern-based NGOs, providing them with grants and seed money (LWR operates in this manner). Although recent trends emphasize working in partnership with local organizations in the South, many of the bigger NGOs (CARE, World Vision, CRS) continue to employ a large overseas staff to carry out their assistance programs.

The first NGOs were established during and just after World War II to respond to the devastation of war. Most of these organizations, such as CRS and Church World Service (CWS),[7] were rooted in a religious tradition and structure. Immediately after the war, secular organizations, such as CARE, emerged to assist in the provision of relief to European victims. During the 1960s and 1970s, a number of new organizations were created that shifted the focus from short-term emergency relief to an almost exclusive focus on longer-term economic and social development in the third world. TechnoServe and Oxfam America are examples of these new organizations.[8] By the mid-1970s, old and new organizations alike began to focus on the root causes of poverty rather than just its symptoms. Unfortunately, especially in the early years, there was a tendency to bring Northern solutions to these newly defined problems, reflecting the paternalistic belief that pushing developing countries to be more like Northern societies would bring about sustained economic growth. Gradually, with the help of articulate and powerful voices from the South, Northern NGOs were forced to acknowledge the enormous human resources that already existed in the South, and they began to shift to a new role of providing service to existing and nascent grassroots organizations and self-help movements. This led to a mushrooming of Southern organizations (described in Chapter 6). Today, it is universally recognized by virtually all Northern NGOs that development is a process in which the primary actors must be the citizens of developing countries.

What Do NGOs Do? (And What Should They Do?)

According to aid analyst Brian Smith, NGOs can be broadly categorized into three main functional roles. First, and most well-known, are the traditional disaster-relief agencies (CRS, CARE, CWS), which are typically the largest and oldest organizations that were founded in the 1940s and have since moved into development assistance. The second group is the technical assistance organizations, which tend to be smaller, more secular, and focused on the transfer of technical resources and skills (TechnoServe, Heifer Project International). The third, and regrettably the smallest, group is the institution and network builders, which typically view development as an indigenous process of self-definition.[9] Trickle Up Program is one example of an organization that puts development squarely in the hands of the people it seeks to help. Focusing on small business development, Trickle Up provides grants of $100 to families or small groups to start or expand businesses they have planned for themselves. Half the grant is given to the group in a first installment, after it has completed a business plan and members have agreed to work a minimum of one thousand hours over three months and reinvest 20 percent of their profits in the enterprise. The second half of the grant is provided upon completion of a business report showing that the conditions of the grant have been met. Trickle Up has helped launch more than fifty-two thousand businesses in 113 countries since its establishment in 1979.

David Korten, an expert on development assistance, also has a tripartite view of NGOs, but instead of categories, he sees NGOs as passing through distinct generations along an evolutionary path toward sustainable development.[10] Beginning as agents that provided emergency and relief aid and only temporarily alleviated the symptoms of poverty, NGOs have evolved into broader development institutions that support community development activities and emphasize self-reliance. However, these agencies have reached only the second-generation phase. The third-generation agencies that Korten would like to see evolve would be less directly involved in implementing projects, acting rather as catalysts in "a foundation-like role . . . facilitating development by other [local] organizations."[11] Here, development becomes synonymous with empowerment or "training for transformation,"[12] and it becomes a process in which Southern citizens hold center stage while Northern NGOs move to the margins. A key difference between this type of NGO and service-provider NGOs is the time frame for involvement. Third-generation NGOs view their role as temporary: "actions are directed toward catalyzing changes that can produce self-directing, self-financing local institutional arrangements that can survive after their departure."[13]

Not surprisingly, many NGOs are often reluctant to step aside. They argue, and not without some validity, that serving the South in a strictly funding role will erode their comparative advantage and set them on a collision course with bilateral and multilateral actors.[14] Additionally, from a fund-raising standpoint, NGOs' financial position could be weakened, because "empowerment can not be reduced to a project"; traditional fund-raising methods and images would be undermined by a more abstract message that would likely be less attractive to donors that are eager to see the tangible results of their contributions.[15]

NGOs' Strengths

The proliferation of NGOs and the growing support from governmental and multilateral sources are a testament to their excellent reputations as providers of assistance to the poor. It is broadly acknowledged that NGOs are in a better position than the larger, multilateral agencies to reach the poor and work at the grassroots level. Whereas NGOs used to promise to reach the poorest of the poor, they now admit that they fail to reach the poorest 5 to 10 percent, but this is still a significant accomplishment, given that, according to UNDP estimates, official and multilateral aid fails to reach the poorest 20 percent.[16] Additionally, NGOs' comparatively small size makes them less bureaucratic, cheaper, and more cost-effective.

Because NGOs are not hampered by political motivations and constraints, as governments are, they have the ability to reach a broader recipient audience, including countries that are deemed hostile and from which official aid is withheld. Ironically, NGOs working in such black-listed countries often report that those are the few countries where the local governments are *not* working against broad-based development.[17] U.S. NGOs also escape the strategic and corporate interests that tend to guide much of U.S. foreign policy and aid, furthering their scope and independence. Many NGOs, such as Oxfam-America and World Neighbors,[18] strictly refuse any U.S. government funds on the grounds that it would compromise their freedom to conduct and fund the projects that they deem most effective and, in essence, would take away their greatest strength—independence.

In addition to a smaller bureaucracy, NGOs' typically small size requires that they limit their focus to a select number of activities and areas of expertise, rather than the broad range typical of the large multilateral agencies, which are often criticized for either spreading themselves too thin or wasting funds on duplicating one another's work (a frequent complaint about UN agencies). Focusing on a single technical specialty

NGO Strategic Networks: From Community Projects to Global Transformation

As we broaden our perspective, we realize that the deepening poverty, environmental devastation, and violence we see in the villages where we work are not local phenomena. They are pervasive and global results of systemic forces that cannot be resolved by action at the village level alone. To achieve the changes of the scope and magnitude required, it is necessary to think of the NGO's people-centered development alternative not as a village project but as a global people's movement for social transformation.

For those who choose to define their role as catalysts in the formation and guidance of strategic networks as elements of a larger movement for global social transformation, there are a number of basic issues to be addressed:

- Moving from protest to proaction. Engaging in protest can make an important contribution to strengthening awareness of issues and building commitment to activism. However, protest actions only pose barriers to the negative forces of the growth-centered development vision. There must be attention to building support for a proactive agenda aimed at transformational change. The question should be continuously in mind: What do we want in place of what we cannot accept?
- Building citizen democracy. Democratization is best thought of as a process of building capacities for and commitment to citizen action through action. Single organizations are rarely successful in taking on significant policy and institutional change agendas. When the issues involve external political and economic forces, strategic networking becomes an essential mode of action.

has proved to have the most sustainable and effective results, as evidenced by Accion International/AITEC, which pioneered microenterprise development in Latin America in the 1970s.[19] With smaller budgets, NGOs are also more likely to finance projects overlooked by the large institutions with grant-size minimums. Many practitioners argue that these small, well-placed grants are far more effective in meeting their goals than are the huge grants that require an inordinate amount of bookkeeping (not to mention the pressure to spend those funds quickly and often thoughtlessly).[20] The size of NGOs also means that fewer people are involved in decision making, thus allowing them the flexibility to experiment and try new approaches with their development assistance projects.

- Forming alliances across social movements. Fortunately, many NGOs that had historically remained isolated and even competitive with one another, focusing almost exclusively on microlevel interventions, are moving beyond their traditional limitations and learning ways of strategic networking. The people-centered development movement is one that embraces the proactive agendas of many existing social movements, including the environment, human rights, peace, women's, social justice, and consumer protection movements.
- Distinguishing between activist and service-provider NGOs. Although it is still too early to say for sure, there are indications that we may be seeing a somewhat permanent division between NGOs that choose to be specialized service providers and those that choose to be social activists working in more catalytic roles.

NGOs no longer enjoy the luxury of being inconsequential actors at the periphery of the development stage. Our choices make serious differences to the global future. We must take our responsibilities seriously and prepare ourselves accordingly. We are only beginning to understand the nature of strategic networks and the critical roles of the catalysts that give them shape and direction. We must make rapid advances in that understanding, in the development of our skills as effective catalysts, and in sharing our insights with others who might assume similar roles.

Excerpt of a paper written by David C. Korten for the Asian Regional Workshop on Strategic Networking for Sustainable Development and Environmental Action, November 26–30, 1990, Bangkok, Thailand. Korten is president of the People-Centered Development Forum, which is dedicated to advancing a people's development movement toward the realization of a people-centered development vision.

NGOs also have the on-the-ground advantage—they typically have more staff people working permanently in the field (not just during emergencies), especially in rural areas, where the poorest populations live, than do the large multilateral agencies. Relationships with local communities are more easily fostered with staff people living and sharing daily routines, which provides NGOs with perhaps their greatest advantage of all: access to local knowledge. As it becomes increasingly clear that the key to sustainable development (which, for aid donors, equates to money well spent) is local participation in all stages, it is obvious that NGOs that know and listen to local populations are in the best position to help achieve it. They can collaborate with local organizations and assist with institution building, training, and staff development—and in the process, be a part of develop-ment that far outlives their presence. Their in-country presence also strate-gically places them in a position to conduct preventive action and implement early warning systems in the increasingly common occurrence of natural and man-made emergencies.

NGOs' Weaknesses

Notwithstanding NGOs' rosy reputation there has actually been little objective reporting or evaluation of NGO projects, and those evaluations that have been done reveal that the NGO comparative advantage tends to be more myth than reality. Judith Tendler conducted one of the most well-known studies of NGOs in 1982 and found that many NGOs do not dif-ferentiate very well among residents of poor communities; the poorest are often overlooked in the hope that the benefits of assisting those who are slightly more well-off will eventually trickle down.[21] Ironically, the World Bank has been loudly criticized by NGOs for its trickle-down approach to development on a macro level, so it is difficult to understand why NGOs would hope that it would work in a micro setting. Tendler also found that NGOs had a tendency to control the decision-making processes and to identify projects according to the sectors and areas in which they had experience, not necessarily according to the priorities of local residents. More recent evaluations have rendered similar findings.[22] An evaluation of a program in Sudan, Ethiopia, and other Sahelian countries to improve local food production and food security found that there is actually little difference in the quality, scope, and approach between NGOs and multi-lateral institutions.[23]

NGOs' comparatively small size is actually somewhat of a double-edged sword, for although it arguably allows them greater flexibility, it also causes a number of weaknesses. Technical capacity is limited by the small staff size and low budgets of NGOs, as is NGOs' capacity to scale up to achieve regional and national impact. As a result, as NGO experts Michael Edwards and David Hulme summarize, "the impact of NGOs on the lives of poor people is highly localized, and often transitory."[24] Related to this is NGOs' failure to understand or even realize the larger context in which they operate and their failure to make the connections between their work at the micro level and the macro systems that are often respon-sible for perpetuating the problems they are working on. This insular thinking can be articulated as follows: "if you see a baby drowning you jump in to save it; and if you see a second and third you do the same. Soon you are so busy saving drowning babies that you never look up to see that

---

What Makes NGO Development Projects Successful?

Most evaluations and impact studies do not attempt to analyze the factors influencing project success. However, one British study did. Though it stressed that project performance was related to a number of different influences, none of which in isolation was sufficient to determine success or failure, it suggested that three factors in particular stood out:

- The participation of the beneficiaries in different cycles of the project;
- Strong and effective NGO management and institutional capacity; and
- The caliber of project staff, their commitment to overall project objectives, their skills, and the degree of empathy with the intended beneficiaries.

R. C. Riddell and M. Robinson with J. de Coninck, A. Muir, and S. White, *Non Governmental Organizations and Rural Poverty Alleviation* (New York: Oxford University Press, and Washington, D.C.: Overseas Development Institute, 1995). Reprinted with permission from ODI Briefing Paper, "The Impact of NGO Development Projects," May, 1996.

---

there is someone there throwing these babies in the river."[25] An example of NGOs' failure to see the "big picture" can be found in their distribution of food aid, where the tendency is to "distribute food first and examine the consequences later" (although bilateral donors are equally if not more negligent in this area). According to a General Accounting Office evaluation of food aid conducted in 1993: "[US]AID and PVOs have generally evaluated food aid projects based on commodity management and outputs, such as numbers of children fed or miles of road constructed, but have not assessed the impact of their projects on long-term food security."[26]

A 1981 study produced by the Center of Concern listed five major criticisms of U.S. NGOs:[27]

1. Many will work in any country, no matter the conditions, transferring a ready-made technical project.
2. They often go where the money is, leading to bad projects and often a negative impact on local populations.
3. Few asked if the project was initiated by the recipient community.
4. There is a growing lack of accountability to taxpayers, Northern constituents, and the Third World poor.
5. NGOs do not challenge one another or engage in self-criticism.

Perhaps NGOs' most egregious flaw, because it is avoidable, is their lack of collaboration with one another. Although it can be argued that "successful"

NGOs win the "market test," in that they must compete among themselves for private contributions, that sense of competition extends into the field, where coordination is vital. The importance of collaboration is never more important than in emergency situations, yet it is during times of crisis that NGOs seem to be most competitive, scrambling to get a piece of the action that will ensure a portion of the flood of donations that begins as soon as the media mobilize the public with graphic pictures of unspeakable pain. David Rieff describes the scene in Zaire in 1996 when genocide in Rwanda sent thousands of refugees fleeing across the border: "Anyone who saw, as I did, the grotesque display of humanitarian agencies' flags flapping alongside each other in eastern Zaire like so many corporate flags in some business park in Purchase, New York, or San Jose, California, realized there was more going on than the simple desire to help. The struggle to stamp out cholera, get shelters built, and dig the pit latrines was simultaneously a struggle for market share."[28] Korten further contends that "one of the most serious barriers to expanding the development roles of NGOs may be the difficulties they face in working with one another. Jealousies among them are often intense, and efforts at collaboration all too often break down into the internecine warfare that paralyzes efforts to work together toward the achievement of shared purposes."[29]

NGOs have been further weakened, many critics argue, by their increasing dependence on government funds. What was once their greatest strength—independence—has been eroded by public funds such as operational program grants, development program grants, matching grants, and other government funds offered since the 1970s. And the trend on the part of governments to work through NGOs has become more popular in recent years, leading many critics to argue that NGOs now package their projects to satisfy USAID's requirements, with little thought of the needs and desires of the intended beneficiaries.[30] This concern was in fact confirmed in a 1982 Government Accounting Office (GAO) study, which found that "financial dependency has led some PVOs to focus on what [US]AID wants, rather than independently identifying and responding to needs through their own networks."[31]

Integration of Women into NGO Projects

When the United Nations declared 1975–85 the Decade for Women, there were high hopes that NGOs and multilateral agencies alike would finally recognize the critical role of women in development. By the end of the decade, Lucille Mair, former undersecretary of the UN, summarized the accomplishments of the past ten years: "The decade has rescued women from statistical invisibility, but little progress has been made in incorporating the statistics into policy analysis and reevaluation."[32] Because NGOs are smaller and can afford to be more specialized, one would assume that they would have a strong advantage over multilateral aid providers in targeting and reaching the group that constitutes 80 percent of the poor in the global South—women. Unfortunately, as found by Tendler, NGOs have been slow "in thinking of women as a poverty group, or being concerned about the exclusion of women from income generating projects."[33] This, she contends, is a function of NGOs' competition for scarce resources, as well as their institutional legacies, especially those influenced by the Catholic Church. Additionally, NGOs sometimes avoid projects that would target women, for fear of being accused of cultural imperialism or tampering with sex roles.

There is some debate regarding which projects produce better, more sustainable results for women—projects with a narrow focus that are set up to provide a single missing ingredient, such as credit, or those projects that promote group-run enterprises, taking into account women's multiple responsibilities. The debate remains unsettled, but consensus has been reached in recognizing that projects that focus on women themselves, rather than on women as members of households, tend to be much more successful in improving women's economic opportunities.[34]

Ironically, it is the very projects that tend to be ignored by both NGOs and multilateral institutions that have the greatest potential for improving the welfare of women. If agricultural programs would more broadly acknowledge and support women's role as farmers and resource managers, women's living standard would rise, as well as that of their entire families. NGOs with microcredit projects that provide loans to women have become acutely aware of the long-term benefits of recognizing women's income-generating roles. However, although microenterprise projects often provide additional integrated services for poor women, including training, health care, and education, they often fail to recognize the unique constraints placed on women microentrepreneurs—their limited access to production information and technology, as well as the scarce resources available to them.[35] And training programs, which hold out the promise for women to learn new income-generating skills, all too often teach women less useful income-generating skills. As Chapter 6 indicates, Southern women have usually achieved the greatest development success by working through their own self-created organizations, such as the Annapurna Mahila Mandal in India. Founded in 1976, this organization of women caterers began selling lunches to workers in local mills. Today, it has organized a number of extremely successful small businesses and has a membership of over sixty-five thousand women. The words of member Asha Bai best articulate its significance: "Nothing I say will fully describe the importance of being an Annapurna. My two daughters will be the future Annapurnas. I can give them education, training, and above all, pride in being a woman."[36]

NGOs and Multilateral Institutions

NGOs' recent popularity in the international aid community is evidenced by their increasing number of partnerships with the World Bank and other multilateral institutions. Although many fear that such partnerships compromise NGOs' independence and integrity in the same way that accepting governmental funding does, the World Bank has undeniably benefited greatly from its contact with NGOs—and developing countries have seen the positive effects of those lessons learned. Indeed, it can be argued that given NGOs' access to local communities, they have a responsibility to provide information to the larger multilateral institutions, which are further removed from their intended beneficiaries and are thus often unaware of the real impact of their programs. NGOs can provide the World Bank and other multilateral aid providers with valuable knowledge about cultures they know little about and assist them in developing relationships they have historically ignored. Whether the World Bank and other institutions will actually heed the advice offered by NGOs and the communities they represent is another question.

NGO environmentalists have had the strongest impact on World Bank policies, capturing international attention and even U.S. government support in the process. In 1983, environmental NGOs persuaded the House Subcommittee on International Development Institutions and Finance to hold the first hearings on multilateral banks and the environment. In addition to reports from scientists and academicians who conducted field studies, the subcommittee heard from representatives of indigenous people's organizations, who charged that many of the projects financed by the World Bank were "a catastrophe for the earth's tribal peoples, verging in some cases on genocide."[37] Among other charges, the World Bank was forced to account for the disastrous Polonoroeste project in Brazil (see Chapter 2). In front of millions of television viewers, the World Bank vice president for external relations admitted that the project had gone ahead despite staffers' warnings of uncontrollable deforestation and virtual genocide of the Indians."[38] As a result of this unprecedented NGO pressure, the World Bank halted remaining disbursements for the Polonoroeste project totaling over a quarter of a million dollars, pending emergency environmental and Indian land protection measures to be taken by the Brazilian government.[39] Since then, the World Bank has also created an inspection panel for public accountability where affected parties can file complaints, and by 1989, the World Bank president proudly announced that more than a third of bank projects had significant environmental components. NGOs had succeeded in creating a public-relations nightmare for the World Bank, and it was that, not new information about widespread destruction and deaths, that finally provoked meaningful change in the institution.

NGOs have been equally vigilant in other areas of World Bank activities, from helping to publicize the human costs of structural adjustment policies to pressuring the bank to assess the poverty impact of its programs. Michael Cernea of the World Bank understated their impact in acknowledging that "international NGOs . . . have repeatedly signaled to the Bank cases when resettlement under Bank-financed projects does not proceed satisfactorily"[40] The fiftieth anniversary of the Bretton Woods institutions prompted an international NGO campaign to bring about profound reform of IMF and the World Bank "through a major restructuring and downsizing of their operations, funding, roles and power."[41] United under the banner "50 Years Is Enough," some 145 NGOs held briefings parallel to World Bank–IMF meetings, mounted demonstrations at UN meetings in cities throughout the world, and accumulated an abundance of data to support their demands, including a change in the World Bank's policy regarding release of reports and access to information, an end to environmentally destructive lending, and a reduction of multilateral debt.[42]

NGO influence in the multilateral arena has been especially evident at the international UN conferences. NGOs have been active at virtually every UN conference, gaining visibility and representation with each event. The United Nations Conference on the Environment and Development held in Rio de Janeiro in 1992 brought together a record number of NGOs, many of which managed to get on national delegations, thus allowing them access to the preconference sessions where much of the policy drafting took place. Largely due to NGO demonstrations and protests, the environment conference chose to vote for a moratorium on commercial whaling, and NGOs had a key role in negotiating an agreement to control greenhouse gases. More than twenty-three hundred NGOs were accredited to the World Summit for Social Development in 1995, and the 1996 UN Conference on Women, held in Beijing, China, included the participation of over four thousand NGOs. Held concurrently with each UN conference is an NGO forum, a typically more vibrant gathering, with far greater diversity of views and people than at the official conference. NGOs also publish daily newspapers during the conferences, providing the best source of information on the progress of the official talks, as well as disseminating the NGO position on key issues under review. The forum and daily newspapers serve as a continuous reminder during the conference that the public agenda is much wider than that discussed at the diplomatic proceedings.[43]

Recent Developments

Regardless of whether NGOs' comparative advantages are real or imagined, NGOs have become the darling of the aid industry in recent years. In fact, it is likely that the popularity of NGOs has less to do with their perceived strengths and more to do with the popular perception of failure on the part of multilateral and bilateral institutions. Another factor contributing to NGOs' surge in popularity, especially during the 1980s, was the political climate in most donor countries that exalted private-sector solutions. Since the New Directions legislation of the 1970s, which directed USAID to spend significant sums to expand the headquarters and field capacities of NGOs, to today's legislation, which stipulates that 12 to 16 percent of the U.S. development and disaster assistance budget go to NGOs, the resources flowing through NGOs have never been greater. In 1993, Title II of the Food for Peace program (PL 480) provided $810 million to U.S. NGOs. During the second half of the 1980s, slightly less than half of all official aid from OECD countries went to the more than two thousand NGOs. Today there are over four thousand NGOs in OECD countries, disbursing over $9 billion annually.

Just as multilateral and bilateral aid institutions' budget allocations have reflected the escalation of emergencies and disasters in the global South, so too have the budgets and operations of NGOs. Thirty-five percent of Catholic Relief Services' budget is now allocated to emergency relief, and the International Committee of the Red Cross spent more than half of its entire budget in Somalia alone during the crisis year of 1993. Not only must NGOs create new paradigms for their work that will link their disaster relief interventions with sustainable development, but they also must face unique ethical challenges working in these emergency contexts. Virtually all NGOs promise neutral assistance, irrespective of political, ethnic, or religious affiliation, but these agencies confront thorny ethical dilemmas when guilty parties show up at the feeding centers, as was recently the case in Zaire: "aid agencies found themselves in the position of feeding not only innocent refugee women and children, but their sons, fathers, brothers, and husbands, many of whom had participated in the 1994 genocide [in Rwanda]."[44] In fact, NGOs' presence during conflicts is usually far from neutral. In Somalia in 1991–92, in an atmosphere of violent anarchy, NGOs' tasks expanded radically from administering relief programs to taking on the responsibilities of diplomats, security experts, and news agents. Ironically, it was an NGO (CARE) that led the call for U.S. military intervention—a questionable act of "neutrality."

Twenty-nine percent of U.S. official (or government) aid is currently administered by NGOs—a statistic that is surely frightening to those who have been warning against the dangers of dependence on government funds for years. Fourteen years ago, then–deputy secretary-general of the United Nations Conference on Trade and Development Jan Pronk warned that "the corruption of NGOs will be the political game in the years ahead—and it is already being played today. . . . It will become impossible for them to criticize governments for decreasing the quality of the overall aid program."[45] The debate wages on regarding the effects of government funds. There is certainly the danger that federal funds could compromise an NGO's project design, pushing it to satisfy government's needs rather than the poor's. Additionally, many argue that government funding inhibits an NGO's ability to critically assess and comment on federal foreign and aid policy, as NGOs fear the possible consequences of biting the hand that feeds them.

Just as real as the dangers of the corrosive effects of government support are the pitfalls of NGOs' expanding role—an unavoidable outcome for many NGOs now charged with carrying on or taking over many of USAID's development programs. Increased funding, whether it be from governmental or other sources, transforms NGOs into large, often bureaucratic agencies with mounting requirements for proper bookkeeping and budget management. A sadly ironic paradox emerges: as NGOs grow, they become more successful in meeting donor requirements of accountability and professionalism (in short, they come to resemble government agencies) and less successful in meeting beneficiary groups' needs as they lose the special advantages of their small size.[46]

At the *World Development*–Overseas Development Institute symposium held in 1987, one of the points raised was that it was no longer acceptable for NGOs to work exclusively at the local level. Southern NGOs were especially vocal in demanding that Northern organizations understand the macro-level public policies that affect the development process. Part of the wider, more macro perspective that NGOs must cast includes recognition of the potential strength, and importance of these Southern-based NGOs. Southern or indigenous organizations have done an exceptional job at forcefully asserting that "the development process is their responsibility—from setting the development priorities to implementing projects to generating more of their own funds."[47] And as it becomes clear that Southern NGOs should, and will, become the central actors on the development stage, Northern NGOs need to realize that they must step aside and focus on their new, equally important role in shaping their own governments' foreign policy and educating their fellow citizens.

Development Education
and Advocacy

Northern NGOs are uniquely situated to play crucial roles in both development education and advocacy. Unlike other educators, their message can be informed by their activities in developing countries, and unlike purely self-interested lobbying groups, they have the relationships that give them the credibility to speak on behalf of the world's poor.[48] Southern NGOs have long been arguing that raising awareness and educating the Northern public about the realities and priorities of the South are international NGOs' most important roles. Based on the simple rationale that many of the causes of underdevelopment lie in the inequality of the world's political and economic systems, Southern NGOs urge their Northern counterparts to use the influence they have to change the misguided policies of governments and multilateral institutions.[49] Northern organizations must look beyond their local role in developing countries and take stock of their own governments' foreign policies and the implications those policies have on global trade, the environment, debt, international security, and peace—in a word, development. Southern NGOs are increasingly challenging their Northern partners to put more resources into education, campaigning, and advocacy—to educate and lobby against the "impediments to just development."[50] Similar to the path NGOs took thirty years ago—moving from relief work that responded to the symptoms of poverty to development work that explored the causes—is the path that lies before them now—leading from what John Clark calls "curative development" to "preventive development."[51]

Development Education

In 1984, *A Framework for Development Education* was published by a number of North American NGOs, representing a commitment by the NGO community to "press beyond overseas programs to address structural aspects of global hunger and poverty."[52] *Framework* stated that development education begins with the recognition of global interdependence and strives to provide information, promote humanitarian values, and stimulate individual and community action.

A few NGOs have been committed to the goals of development education for years and have impressive programs and publications to show for it: CWS's Office on Global Education develops global education material for use in primary and secondary schools and colleges; CARE, in cooperation with the Overseas Development Council, publishes a series of briefs on various development issues; and World Neighbors offers a number of study visits to countries where participants can meet and learn from World Neighbors' program partners around the world. Over the years, a number of new NGOs have been created that work exclusively in the development education (and advocacy) arena: Bread for the World, Results, and World Resources Institute, to name a few. A significant development education success story is the expansion of the U.S. National Committee for World Food Day, which began in 1983 as a collaborative effort with the UN's FAO to raise awareness in the United States of the needs of the poor in the third world. Today, the U.S. National Committee (other countries have national committees that are engaged in similar efforts) includes 450 member organizations and reaches thousands of Americans who dedicate each October 16 to activities with themes relating to food and hunger, including a nationwide teleconference focusing on hunger policy issues shown at hundreds of universities and high schools.

Although NGOs are generally regarded as the best hope for improved public information and better education about development issues, multilateral and bilateral aid providers have come to realize the importance of an informed citizenry as well. From FAO's role in the creation of World Food Day to the recent proposal by UNDP that a small portion of aid (2 percent, or $1 billion a year) be earmarked to cultivate public support and awareness about the objectives of aid, it is becoming universally accepted that donors have an obligation to inform and educate citizens about where aid dollars go and why. In 1981, the Biden-Pell Amendment to the 1981 foreign aid bill mandated that USAID provide matching grants to NGOs toward the goal of generating "widespread discussion and analysis of the root causes of world hunger and poverty . . . and to expand the network of organizations involved in development education."[53] From 1982 to 1993, eighty-eight organizations, including Interfaith Hunger Appeal, received modest grants, which designed a national curriculum development program that assists faculty in teaching about development and global issues.[54] A detailed 1993 evaluation of the Biden-Pell program found that an estimated thirty-seven million U.S. citizens had been reached by these projects in some fashion and that, compared with the general American public, these audiences "have much stronger support for foreign assistance and understanding of the U.S. stake in the Third World."[55] Unfortunately, since then, the grant program has come under sharp attack and was nearly cut entirely by the Republican Congress in 1994. It has managed to survive, with a slashed budget, offering a fraction of its original grants.

The potential and the need for effective development education are enormous, and international NGOs' access to grassroots knowledge remains the brightest hope for a type of education that engages, even transforms, the learner. In the current age of misinformation through overinformation, the challenges facing development education are great and require innovative thinking as well as real lessons from the South. Although certain international NGOs have an unfortunate tendency to simply promote their own programs under the guise of development education, domestic NGOs engaged exclusively in education and advocacy provide inspiring examples of high-quality programs and publications that educate and advise citizens and policy makers alike.

Advocacy

From the Southern perspective, Northern NGOs' role in advocacy, even more than in education, is crucial in creating a true partnership between Northern and Southern NGOs. One of the first successful illustrations of such a partnership occurred in the late 1970s when North-South networks of advocacy groups began to speak out against the dangerously misleading marketing tactics of baby-formula companies. The original group of seven NGOs rapidly grew to 150 organizations from all over the world. This International Baby Foods Action Network worked together to lead a successful campaign for an international governmental agreement on a code for baby-food marketing that is monitored by WHO.[56]

Perhaps the most well-known and respected organization in the advocacy arena is Bread for the World, a Christian citizens' movement of forty-four thousand members that effectively combines constituency education programs on public policy issues with an action agenda on international and domestic hunger issues. Established in 1973 by a committee of seven Catholics and seven Protestants, Bread for the World proposes legislative initiatives on hunger policy issues and rallies support for them through petitions to Congress. Although some hunger experts argue that Bread for the World often fails to adequately challenge the biases of middle America and address the political and economic structures at home that perpetuate underdevelopment, the thousands of letters that flow into Congress as a result of Bread for the World's initiatives have often represented real, albeit slow, progress.[57]

For the most part, development-oriented lobbying campaigns focus on trade, international finance, and foreign aid. Advocacy NGOs' strategies in effecting change range from direct lobbying of key individuals within governmental or multilateral agencies, to distributing publications and press releases, to staging protests or demonstrations that will win them a spot on the evening news. The question of which is the most effective strategy is a hotly debated one among activist NGOs, pitting proponents of "constructive dialogue" against those who prefer to "shout from the sidelines."[58]

Oxfam UK conducted a highly successful campaign in 1987 that pushed the debt crisis into the national consciousness. In response to the high levels of debt service that developing countries were required to pay their creditors, Oxfam UK, in a very public statement, posed the following challenge to the British public: "The scandal of the money that Africa gave to us: For every £1 we all gave for famine relief, £2 came back in debt payments. Don't stop the giving, stop the taking." The response was tremendous, and the British government, in an effort to respond to public outrage, proposed a debt relief initiative that was eventually accepted.[59]

In the United States, Interaction, an umbrella group consisting of virtually every major PVO involved in humanitarian work overseas, is the dominant player in the field of advocacy. Being the voice, so to speak, of the more than 150 organizations it represents makes Interaction's a difficult voice to ignore on Capitol Hill, and NGOs certainly benefit from their membership in such a potentially powerful consortium. Unfortunately, Interaction rarely advocates for issues beyond somewhat self-interested ones; priority is placed on encouraging legislators to support (increase) the foreign aid budget, especially as it relates to funding for NGOs. To a lesser extent, Interaction also advocates for reform of U.S. foreign assistance policies or, at a minimum, for the thoughtful consideration of the goals and accomplishments of development assistance.[60]

Recently, three organizations known for their less self-interested advocacy work released a proposal that squarely focused on improving (reforming and restructuring) U.S. international aid, specifically USAID. The Development Gap, Oxfam America, and Friends of the Earth released a proposal that would transform USAID into a free-standing agency called the U.S. Agency for Cooperation.[61] Within it, argues the proposal, should be established an Agency of Development Assistance Administration, which would be protected against political interference; all other programs and activities that promote strategic, commercial, and short-term foreign policy objectives could be left under the control of the State Department.

Fund-Raising Issues

For those organizations dedicated exclusively, or even partially, to improving development education and advocacy efforts, funding is a constant problem. Foundations rarely fund projects that aim to change public policies, and if they do, support is usually limited to one-year grants. In the United States, funding levels for development education represent a mere

0.2 percent of all funding to NGOs. Furthermore, raising funds for advocacy or education via NGOs' usual methods (solicitation newsletters or ads) is a hard sell for an audience that demands visible results for the dollars they put into a return envelope.

Although operational NGOs that are active in developing countries have a far easier time raising funds from the general public, they face different, equally challenging fund-raising issues. Twenty years ago, it was all too common for NGO contributors to open their mail and see pictures of skeletal mothers holding limp babies in their arms. This imagery is commonly referred to today as "the pornography of poverty," and fortunately, NGO fund-raising has evolved over the years to the point where such images are no longer a necessary or acceptable fund-raising ploy. Interaction requires that members' "communications shall respect the dignity, values, history, religion, and culture of the people served by the programs." Urged by their counterparts in the South, NGOs have been forced to realize their responsibility for portraying life in developing countries honestly and respectfully. For the thousands of Americans who receive monthly appeal letters from their favorite international organizations, the words they read and the pictures they see there are usually their primary source of information about developing countries, especially crisis-free countries that do not capture the media's attention.

Although manipulative and exploitive fund-raising has generally been abandoned by most NGOs, it continues to be a temptation for some. Clark observed that some NGOs "go straight for the artery connecting the heart and wallet. No image is too harrowing for them; no technique too tacky. This, coupled with the rapid rise of mass media evangelicalism, particularly in the United States, leads to a very steep growth curve for these agencies."[62] The media have actually obviated much of the need to engage in such fund-raising tactics; all too often, feature stories on third-world crises depict images of the South that most NGOs would reject as manipulative and exploitive, with the end result being that donors, responding to heart-wrenching scenes, are eager to contribute to the agencies working in those front-page-story countries. NGOs, however, must bear some responsibility for the media's depiction of Southern realities, as they play a key role in guiding international journalists to their newsworthy stories. Returning from Somalia in 1992, BBC correspondent George Alagiah spoke of the "unspoken understanding" between NGOs and journalists: "We try not to ask the questions too bluntly, 'Where will we find the most starving babies?' And they never answer explicitly. We get the pictures all the same."[63] The controversy regarding fund-raising tactics only underscores the difficulty in raising funds for advocacy and education efforts. Activists lobbying for change in the way the United States allocates its foreign aid, or educators teaching Americans about the little-known progress occurring at the grassroots level in many developing countries, are unfortunately not the images that inspire a flow of donations.

The shortage of funds for education and advocacy is only one reason that NGOs and the American public have been so slow to see the importance of these efforts. Another contributing factor is certainly the complexity of hunger and poverty issues; unlike some of the popular causes that rally public support these days, there are no easy answers to the monumental problems of underdevelopment, and this often leads to a paralyzing form of apathy. Although Americans continue to donate generously to many of the large NGOs working in the third world, Larry Minear points out that "the flip-side of American generosity may be an unwillingness to take time to understand the underlying causes of suffering and an impatience with intractable problems. For Americans perhaps the adage should be: 'Don't just do something. Stand there!'"[64]

The growth and expansion of NGOs over the past decade have been tremendous. It is estimated that NGO activity now touches close to 250 million people.[65] Although objective evaluation is difficult due to the lack of substantive analysis, there are clear areas where NGOs have made, and continue to make, enormous contributions to the process of development in the South. One such area is emergency relief. In a time of unprecedented civil strife and war, NGOs have been able to act faster and more effectively, though admittedly on a smaller scale, than the large multilateral institutions. Their permanent presence in developing countries further facilitates their ability to provide early warning and disaster preparedness. Another area of success is in the provision of credit to the poor who would be ineligible for any form of credit from official institutions. Since more than half of the developing world's labor force is self-employed, these small loans are crucial in creating long-term self-sufficiency, especially when they are accompanied by training and financial services.

However, notwithstanding NGOs' growing reach and empowering success stories, it is important to take stock of their limitations. UNDP argues that NGO interventions, although effective at reducing some of the worst forms of poverty, are not generally capable of helping people escape from structural poverty. Additionally, NGOs are unlikely to play more than a complementary role in providing social services and eradicating poverty.[66] Although NGOs' ability to effect profound structural changes in eradicating poverty may be limited, their influence and importance should hardly be dismissed. Northern NGOs have already made arguably the greatest contribution to development by being the first to point out that poverty can and should be addressed.

Notes

1. The actual number of NGOs is a contested issue, with most experts agreeing that it is virtually impossible to accurately determine how many there are. These figures come from Ian Smillie, "Mixed Messages: Public Opinion and Development Assistance in the 1990s," in *Public Support for International Development*, ed. Colm Foy and Henny Helmich (Paris: Development Centre of the Organization for Economic Co-operation and Development, 1996), 32.
2. "Aid: Falling Fast," *Economist*, June 22, 1996, 43–4.
3. Catholic Relief Services was founded in 1943 by the Catholic bishops of the United States. Today, CRS is one of the largest U.S. NGOs, active in over eighty countries, with a budget of over $260 million (FY 1995). Lutheran World Relief works on behalf of the Evangelical Lutheran Church in America and the Lutheran Church–Missouri Synod. Founded in 1945, LWR works in forty-eight countries, primarily in partnership with local organizations. Its 1995 budget was over $12 million.
4. TechnoServe Annual Report, 1995, 2.
5. Thomas F. Fox, "NGOs from the United States," *World Development* 15 Supplement (1987): 11–9.
6. CARE began in 1945 to assist the victims of World War II. Today, CARE is one of the largest NGOs; it provides assistance in fifty-three countries worldwide with an annual budget of nearly half a billion dollars (1994).
7. Church World Service was founded in 1946 as the international relief and development agency of the National Council of Churches in the United States.
8. Oxfam America is one of the seven autonomous Oxfams that provides assistance for self-help efforts throughout the world.
9. Stephen Hellinger, Douglas Hellinger, and Fred M. O'Regan, *Aid for Just Development: Report on the Future of Foreign Assistance* (Boulder, Colo.: Lynne Rienner, 1988a).
10. David C. Korten and L. David Brown, "Working More Effectively with Nongovernmental Organizations," in *Nongovernmental Organizations and the World Bank*, ed. Samuel Paul and Arturo Israel (Washington, D.C.: World Bank, 1991).
11. Henrik Secher Marcussen, "Comparative Advantages of NGOs: Myths and Realities," in *Foreign Aid towards the Year 2000: Experiences and Challenges*, ed. Olav Stokke (Portland, Ore.: Frank Cass, 1996), 264.
12. Charles Elliot, "Some Aspects of Relations between the North and South in the NGO Sector," *World Development* 15 Supplement (1987): 57–68.
13. Korten and Brown, "Working More Effectively," 59.
14. Marcussen, "Comparative Advantages of NGOs," 264.
15. Elliot, "Some Aspects of Relations between the North and South," 57–68.
16. Kunnibert Raffer and H. W. Singer, *The Foreign Aid Business: Economic Assistance and Development Co-operation* (Brookfield, Vt.: Edward Elgar Publishing, 1996), 139.
17. According to Frances Moore Lappé, Joseph Collins, and David Kinley, *Aid as Obstacle: Twenty Questions about Our Foreign Aid and the Hungry* (San Francisco: Institute for Food and Development Policy, 1980), 137.
18. World Neighbors is a nonsectarian agency that works throughout the world to establish and assist self-help programs. In 1994 it was active in twenty-one

countries with eighty-seven development programs, ranging from technology extension to small business development.

19. Hellinger, Hellinger, and O'Regan, *Aid for Just Development*, 108.
20. Lappé, Collins, and Kinley, *Aid as Obstacle*, 138.
21. Judith Tendler, "Turning Private Voluntary Organizations into Development Agencies: Questions for Evaluation," Program Evaluation Discussion Paper no. 12 (Washington, D.C.: USAID, 1982).
22. See Welland and Copestake, 1993; and Bebbington and Thiele, 1993.
23. Marcussen, "Comparative Advantages of NGOs," 278–80.
24. Michael Edwards and David Hulme, "Scaling up the Development Impact of NGOs: Concept and Experiences," in *Making a Difference*, ed. Michael Edwards and David Hulme (London: Earthscan Publications, 1992), 13.
25. Quoted in ibid. (original quote from Ellwood).
26. Quoted in Michael Maren, *The Road to Hell: The Ravaging Effects of Foreign Aid and International Charity* (New York: Free Press, 1997), 202.
27. Ian Smillie, "Changing Partners: Northern NGOs, Northern Governments," in *Non-Governmental Organisations and Governments: Stakeholders for Development*, ed. Ian Smillie and Henny Helmich (Paris: Development Centre of the OECD, 1993), 316.
28. David Rieff, "Charity on the Rampage," *Foreign Affairs* 76, no. 1 (1997): 134.
29. David C. Korten, "Third Generation NGO Strategies: A Key to People-Centered Development," *World Development* 15 Supplement (1987): 157.
30. Hellinger, Hellinger, and O'Regan, *Aid for Just Development*, 103.
31. Quoted in Smillie, "Changing Partners," 315.
32. Sally Yudelman, "The Integration of Women into Development Projects," *World Development* 15 Supplement (1987): 179–87.
33. Judith Tendler, as cited in Sally Yudelman, "The Integration of Women into Development Projects," *World Development* 15 Supplement (1987).
34. Mayra Buvinić and Margaret A. Lycette, "Women, Poverty, and Development in the Third World," in *Strengthening the Poor: What Have We Learned?* ed. John P. Lewis (New Brunswick, N.J.: Transaction Books, 1988), 157.
35. Ibid., 160.
36. Quoted in Oxfam America pamphlet "Women Taking the Lead."
37. Raffer and Singer, *Foreign Aid Business*, 145.
38. Ibid.
39. Bruce Rich, *Mortgaging the Earth: The World Bank, Environmental Impoverishment, and the Crisis of Development* (Boston: Beacon Press, 1994), 126.
40. Quoted in John Clark, *Democratizing Development: The Role of Voluntary Organizations* (West Hartford, Conn.: Kumarian Press, 1991), 77.
41. Quoted in Gerald Fraser, "Fighting for a More Open Bank," *Earth Times News Service*, September 25, 1996.
42. Among the members of the NGO coalition were Environmental Defense Fund, Oxfam America, United Church of Christ Board for World Ministries, and Maryknoll Fathers and Brothers.
43. Peter Willetts, "Consultative Status for NGOs at the United Nations," in *The Conscience of the World: The Influence of Non-governmental Organizations in the UN System*, ed. Peter Willetts (Washington, D.C.: Brookings Institution, 1996).
44. Rieff, "Charity on the Rampage," 134.
45. Quoted in Doug Hellinger, "NGOs and the Large Aid Donors: Changing the Terms of Engagement," *World Development* 15 Supplement (1987): 137.
46. Marcussen, "Comparative Advantages of NGOs," 264.

47. Anne Gordon Drabek, "Development Alternatives: The Challenge for NGOs—An Overview of the Issues," *World Development* 15 Supplement (1987): x.
48. Larry Minear, "The Other Missions of NGOs: Education and Advocacy," *World Development* 15 Supplement (1987): 209.
49. Edwards and Hulme, "Scaling up the Development Impact of NGOs," 20.
50. Clark, *Democratizing Development*, 126.
51. Ibid., 127.
52. Minear, "Other Missions of NGOs," 201.
53. Quoted in ibid., 202.
54. Interfaith Hunger Appeal (IHA) was unique in that it represented four international NGOs' commitment to development education—CRS, CWS, LWR, and the American Jewish Joint Distribution Committee jointly sponsored the program. Perhaps indicative of an unfortunate changing tide in terms of NGO support for development education, these four agencies recently decided to cease their support and shut down all of IHA's education programs.
55. Quoted in Smillie, "Mixed Messages," 43.
56. Clark, *Democratizing Development*, 32.
57. Patricia L. Kutzner, "Thirty Years of Anti-Hunger Advocacy," in *Hunger 1994* (Silver Spring, Md.: Bread for the World Institute, 1993), 90.
58. Edwards and Hulme, "Scaling up the Development Impact of NGOs," 21.
59. Clark, *Democratizing Development*, 141.
60. Interaction recently released a policy paper detailing its proposal for a refocused development assistance program and presenting the options under consideration for organizational restructuring. "American Values—National Interest," Interaction, March 1997.
61. Press release, "NGO Proposal on Foreign Aid Reform," May 5, 1995 (issued by Development Gap, Oxfam America, and Friends of the Earth).
62. Clark, *Democratizing Development*, 38.
63. Quoted in Alex De Waal and Rakiya Omaar, "Doing Harm by Doing Good?" *Current History* 92 (1993): 202.
64. Minear, "Other Missions of NGOs," 204.
65. UNDP, *Human Development Report 1993* (New York: Oxford University Press, 1993), 98.
66. Ibid.

6

Southern NGOs

T HE NGO EXPLOSION was not solely a Northern phenomenon. Organizations based in the South have proliferated in recent years on an even greater scale than in the North. Southern NGOs are known by a number of names—grassroots organizations, base groups, people's organizations, indigenous or local organizations—but they all refer to locally based groups working to improve and develop their own communities in a variety of ways. Like their Northern counterparts, their diversity defies generalization; perhaps the only common characteristic that binds this vibrant community is that Southern NGOs are born of and reflect the culture of the people they aim to assist.

Origins

Peggy Antrobus, a founding member of a network of third-world feminists promoting development alternatives,[1] views Southern NGOs as an expression and outgrowth of the ending of colonial rule, "a symbol of a people's new-found confidence in defining their own needs and priorities and in taking responsibility for addressing these."[2] Many organizations grew out of independence struggles; for example, the Gandhian movement in India, which encouraged Indian youth to work among the poor, had many offshoots that continue to flourish today, such as hand-loom centers and cooperatives.[3] In most developing countries, NGOs are built on the foundation of traditional practices and forms of organizing. Cooperative lifestyles have a strong history in many countries in the global South, where tribes typically organized into informal work groups and kinship organizations dating back centuries in some cases. Communal land ownership has also been extremely common for decades, if not centuries. In many countries, NGOs are far from new on the development scene. In Nepal, for example, Southern NGOs have maintained irrigation systems, built roads, planted trees, and built schools for generations, filling the void left by the weak central government, and similar examples can be found in Thailand and Sri Lanka.

As in the North, the 1970s witnessed a huge growth in Southern NGOs, many of them fueled by a combination of escalating demands from below and an increased supply of funds from above—from Northern NGOs as well as multilateral donors. Often, organizations sprang up in response to natural disasters, as in Bangladesh after the floods of 1975 and in Mexico City following the earthquake in 1985. In Africa, the drought and famine of 1984 and 1985, combined with the "brutal disengagement of the state," acted as an impetus for hundreds of organizations to develop.[4] Many Southern NGOs became increasingly politicized during the 1970s, influenced by new political concepts emerging at the time, such as the theology of liberation, which viewed development as a process of liberating the poor. The writings of Paolo Freire had a great impact on Brazilian NGOs, with his approach of "conscientization"—a combination of political education, social organization, and grassroots development that was designed to not only raise living standards but also help the poor perceive their exploitation and realize the means for overcoming it through mass organization.[5] Additionally, the political repression that was all too common during the 1970s, especially in Latin America, spawned thousands of women's organizations and human rights groups.

Although the incredible growth of Southern NGOs is a well-known story, there are no reliable statistics on their actual numbers. Because they are growing so quickly, information that is collected tends to be out of date before it is even published. Most estimates place the number at upward of a million, with a growth rate far exceeding that of their Northern counterparts. Thomas Dichter estimates that there are tens of thousands of crafts cooperatives worldwide, tens of thousands of agricultural cooperatives, at least twenty thousand squatter neighborhood-improvement associations in Latin America, twenty-four thousand development organizations in India alone, and more than two thousand small farmer development groups in the small country of Nepal.[6] The Indian state of Tamil Nadu is now famous the world over for its twenty-five thousand grassroots organizations.

Even more difficult to estimate than their numbers is the impact that these thousands of organizations have on their communities and countries. One source estimates that at least 100 million people benefit from Southern NGOs of all types: 25 million in Latin America, 60 million in Asia, and 12 million in Africa.[7] A study of agricultural development in tribal areas of Zimbabwe found that nearly half of the five hundred randomly selected households were members of local agricultural associations.[8] However, notwithstanding these staggering figures, the rate of population growth in most developing countries causes a dilution of the effects of NGOs, as their programs have to respond to a growing number of needs. Even the most famous NGO, the Grameen Bank, reaches only

6 percent of the population below the poverty line.[9] Whatever the exact number of people reached by NGOs, it is clear that countries with a strong nongovernmental sector have been indelibly impacted. In Latin America, NGOs have often been the sole channel for public concern when governments have remained silent. In Mozambique and Kampuchea, local NGOs, not official aid institutions, are the main development partners of the government. And in Bangladesh and India, they have had a significant impact in forcing through legislation concerning minimum wages, environmental protection, and labor conditions.

What Do Southern NGOs Do?

Southern NGOs respond to local needs and thus are engaged in an enormous range of activities, from community-based sewing cooperatives to regional entrepreneurial assistance. They range in size from tiny, three-member cooperatives to large, national networks, and in activities from a single function to broad-ranging activities in almost every sector. The one similarity that virtually all indigenous organizations share is the view of development as a holistic process; thus, even small organizations that begin as a response to a single specific need usually expand as their collective strength grows to tackle a number of issues and become broad-based development organizations. Linkages between the structural causes of poverty and development work at the local level are readily made by many of the strongest Southern NGOs, which view their work as a process of empowerment: "We should not only tend the wounds of those who have been run over by the cart, we have to stop the cart as well. We will have to drive a stick into its wheels."[10] So it should be understood, in looking at the various organizations listed below, that few, if any, are exclusively enterprise development or cooperative organizations; more often, they are an amalgam of a number of these loosely defined categories.

Enterprise Development Organizations

The provision of small loans has enabled thousands of low-income people to start their own small businesses. Microenterprise has existed for generations in the South, funded primarily from outside sources (Northern NGOs) but also from increasingly self-sufficient Southern NGOs. In 1992, the Asian Development Bank report noted Southern NGOs' remarkable success in the area of enterprise development: "In the area of rural credit, formal credit institutions have been singularly unsuccessful in either recovering loans, or in even reaching the poor. In contrast, the success of Grameen Bank, BRAC and other projects has meant that around one third of assetless rural households are now being covered by sustainable credit programmes."[11] Even many local organizations that are not enterprise development organizations per se promote it as part of an integrated development strategy.

The Grameen Bank in Bangladesh is probably the most well-known of all Southern NGOs and has become a model for microenterprise programs throughout the world, including in the United States. It began in 1976 as a modest grassroots initiative by a university professor interested in providing credit to the landless poor who had never before received a loan and likely never would. The bank loans, which have to be repaid within one year, are provided only to self-formed groups; each group is allocated a capital sum, and each group allocates two members who will receive the loan. The bank will not issue any other members loans until the first two members have started their weekly repayments. These strict rules have yielded a repayment record of 98 percent. Development lessons are also handed out with the loans—clients are required to pledge to boil their drinking water, keep families small, and maintain good health practices. By 1983, the bank had extended its operations to a national level, developing an enormous network of bankers on bicycles who start at 6:00 A.M. and cover fifteen miles a day. The following year, the bank received more than $25 million from the International Fund for Agricultural Development to assist its expansion to a targeted five hundred branches. Beneficiaries of Grameen Bank loans have used these funds for the development of such enterprises as weaving, pottery, cycle repair, rice husking, and garment manufacture. The bank has been especially successful in providing loans to women; of the bank's 2.1 million borrowers, 94 percent are women. Today, the Grameen Bank is operational in more than half the villages of Bangladesh, providing loans totaling more than $400 million a year.

In Ahmedabad, India, a trade union of women in the informal sector, mostly construction laborers and street vendors, established the Self-Employed Women's Association (SEWA) in 1972. The women began the group as a collective front against the all-too-common police harassment inflicted on them. SEWA rapidly grew to the point where it set up its own cooperative bank, owned by the members, and it now has nearly forty-seven thousand depositors. The bank provides its clients with insurance, housing financing, and the capital that allows them to increase their daily incomes and gives them the security to defend their rights against unfair fines and other marginalizing practices. SEWA also supports a system of cooperatives for artisans, dairy workers, trading and vending workers, and service workers. Almost half of its members—and the majority of women in India—are home-based workers. Exact numbers are unknown, because home-based work is not considered employment by the official census. SEWA provides an invaluable service to its nearly 150,000 women members, not only through loans, cooperatives, and other supporting services such as day care and literacy classes, but perhaps more profoundly in the empowerment it instills.

Cooperatives

Examples of cooperative organizations abound in virtually every country in the global South, where the importance of collective strength, especially in the face of unwelcome governmental or Northern policies or advice, has secured their future as a vital force in any developing context. The Matsvaire Village Development Program in Zimbabwe is a good illustration of this collective strength in action. Villagers in Matsvaire found that the technical production package of hybrid maize seed, chemical fertilizers, and pesticides that Northern funding agencies were promoting was not producing results. Instead of deferring to Northern expertise, as they were encouraged to do, they collectively sought alternatives. The technical package was replaced with the creation of cereal banks to store cooperative grain for distribution throughout the year—and, in the process, a new respect for traditional crops and seeds was acknowledged.[12]

One of the most successful cooperatives in the global South began in the Kaira District Dairy in the 1960s in Gujarat, India, to help women and the landless acquire milch stock. With the assistance of Northern funds, the cooperative was able to introduce technological innovations in animal feeding and gradually saved enought to invest in a factory. This factory is known today throughout India as the Amul Dairy, and it produces a wide array of milk products on a national level. When in the mid-1970s the European Economic Community (EEC) offered the government of India surplus dairy products as food aid, the leaders of the Kaira Dairy cooperative saw how this could sweep away the market they had built up. They quickly mobilized and negotiated with the government to reconstitute the EEC's dairy products as whole milk and then use the income from the sale of this milk to finance dairy production throughout India based on the Amul model.[13]

Following a famine in the Casamance region of Senegal in 1984, the Committee for the Fight for the End of Hunger (COLUFIFA), a community self-help organization, was created. COLUFIFA's strategy respects and relies on local traditions, including a sense of community, to feed the people in the area. Members with positions of responsibility must pledge a traditional allegiance, and a committee of village elders is the authorized body to settle disputes and internal conflicts. Reflective of its self-respect and self-reliance, COLUFIFA accepted no outside funds between 1985 and 1990, sustaining its members through its independently created collective food banks and granaries. COLUFIFA is a perfect example of an organization that has expanded to address the many challenges of development. A credit system was created with the revenue earned by commercializing agricultural products, and it now provides loans to needy members at low interest rates. It also provides training in nutrition and health. Today, COLUFIFA has over twenty thousand members, and it is often asked by peasants in neighboring countries to provide assistance in organizing committees. Its long-term objective remains the elimination of hunger in the villages of the Casamance region by the turn of the century.

Mouvan Peyizan Papaye (Creole for Peasant Movement of Papaye), or MPP, was established in Haiti by a group of peasant farmers eager for greater cooperation and dialogue. A discussion of the government's failure to meet the farmers' growing needs led to the establishment of this small agricultural collective in 1973. By the late 1980s, MPP enterprises engaged more than twelve thousand peasants in cooperative processing and distribution of crafts and produce. Among the activities that MPP is involved in are the raising of small livestock, honey production for local use and export, grain storage, and credit and marketing programs. Additionally, educational and environmental programs work to offset the region's high illiteracy rate and the erosion of croplands. MPP is often noted for its ability to scale up politically.[14] Initially shying away from any political involvement out of a well-placed fear of repression, MPP became one of the main forces behind Operation Lavalas, a national peasant movement with over 100,000 members whose direct aim was to challenge the government. Lavalas was instrumental in bringing Jean-Bertrand Aristide to power. During the 1992 military coup, MPP offices were destroyed, assets were stolen, and members were attacked. The recent return of a peace to Haiti has allowed MPP to begin to restore seed and tool reserves, though like the peace itself, its future is not secure.

Protest Movements: Environmental Organizations

Protest movements are usually associated with a political struggle to overcome a repressive regime or governmental practice. In Latin America, protest movements have a particularly strong history. For instance, peasant rebellions in Mexico date back to the seventeenth century. In Colombia, between 1971 and 1980, 128 demonstrations occurred in communities representing 18 percent of the national population.[15] However, a defining feature of rural peasant movements has been not only a reaction to political repression but also, and even more frequently, a means for the poor to demand access to natural resources. Most protest movements are led by environmental organizations, which often go on to lobby for or work toward environmental goals far beyond their original focus. Environmental protest movements have been, and continue to be, a driving force in Brazil, where they originally sprang up to protest the displacement of peasants by large landowners and the ravaging of the land, especially the rain forest. The rubber tappers union captured international attention when its leader, Chico Mendes, was murdered in 1988. Between 1975 and 1988, fifteen rubber tappers movements formed, and in alliance with indigenous tribal peoples, they managed to preserve 1.2 million hectares of forests.[16] Asia also has an extremely vibrant community of environmental activists; as of 1990, there were five hundred environmental organizations in India alone. A common characteristic of many of these movements and groups, from Brazil to India, is the effort to regain local management and control of natural resources.

Perhaps the most famous Indian environmental group is the Chipko movement of northern India, which provides a powerful example of a relatively small community group's successful battle against the forces of state and private capital. In 1964, a workers' cooperative, the Dasholi Gram Swarajya Mandal, which organized unskilled and semiskilled construction workers, started a new enterprise involving the collection of roots and herbs from the forest. This activity employed over a thousand people between 1969 and 1972 and allowed the cooperative to open a small manufacturing plant that produced turpentine and resin from pine sap. However, the plant was forced to close down when the Indian Forestry Department refused to allot adequate supplies of pine sap. Further outraging the members of the cooperative was the government's decision to allot three hundred ash trees to the Simon Company, a sporting goods manufacturer. When agents from the Simon Company arrived to supervise the cutting of the trees, villagers organized in the most powerful yet peaceful of ways: beating drums, marching, and singing traditional songs, they drove the company employees away without a single tree falling. Later, when the Forestry Department announced that it would auction almost twenty-five hundred trees in the Reni forest, villagers, aware of the landslides and floods that this deforestation could cause, hugged the trees as a tactic to save them. Thus the most poignant image of the Chipko movement was born—masses of villagers, mostly women, embracing their trees to save them. (Chipko comes from the Hindu word meaning "to hug.")

The Chipko movement continues to spread to this day, connected horizontally through runners who carry messages of Chipko happenings from village to village—and even at times to the national government. In 1981, Indian Prime Minister Indira Gandhi declared a fifteen-year ban on tree felling in the Garwahl Himalayas. Today, the Chipko movement is led primarily by women and has a diverse membership, from poor villagers to intellectuals and scientists.

An equally well-known environmental group in East Africa is also driven by the activism of women. The Green Belt Movement of Kenya originated in 1977 from a project of the National Council of Kenyan Women. The principal aim of the movement is to work in cooperation with women's organizations in opposing deforestation and, in the process, support women's rights. The Green Belt Movement's goal is "to improve the environment, and in the process, raise public awareness about the basic role of our natural environment at the family, regional and national level."[17] Targeting primarily poor rural women, the movement has planted over ten million trees with the participation of more than fifty thousand women.[18] Almost all of the movement's financial resources come from the North; local contribution occurs in the form of labor and some voluntary services.

Women's Organizations

The liberation and channeling of women's energy has been called the "single most important force fueling the grassroots explosion."[19] Women-run NGOs have witnessed the most dramatic growth of all. In 1975, eighty NGOs, from both North and South, attended the UN Conference on Women in Mexico; in 1985, nine thousand participants came to Nairobi for the third women's conference, representing several thousand organizations. Like all NGOs, women's NGOs embrace an enormous range of issues and activities, similar only in that they virtually all share a strong philosophy of participatory development and tend to view themselves as part of the broader grassroots movement rather than as separate institutions. The growth and success of women's groups have led to an awareness and even appreciation by men, who initially disregarded and sometimes opposed them. As one male leader of a peasant movement in Burkina Faso commented, "development without women is like having ten fingers and only working with five."[20] Research has shown that organizations that start off as strictly women's groups have been able to expand their scope and include men at a later stage without costing women their leadership positions or voice. In contrast to what might be considered "women's issues" in the North, the issues addressed by Southern NGOs led by women are not about personal rights but about community or environmental problems, as seen with the Green Belt and Chipko movements. A cofounder of a women's self-help group in the Peten region of Guatemala describes how environmental issues are intimately tied to the personal: "Our object is to teach self-esteem, promote health, and help bring home cash so men don't have to knock down the forest to support the family. If the rainforest disappears, drought will come, and that will be the most terrible of things."[21] The group, called Ixchel, after the Mayan goddess of corn and birth, began with thirty women who taught one another dressmaking and shared information about plants and kitchen gardens. Its participatory organizational structure was recently recognized with an award of external funding to raise tepesquintle, a prized jungle rodent high in protein and in danger of extinction.

One of the largest of all Southern NGOs is the All Pakistan Women's Association (APWA), established in 1949 to facilitate the total involvement of women in the process of development and to restore women's legal rights. APWA successfully spearheaded national campaigns in education and health, establishing over seventy institutions of higher and primary education, as well as hospitals and health clinics that benefit over 250,000 women and children annually. Priorities are placed on education, health, and training in income-generating and vocational skills. With sixty-one provincial branches and five affiliates, APWA is a national force capable of mobilizing huge numbers of volunteers.

Independencia, an impoverished suburb of Lima, Peru, known as the "poverty belt," is home to a small grassroots group of women called the Women's Organization of Independencia, or WARMI. The organization operates an extensive network of community kitchens where members donate their time and talents to cooking. Recently, WARMI developed an alternative food purchasing and distribution network and began to offer basic health care services in an attempt to meet the needs of community members in a holistic way. The organization is sustained by funds generated from the sale of meals (at cost) to those who can pay, as well as the voluntary labor of its staff.[22]

DAWN (Development Alternatives with Women for a New Era), based at the University of West Indies in Barbados, is proof that Southern NGOs are not only addressing local needs but also working on a global policy scale, as they have encouraged their Northern counterparts to do. DAWN was established in 1984 for the purpose of analyzing third-world issues and providing the worldwide women's movement with the tools to politicize the role of women in development. Recognizing that the UN Decade for Women (1975–85) had fallen short of its targeted goals, this network of third-world women activists and researchers set out to publish an instrument for the International Women's Conference in Nairobi that would define the issues of development from the vantage point of women.[23] DAWN continues to fulfill its mandate of the empowerment of women, seeking alternative development strategies and improving North-South dialogue through its first-rate research, advocacy, and training programs.

National or Network NGOs

As Southern NGOs grow in size and scope, tackling ever larger impediments to their community's development, many of them have expanded into national-level institutions, providing services needed by grassroots groups while also inducing social change. Many of the organizations already listed above, such as APWA, SEWA, and MPP, are examples of national networks. Frequently, national governments and Northern NGOs establish large intermediary NGOs with national scope that channel aid from Northern funders to smaller, local organizations.

The Bangladesh Rural Advancement Committee (BRAC) is arguably the largest NGO in the global South, reaching over eleven million households in fifty thousand villages, with a staff of over seventeen thousand field-workers.[24] Similar to many of the oldest Northern NGOs, BRAC was founded in 1972 by F. H. Abed as a relief organization to provide services to refugees in the wake of the War of Liberation. Gradually, its relief-oriented approach was replaced with longer-term objectives, primarily integrated rural development for the assetless poor. As such, its major program, the Rural Development Program, supports the rural poor by assisting them to set up rural institutions, headed by local leadership, where they can assert their rights and improve their socioeconomic condition.[25] Each village participating in the Rural Development Program actually sets up two organizations, one for each gender. BRAC has found that the "lack of exclusiveness in mainstream programs has resulted in biases against the poor and women."[26] In concentrating on women separately, BRAC has achieved some of its most significant successes. Its Child Survival Program, which has attracted the participation of the government of Bangladesh, aims to provide oral rehydration therapy, immunization, nutrition, health education, and family planning and to enhance the professional development of rural midwives. Its Oral Therapy Extension Program, which teaches about the causes of and preventive measures for diarrheal diseases, has taught at least one woman from each household (or nearly ten million people).[27] Additionally, its Primary Education Program has created model schools where students are engaged in education that is accessible and relevant to their needs. The program, which won international accolades from

UNICEF,[28] consists of over twenty-five hundred schools, with attendance rates of over 95 percent. Another principal area for BRAC is its Credit Program, a self-sustaining, nationwide banking operation that has tested the ability of the landless poor to use their own resources.

With its emphasis on empowerment and self-reliance, BRAC's stance on external assistance is unsurprising. The rapid growth and notable achievements of the organization have won it hearty support from a range of international donors, from Northern NGOs to multilateral institutions. However, BRAC maintains a strict policy of limiting foreign assistance to no more than 40 percent of its income, and consequently, it engages in a number of efforts to generate its own funds. It has been successful in establishing a string of retail outlets to market crafts and textiles produced by rural artisans and has also established two commercial projects—an ice plant/cold storage and a printing press. With a budget of over $20 million, BRAC continues to spur real development among Bangladesh's poorest groups, especially women and the landless.[29]

The Sarvodaya Shramadana Movement (SSM) in Sri Lanka is one of the oldest and most successful rural development networks in the world, reaching roughly three million villagers with its rural development programs. Begun in 1958, SSM uses Buddhist values to promote moral, personal, and social improvement and to encourage nonviolent change in all fields of development. SSM's work is grounded in the belief that development can come about only through self-fulfillment, nondependence, and, above all, awakening from the ignorance that perpetuates underdevelopment.[30] The word *Sarvodaya* means "the awakening of all," a term coined by Mahatma Gandhi. To bring about this awakening, SSM works with villages, guiding them through five stages of development toward complete self-reliance. The first stage is the Shramadana work camp, where SSM volunteers and villagers join to meet a specified need of the community together and voluntarily. The next stage occurs when the village forms one or more Sarvodaya groups, which then go on, in stage three, to conduct a village survey and draw up a development plan. Stage four is achieved when the village, having established some income-generating activity, becomes completely self-financing and is ready and willing (in stage five) to turn to neighboring villages to offer support and assistance.[31] SSM was the target of negative publicity during the 1980s when conflict erupted between the Tamils and Sinhalese. The organization was accused of hostile treatment of the Tamils, which prompted its principal international funder to threaten to cut off all support, thereby eliminating the group. The unsettling experience pushed the agency to diversify its funding sources; today, UNICEF and USAID are among its biggest supporters.

In Bolivia, a group of young university graduates created INEDER (Educational Institute for Rural Development) in 1973 to improve the standard of living for farmers by effecting structural social change. Today, INEDER is active with farmer unions throughout Bolivia, helping to organize and coordinate networks in which grassroots organizations, the local civil government, state development projects, churches, and other NGOs all work together to define a development plan for a given region. INEDER conducts programs in the areas of farming and animal husbandry, fostering of popular peasant organizations, promotion of women, rural radio, agricultural education, health, and research. INEDER faced significant obstacles in its early years due to a repressive dictatorial government that prohibited political activity in rural areas, but today it is thriving, growing rapidly in pursuit of its long-term aim: "to contribute to the macroeconomic and political change of society."[32]

The 6-S Association of West Africa is perhaps the largest and most innovative network of peasant groups in the world.[33] 6-S came into existence in 1977 when it received funding from the Swiss Development Cooperation (the Swiss equivalent of USAID), which took the bold and unprecedented step of providing flexible, long-term funding rather than the typical project-to-project funding usually offered by bilateral donors. The 6-S Association's broad goals are to provide training and funding for organized peasant groups. Its approach is unique: before providing any funding, it helps groups organize into federations and develop networks that include all members of the community. It also assists with the teaching of elementary concepts of management and lays the groundwork for literacy training. Only after the federation has proved its ability to save, manage, and communicate effectively will 6-S provide funding, usually in the form of loans. 6-S assistance ends when the federation reaches a point where it is able to attract external funds from banks or other agencies. What makes the 6-S Association even more distinctive is the fact that it provides funds to federations without advance knowledge of the projects for which the funds will be used, thus giving the groups the autonomy and responsibility to carry out the projects that they, not outside donors, deem most necessary. With 6-S support and other loans, one federation in Mali implemented such wide-ranging projects as construction of wells and stoves, training of grassroots communicators, and the creation of a young people's theater group. As one federation leader expressed, "[6-S] is the only NGO to have really accepted the way peasant organizations function."[34] Farmers' voices, concerns, and vision guide the development process from all levels; the 6-S General Assembly is composed almost entirely of peasant representatives, and farmers are trained in the basic elements of management and communication for the very purpose of improving their ability to voice their needs and demands in ever-widening spheres. Each year, over $2 million is distributed to the roughly four thousand federations in countries such as Burkina Faso, Senegal, Mali, and Mauritania.

Although the flourishing of Southern NGOs into national networks and federations provides an inspiring example of development from the bottom up, it is important to bear in mind the dangers of rapid growth and expansion. Like NGOs in the North, Southern NGOs that grow quickly, often with the assistance of government funds, run the risk of being co-opted by the government and losing the unique strengths that their small size and community base provide. Rapid growth and networking also tend to generate a bureaucracy that is absent in small organizations. One large Senegalese peasant federation is already "generating bureaucrats," claims Pierre Pradervand. Communication can also be jeopardized by the rapid expansion of an organization across regions that do not even have roads, much less members with vehicles.[35] Additionally, it is important to bear in mind that most national networks depend on large subsidies from external donors, leading some critics to question whether ministries of health and education would not meet with similar success if their budgets were augmented so significantly.

North-South Relationships

Northern influence and intrusion in the South are nothing new. From colonial governments to Christian missionaries, Northern interventions have ranged from repressive to paternalistic to participatory. Although the dynamic of North-South relationships continues to cover a broad range, the opportunity for change and innovation in those relationships is being made possible due to the autonomy rendered by the growing economic strength of Southern organizations. Never before has so much money been directed from the North to Southern NGOs. Between 1970 and 1990, grants by Northern NGOs increased from just over $1 billion to $5 billion.[36] And multilateral institutions have also sought new development partners; the World Bank as well as many UN agencies are increasingly working through local organizations and associations. But nowhere is the current philosophy (and popularity) of partnership building stronger than in Northern NGOs' rhetoric. However, the nature of these partnerships deserves close scrutiny—as the 1993 UNDP report pointed out, "the one-sided control of the wallet gives lie to the equality implied in the term."[37]

Obviously, the relationship that develops between Northern and Southern NGOs varies, depending on the internal philosophies and dynamics of the individual agencies. Some Northern NGOs, in an effort to fulfill their mandate to work with local organizations, simply create brand-new organizations, ignoring existing ones. Although some very capable Southern NGOs that have grown into their own autonomy have been created by outsiders, the paradigm of empowerment from above, rather than from the grassroots, is generally less sustainable and far-reaching. Other Northern NGOs believe strongly that their principal function is to strengthen the capacity of existing local NGOs, and these Northern organizations carry out programs of institution building and empowerment, rather than operational projects. Regardless of the specific arrangement governing the relationship between Southern and Northern NGOs, tensions between the two are inevitable due to their contrasting priorities and philosophies.

U.S. PVOs, and Northern NGOs in general, tend to be far more bureaucratic than their Southern counterparts, placing more value on accountancy and reporting. When Northern organizations fund Southern NGOs to carry out specific projects, as is usually the case, this often imposes a limited, Western concept of time and efficiency that values met deadlines more than the learning or organizing process, which, from the Southern perspective, is often the most valuable aspect of the entire project.[38] This project aid is becoming more common with the growth of Northern NGOs' budgets (due to increasing government support) and the increasing demand for more and more projects on which to spend their money. Project funding is also criticized by Southern NGOs for the lack of long-term commitment it suggests. Members of BRAC accurately complain that "as long as you are merely dependent on single projects which you have to sell in the charity business, you will never get around to programming or to long-term planning."[39] Indeed, the Northern practice of channeling funds to Southern NGOs on a project-by-project basis contradicts their own definition of development as a complex process involving the interaction of economic, political, social, and cultural processes. Furthermore, examples such as the 6-S Association's funding policy suggest that isolated project grants have a far more limited impact than those that provide flexible funding and concentrate on strengthening local institutions. Southern NGOs are eager to balance the asymmetry of power that continues to dominate the relationships with their Northern counterparts; it is time for Northern agencies to share that commitment to a true partnership.

NGO-Government Relationships

The creation of Southern NGOs is often a direct reaction to the national government's failure to meet communities' demands or, in some cases, a response to government repression. Military regimes, especially in Latin America, sparked the creation of hundreds of popular organizations rooted in political opposition, which were often the only voices challenging state policies. Meanwhile, Asian NGOs have proved to be adept at building alliances with national governments, which has secured them a voice in advocating for constructive domestic policies.

Although democratization is taking place on every continent, the most common form of governance, especially in Africa, continues to be somewhat Marxist-oriented, single-party rule. Although these governments claim to have incorporated a pro-development view into state policies, their definition of development is usually blind to considerations such as gender and the environment. NGOs in such political atmospheres are tolerated, but generally only insofar as they complement welfare-oriented government programs, and external funding has scarcely a chance of reaching them when governments exert foreign exchange control. Liberal democracy, a growing phenomenon in developing countries, is the most complicated environment in which NGOs operate. Relationships between NGOs and liberal democracies range from overwhelming governmental support to harassment and intimidation by government officials who view NGOs' existence as an implicit criticism of them.[40]

As Southern governments witness the sudden popularity of domestic NGOs and the funds that they attract (largely a result of bilateral aid programs' requirements that a portion of official aid be channeled through NGOs), many politicians have sought to set up their own NGOs to get a portion of that aid. These not-so-nongovernmental NGOs (sometimes called GRINGOs, for government-inspired NGOs, or GONGOS, for government-organized NGOs) have occasionally proved to be effective providers of assistance, though rarely reaching out to the poorest populations. For the most part, however, government-organized NGOs tend to be intimately linked to the ruling party and are generally set up to further the aims of national and local politicians.[41] A former prime minister of the Republic of Congo, for example, promoted a fictitious village group to international donors and pocketed the proceeds.[42]

There have also been positive examples of effective and positive collaboration between governments and local organizations, especially in the area of urban services. In Mexico City, for example, a low-income housing authority called FONHAPO, established in 1981 by the Mexican government with World Bank support, has created a new model for relations between community groups and the government. Involving activists from the urban NGO sector, FONHAPO has augmented the provision of housing credit to barrio associations, cooperatives, and community groups, reaching segments of the population that the government had previously been unable to reach.[43] When governments view NGOs less as adversaries and more as a source of valuable information, the entire country benefits. The Amul Dairy in India proved to be inspirational for the

Indian government, which drew on the Amul experience in the mid-1960s for the design of the country's National Dairy Development Program, known as Operation Flood. Similarly, the government of Bangladesh has replicated many of the Grameen Bank's strategies on a national basis.[44]

Because their survival is often at stake, Southern NGOs tend to learn from their mistakes much faster than do international organizations that do not suffer the direct consequences. And much has been learned in the past decade of dizzying growth and expansion. As their economic sustainability becomes possible as a result of their income-generating projects and their own fund-raising, Southern NGOs are already changing the dynamic of their relationship with Northern aid providers and moving center stage in the development arena—changing their own communities, improving their own systems, and providing a model of real, sustaining development.

Notes

1. This group is called DAWN and is described in further detail in the section "Women's Organizations."
2. Peggy Antrobus, "Funding for NGOs: Issues and Options," *World Development* 15 Supplement (1987): 96.
3. John Clark, *Democratizing Development: The Role of Voluntary Organizations* (West Hartford, Conn.: Kumarian Press, 1991), 29.
4. Pierre Pradervand, *Listening to Africa: Developing Africa from the Grassroots* (New York: Praeger Publishers, 1989), 47.
5. Clark, *Democratizing Development*, 31.
6. Thomas W. Dichter, "The Changing World of Northern NGOs: Problems, Paradoxes and Possibilities," in *Strengthening the Poor: What Have We Learned?* ed. John P. Lewis (New Brunswick, N.J.: Transaction Books, 1988), 184.
7. Julie Fisher, *The Road from Rio: Sustainable Development and the Non-Governmental Movement in the Third World* (Westport, Conn.: Praeger Publishers, 1993), 95.
8. Ibid., 23.
9. Ibid., 96.
10. Quoted in Sjef Theunis, ed., *Non-Governmental Development Organizations of Developing Countries: And the South Smiles* (Dordrecht: Martinus Nijhoff Publishers, 1992).
11. Quoted in Ian Smillie, "Mixed Messages: Public Opinion and Development Assistance in the 1990s," in *Public Support for International Development*, ed. Colm Foy and Henny Helmich (Paris: Development Centre of the OECD, 1996), 15.
12. Bill Rau, *From Feast to Famine: Official Cures and Remedies to Africa's Food Crisis* (London: Zed Books, 1991), 173.
13. Clark, *Democratizing Development*, 34.
14. Peter Uvin, "Fighting Hunger at the Grassroots: Paths to Scaling Up," *World Development* 23 (1995): 934.

15. Fisher, *Road from Rio*, 66.
16. Ibid., 67. Bruce Rich, in *Mortgaging the Earth: The World Bank, Environmental Impoverishment, and the Crisis of Development* (Boston: Beacon Press, 1994), points out that this alliance was especially noteworthy, as the relationship between rubber tappers and indigenous groups had historically been laden with conflict.
17. Theunis, *Non-Governmental Development Organizations*, 202.
18. UNDP, *Human Development Report 1993* (New York: Oxford University Press, 1993), 97.
19. Fisher, *Road from Rio*, 48.
20. Quoted in ibid., 101.
21. Quoted in Mary Jo McConahay, "Wise Women of the Rainforest," in *Choices* 4, no. 2 (August 1995): 21.
22. William Savitt and Paula Bottorf, *Global Development: A Reference Handbook* (Colorado: ABC-CLIO, 1995), 264.
23. See Gita Sen, *Development, Crises, and Alternative Visions: Third World Women's Perspectives* (New York: Monthly Review Press, 1987).
24. "NGO of the Year," *Earth Times*, December 27, 1996.
25. Theunis, *Non-Governmental Development Organizations*, 54.
26. Ibid.
27. Ibid.
28. UNICEF, "Education: Breakthrough in Bangladesh," in *State of the World's Children 1990* (New York: Oxford University Press, 1990), 60.
29. Savitt and Bottorf, *Global Development*, 258.
30. Theunis, *Non-Governmental Development Organizations*, 280.
31. Ibid.
32. Ibid., 244.
33. Pradervand, *Listening to Africa*, 99–109.
34. Quoted in ibid., 103.
35. Ibid., 171.
36. UNDP, *Human Development Report 1993* (New York: Oxford University Press, 1993), 88.
37. Quoted in Clark, *Democratizing Development*, 60.
38. Pradervand, *Listening to Africa*, 187.
39. Quoted in Theunis, *Non-Governmental Development Organizations*, 311.
40. Theunis, *Non-Governmental Development Organizations*, 316.
41. UNDP, *Human Development Report 1993*, 88.
42. Fisher, *Road from Rio*, 33.
43. Samuel Paul, "Governments and Grassroots Organizations: From Co-Existence to Collaboration," in *Strengthening the Poor: What Have We Learned?* ed. John P. Lewis (New Brunswick, N.J.: Transaction Books, 1988), 66.
44. Ibid.

7

Critical Perspectives

THE INTERNATIONAL AID DONOR community is as large as it is
diverse—from bilateral donors providing multi-million-dollar loans
to correct balance-of-payment difficulties in an emerging market to small
NGOs conducting community development programs. Aid donors face
different challenges in their attempt to provide aid that will succeed in
stimulating economic growth and development. However, the negative attitudes about aid that are prevalent today, especially during this period of
economic strength in the United States, underscores a growing perception
that aid has failed. Aid critics, especially well-known conservative members of Congress, often complain not only that foreign aid has failed to
accomplish its objectives but also that it was an exercise in futility all
along. When critics describe developing countries as "foreign rat holes"
they are placing the blame for aid's uneven record squarely on the shoul-
ders of the global South. Although in some cases blame must be shared
with corrupt Southern governments or unsound economic policies, the
accusation is a classic blame-the-victim argument, laden with ignorant
assumptions that make the necessity of understanding aid and the key aid
institutions all the more acute.

This book has attempted to facilitate that learning process by introducing the primary institutions involved in the provision of aid and discussing
the various challenges and accomplishments associated with them. Clearly,
none is perfect. However, notwithstanding their flaws, each donor in different ways is tackling the problems of poverty and underdevelopment.
Significant progress has been made, and all donors deserve to share the
credit for the accomplishments of the past half century. Real per capita
GNP tripled for all developing countries between 1960 and 1989. China
accomplished in ten years what it took the West fifty years to do in the
nineteenth century: average life expectancy has increased by sixteen years,
adult literacy has increased by 40 percent, and child mortality rates have
been cut in half.[1] Additionally, foreign aid has played a critical role in significant medical advances of the past few decades, including the elimination of smallpox and the near universal immunization of children under
five. If this book appears to close on a critical note, it is not to join the

chorus of critics but to suggest an agenda for a new aid policy, one that will foster and support sustainable development and, as such, have a hand in the creation of a more just and equitable global tomorrow.

The aid agenda of the United States inevitably impacts the policies of other bilateral donors and multilateral agencies. The recent cuts in the U.S. aid budget predict a grim future for overseas aid more generally. However, the shortcomings of international aid are due not only to inadequate resources but also to donors' weaknesses in allocating those limited funds. The success of the Asian "tigers" offers compelling lessons of how poor countries with good economic policies can benefit from increases in aid. Taiwan and South Korea, for example, productively absorbed at least $50 per capita per year over roughly two decades and today are widely recognized as part of the "East Asian miracle" in terms of sustained economic growth. A bill will soon be introduced in Congress that proposes a different approach to economic development in Africa.[2] The proposal is hardly innovative; it calls for selective aid that rewards countries with good economic policies with more aid. As obvious as this sounds, the principle of selective aid has rarely been applied, especially during the cold war, when recipients' politics were deemed more important than their economic policies. U.S. foreign aid policy now has the opportunity to influence other donors by setting an example that actively encourages reform and sound policy frameworks. The new initiative proposed by the Clinton administration will concentrate efforts (and aid) on those African countries such as Uganda and Ghana that have shown serious commitment to market-based reform.

Whether economic liberalization is truly the means to achieve economic growth and development, or whether it has merely replaced the solutions of previous decades (such as basic needs or structural adjustment), remains to be seen. Although the notion that globalization is an inevitable process that will bring about economic growth, and hence development, seems to have been accepted by official aid donors, it remains a hotly debated issue, as David Korten reveals below. The U.S. government, for the most part, has eagerly accepted globalization as the "answer," leading some to suggest that USAID has gone from furthering the U.S. government's strategic and political goals to promoting U.S. business interests abroad. Whatever the motivating factors, USAID is clearly hampered in its efforts to work toward development and poverty alleviation by its dependent relationship to the Department of State. Despite its claims of independence, USAID's autonomy is repeatedly called into question when its development-oriented goals conflict with foreign diplomacy, trade interests, or political goals. For example, USAID's mission to empower the poor often clashes with U.S. embassies' goal of strengthening friendly governments—including governments that would prefer to stifle rather than empower vocal opposition movements that challenge their authority or legitimacy.[3] As the debate regarding the future disposition of USAID continues, the bureaucratic and political competition over aid disbursements is certain to figure prominently.

Multilateral aid is also popularly perceived as having failed to spur economic and development progress in the global South. However, notwithstanding the high costs, important lessons have been learned. The World Bank and International Monetary Fund have admitted that structural adjustment and stabilization policies have, even in the best cases, led to stable but stagnant economies. Gradually, the Bretton Woods institutions have realized that imposing particular economic growth models on recipients is counterproductive, as is the attempt to micromanage developing countries' economic policies. If development is truly a goal, multilateral aid must break the vicious circle of providing new aid to pay for the interest owed on old aid. The accumulation of unending debt perpetuated by such a model has forced the international financial institutions to recognize the need for debt reduction, if only to bring impoverished nations' debt to sustainable levels. Although the agencies of the United Nations have certainly been less encumbered by political and economic considerations, they too could stand improvement. Recent charges of mismanagement and wasted funds demand efficiencies, including the possibility of merging those agencies that share mandates yet compete for funds. The rising incidence of emergencies flaring up around the globe also presents new challenges to the UN agencies, as they must struggle to retain their commitment to development as resources are shifted to cope with urgent short-term needs.

Declining support for multilateral solutions accounts in large part for the rise in popularity of unofficial aid donors. However, although Northern and Southern NGOs may have become the darlings of the aid industry in recent years, they are far from the silver bullet for development. The scarcity of evaluations of Northern and Southern NGOs makes it difficult to comparatively assess these aid providers. Certainly success can be (and is) claimed in achieving short-term goals—people trained, equipment provided, food distributed—but the results are less conclusive when evaluating how NGO interventions alter the status quo and affect long-term sustainable change. In the current climate, NGOs are forced to compete fiercely for ever-scarcer funds. As a result, they often shy away from evaluation, for fear that any hint of underachievement could result in a reduction in contributions.[4] Thus a vital learning tool is lost, for without evaluation, Northern and Southern NGOs cannot measure progress or improve effectiveness. Evaluation would also provide an important pool of collective information about what works and what does not. If ever there were a time for close collaboration among NGOs, it is now. The process of globalization is not only shrinking the world but also making the development lessons learned in one region all the more applicable in regions halfway around the globe.

As the challenges of development increase, NGOs play a crucial role in mobilizing public attention and action. However, even in an ideal world, where Northern NGOs accepted the responsibility of educating and advocating in the North for the prerequisite conditions for development in the South, while collaborating with their Southern partners (in the true sense of the word) on the indigenous process of development, it would not be enough. Governments, financial institutions, and multilateral agencies must be equally committed to providing aid that it is focused, above all, on economic *and* human development.

Understanding the complexities of international assistance has become more difficult in the post–cold war era. Most Americans grossly overestimate how much their government spends on aid, and they perceive that that aid has failed to achieve its objectives. But the objectives of aid have always been multiple and, in many cases, conflicting. Thus it is important, albeit difficult, to determine in whose terms that failure is defined. Throughout its history, U.S. international aid has had such broad-reaching objectives as the containment of communism, the appeasement of strategic allies, the provision of humanitarian relief, and most recently, the liberalization of global markets. Although political interests continue to play a role—most clearly evidenced by the ongoing, overwhelming allocations received by Israel and Egypt—economic motivations have replaced cold war concerns. Consensus appears to have been reached by aid donors, bilateral and multilateral alike, that the primary goal of international aid ought to be to help developing countries enter the global marketplace. Most bilateral donors, especially the United States, are eager to widen the consumer base for their goods, whereas the international financial institutions have long been advocates of allowing the market to solve economic woes. Although economic liberalization is only the latest prescription, economic growth has always been the primary objective for all aid donors. However, as UNDP has indisputably shown, economic growth is not enough. Only development, economic and human, can lessen the risks of the coming millennium—the international dangers of disease, violence, and environmental decay from which no one anywhere is immune. International aid alone cannot solve any of these problems, just as it, alone, cannot bring about development. However, aid can play a critical role in assisting Southern governments to make the economic and political changes that development demands and in supporting the grassroots movements and organizations that are key to a strong civil society.

In 1995, Senator Jesse Helms and others in the Senate proposed a plan to reorganize and revitalize the United States' foreign affairs institutions.

It called for the dissolution of USAID and a sharp reduction in the foreign aid budget. Not surprisingly, the proposal elicited strong reactions from both proponents and critics of international aid. At the Senate hearings, a few of these voices were heard. Reprinted below are excerpts from the testimony of USAID administrator Brian Atwood and the comments of Senator Helms—two voices that represent opposing sides of the heated debate that continues to be waged on Capitol Hill, as well as (it is hoped) in U.S. classrooms. When opinions differ as sharply as these two do, the debate often appears to be a deaf one, with little substance being brought to light. For this reason, excerpts of the testimony of John Sewell, president of the Overseas Development Council, is also included, as he provides a more balanced assessment of the divergent positions while making a compelling case for the continuing necessity for foreign aid.

Following the excerpts from the Senate hearings is an article by David Korten that places the conflicting arguments in critical perspective. Whereas politicians and development specialists argue about budgets and administrative structures, Korten raises important questions about the very framework and assumptions on which international aid is based. Arguing that aid spending can be dramatically cut and still benefit the poor, Korten offers a number of suggestions for how this could be achieved. Although his recommendations are certainly ambitious and perhaps even unrealistic, they envision a new aid agenda. And as all idealists know, it is necessary to imagine the impossible if we are ever to make it come true.

Notes

1. John Sewell, testimony before the Committee on Foreign Relations, U.S. Senate, March 30, 1995.
2. "Out of Africa," *Economist*, March 15, 1997.
3. Denis Sullivan, "The Failure of US Foreign Aid," *Global Governance* 2, no. 3 (1996): 401–15.
4. Ian Smillie, "NGOs and Development Assistance: A Change in Mind-Set?" *Third World Quarterly* 18, no. 3 (1997): 563–78.

United States Senate, Committee on Foreign Relations
Hearings, Thursday, March 30, 1995*

Comments by Sen. Jesse Helms, Chairman
Committee on Foreign Relations

We meet this afternoon to explore the existing program by which the enormous sums of taxpayers' money is distributed by the Agency for International Development. Now, the Federal Government, I will say to the people here and who are watching television, is $4,800 trillion in debt, and as I have said repeatedly, foreign aid will be cut this year. Read my lips it will be cut.

Many of us have concluded that the Agency for International Development with its 9,000 full-time employees has very little, if any, purpose when there are fewer and fewer countries to which to hand out aid around the world. Bear in mind that since 1945, which was the year that foreign aid started, the United States has given away more than $451 billion in foreign aid, every bit of it borrowed money, and of that amount, $282 billion was for so-called development assistance. Americans have been required to give billions of dollars more in aid through the UN and the World Bank.

Now, I have never supported these giveaways. I had a distinguished colleague when I first came to the Senate and I was blessed to serve as his colleague for 2 years before he retired, Senator Sam J. Ervin. Senator Ervin used to say I have never voted for a dime in foreign aid.

All of us are for economic development. Make no mistake about that, but the American people do not support this business of handing over billions of dollars to corrupt dictators in faraway countries in which the United States has little, if any, national interest.

I do not support foreign aid. Most Americans do not support it largely because many of the programs which have been undertaken in developing countries have brought few tangible results for those they were designed to benefit. In fact, billions of dollars in foreign aid spending have been counterproductive. This aid has gone to nations which sanction drug trafficking; which rule undemocratically; which abuse the rights of their citizens and the rights of Americans; which oppose the United States in international forums; and which stifle economic growth and shield their markets from US exports. It is incomprehensible how a nation which is $4.9 trillion in debt can continue to spend nearly $14 billion annually on foreign aid.

---

* U.S. Senate Committee on Foreign Relations, *Hearings and Markup before the Committee on Foreign Relations and the Subcommittee on International Operations of the Committee on Foreign Relations*, 104th Cong., 1st sess. (Washington, D.C.: U.S. Government Printing Office, 1995).

Statement of Hon. J. Brian Atwood, Administrator
U.S. Agency for International Development

I appreciate the opportunity to join my colleagues to discuss the future of America's foreign policy institutions before this Subcommittee.

Our new post–Cold War foreign assistance program isn't about charity. It is about US self-interest. That is why USAID's operating principles are integration and coordination. A successful foreign assistance program must be an integrated program, one that recognizes that you only advance US interests by battling on all fronts simultaneously—through efforts which reinforce each other—and in sync with other agencies, public and private, that are working toward the same goal.

Furthermore, an effective foreign assistance program must recognize that nations cannot simply be categorized as developed or undeveloped; that you trade with the first, and give aid to the second. There is, in fact, a development continuum.

At one extreme are natural and human-created disasters. The continuum runs from such disasters to civil conflict and to problems of development, such as unsustainable rates of population growth, endemic poverty, environmental damage, and the absence of democratic institutions; through periods of transitions; all the way to sustainable development and trade. USAID's goal is to move countries on that continuum from, at worst, the collapse of civil society all the way to self-sufficiency and trade.

Today, other donors, as well as the countries receiving aid, recognize that the USAID mission, flying the American flag, is an extension of the world's only superpower. They are responsive to the concerns of our people in the field because they know that USAID's representatives speak for the US government. That is also why we have been so successful at coordinating assistance from other donors. We are able to maximize the impact of our aid, an amount that is declining, by using US influence to bring leverage funding from other sources. We can do that because we are part of the US government and an extension of the Secretary of State.

Statement of John W. Sewell, President
Overseas Development Council

Mr. Senator, thank you very much. I appreciate this opportunity to testify.

Before one can engage in any effective discussion of the future organization of the US foreign assistance apparatus, a number of broader questions must first be answered. The first question is what principles and interest should guide US involvement in the developing world and why? The second, the effectiveness of aid programs. The third question concerns how much of our limited budget resources are we willing to devote to promote those interests. Let me summarize briefly my conclusions:

1. Although the Cold War is over, and with it the old rationale for development assistance, the United States has a range of important long-term interests in global development that should drive policy makers to give development cooperation programs priority for attention and resources. These include the expansion of exports and jobs in this country, and the attack on problems such as drugs, migration, and direct health threats. The proposals now under discussion in the Congress on reorganization fail to adequately encompass these interests.

2. Development assistance remains very important in dealing with these issues. It is often asserted that development has been a failure and that foreign aid has been a waste of taxpayers' money. That view is at odds with the impressive accomplishments of the development process that have taken place over the past four decades. Aid has played an important role in those achievements.

3. Current development cooperation programs are threatened with budget cuts over the next five years that jeopardize their existence. If these cuts are made, important global and American interests in sustainable development will be harmed and proposals for reorganization of the executive branch development programs will be rendered moot.

4. Congress is correct that successive administrations have failed to adequately coordinate international development policies. However, neither this Congress nor this Administration have developed mechanisms to coordinate the policies of the range of government agencies whose policies have an important impact on long-term global development and the management of related global problems.

5. The proposals to reorganize by merging AID into the State Department move in the wrong direction. The State Department cannot coordinate the various agencies that are involved in global development issues, and has shown no interest or capability for managing complex development programs.

6. The management changes that have been made by the new AID Administrator are moving the agency in the right direction. AID now needs to be pushed further to focus its program on a selected number of critical *development* goals where US leadership can have a major visible impact in a measurable time frame. AID should be allowed to implement its changed directions and should not have its budget cut so severely as to cripple the reforms. Organizationally, AID should be made more independent of the State Department and its programs should be coordinated with other agencies' development related decisions through a new White House coordinating group.

Clearly, a government's primary responsibility is to its own people. The United Sates first must aggressively address the challenges within its own borders. When the country with the world's largest GNP ranks twentieth in child mortality and has 36 million people without health care coverage, a shortage of low-income housing, and a budget deficit of almost $200 billion, claims to a global leadership ring hollow.

Nevertheless, the United States cannot afford to ignore the world beyond its shores. Many of the economic, environmental, and social challenges facing the United States can only be dealt with through cooperation with other nations, including those in the developing world. There are very few problems or opportunities that this country faces that can truly be called "domestic."

The end of the Cold War makes it possible for perhaps the first time to envision a world characterized by peace, economic growth, environmental sustainability, and widespread democratization and human development. In this world, the traditional dichotomy between "domestic" and "international" issues is an anachronism. Global action is needed to address successfully the majority of so-called domestic concerns as well as to advance longer-term US interests in building a better world and promoting American humanitarian ideals. The United States must learn to think strategically—helping to frame the new international agenda while sharing responsibility for its implementation and using available resources to leverage participation by other nations.

The Poverty of Foreign Aid*
by David C. Korten

Progressive groups persistently hold up the percentage of a country's total national output it allocates to foreign assistance as a measure of national compassion for the poor. Yet countless progressive groups deeply concerned about the plight of the poor have presented tale after documented tale of how foreign aid has been actively harmful—from the structural adjustment programs of the World Bank and International Monetary Fund that turn over national economies to foreign creditors to food aid programs that undermine small local farmers. There is almost no one—with the possible exception of agencies directly dependent on the aid system—prepared to argue that more than a tiny fraction of current foreign aid actually benefits the poor. As one who cares deeply about the poor and spent nearly 30 years working in one way or another within the foreign aid system, I have come to an uncommon conclusion: it is entirely within our means to dramatically cut foreign aid spending and benefit the poor and the environment in the process.

Saying that existing foreign aid programs are on balance harmful or useless is not the same as saying rich countries have no obligation to help poor countries. That obligation is substantial. But this obligation is not appropriately defined in terms of financial transfers and we do no service to the poor and the environ-

* International Journal of Technical Cooperation 2, no. 1 (Summer 1996): 99–105. Reprinted with permission from Frank Cass and Co., Ltd., Essex, England.

ment by defending the whole aid system in the belief that this is necessary to protect the small pieces of it that may be doing good.

Revealing Statistics

Bread for the World has been taking a hard look at foreign aid allocations for several years. Of the total US foreign aid budget of $15.2 billion for FY 1994, only $8.3 billion made even a pretense of being for development. The remainder was for a combination of military aid, security related economic aid, promotion of US exports, and other forms of nondevelopment economic spending. The bias toward military security is evident in the listing of the top ten recipients of US foreign aid between 1982 and 1991. They are in order of the total billions of dollars received: Israel ($29.9), Egypt ($23.2), Turkey ($6.9), Pakistan ($5.4), El Salvador ($4.0), Greece ($3.7), Philippines ($3.5), Spain ($1.9), Honduras ($1.9), and India ($1.7).

The political impetus for foreign aid came largely from the cold war. Stable dictatorships were favored so long as they professed to be anti-communist. The majority of US assistance was earmarked for military assistance and economic payoffs for political favors such as military base rights. The cold war is over and these categories of aid have properly declined as a percentage of the total. Yet such forms of aid continue—including to repressive regimes.

The Bread for the World study disaggregated the remaining $8.3 billion of aid to identify those portions that might arguably be devoted to the addressing long-term causes of poverty, hunger, and environmental deterioration. It classified these as sustainable development expenditures. Using highly generous criteria, it found that at most $2.6 billion of the FY1994 aid budget (17 percent of the total) supported sustainable development. An additional $1.7 billion was allocated to migration, refugees, disaster assistance and food aid—humanitarian aid which may help the poor, but without addressing the underlying causes of their plight.

Flawed Premises

Revealing as the budget numbers are they do not take us to the heart of foreign aid's problem—the fact that is based on flawed premises. For example:

- *The presumed goal of aid continues to be to bring poor countries up to an American standard of material consumption by accelerating economic growth*—notwithstanding evidence that the current American standard is unsustainable even for Americans and that economic growth often enriches the already wealthy at the expense of the poor. Indeed, much of our aid continues to be channeled to the rich and powerful on the discredited trickle down theory that this will ultimately benefit the poor. The fact that poverty is deeply imbedded in institutional structures is actively ignored.

- *Aid implicitly assumes that development is advanced by increasing external economic dependence.* Foreign aid provides a country with unearned foreign exchange to buy more things from abroad. Countries that want to keep their military weaponry up to date and provide their wealthy elites with the latest in brand name consumer goods need to orient their economies to the needs and goods of the global economy. However, where the primary goal is to create societies able to provide adequate food, clothing, shelter, basic health care, and education for their own people based on their own resources, then foreign purchases—and thereby foreign aid—have a more limited role. The primary expenditure needs are local and a country is better advised to create its own money, borrowing nationally if necessary.
- *A substantial portion of assistance has been loan funded.* Debt service payments on public foreign debt from both official and commercial sources have placed poor countries in virtual debt bondage to their creditors and allowed the World Bank and IMF to impose structural adjustment programs that have stifled poverty alleviation efforts all around the world. It is time to reverse this process, recognizing that for most poor countries the elimination of foreign debt would free far more foreign exchange to meet necessary and appropriate import needs than would be provided even by significant increases in development assistance.

Dangerous Myths

Indeed, most contemporary development practice in both North and South is based on dangerously inaccurate myths that are treated as self-evident truths.

- The myth that growth in GNP is a valid measure of human well-being and progress.
- The myth that free unregulated markets efficiently allocate a society's resources.
- The myth that growth in trade benefits ordinary people.
- The myth that economic globalization is inevitable.
- The myth that global corporations are benevolent institutions that if freed from governmental interference will provide a clean environment for all and good jobs for the poor.
- The myth that inflows of foreign money are a path to local prosperity.

The Growth Myth To begin with, measures of growth are deeply flawed in that they are purely measures of activity in the monetised economy.

- Divorce is good for the national economy. It generates lawyers' fees and creates the need to buy and outfit an extra house—generating real estate brokerage fees and retail sales.

- If a young parent stays home to care for his or her own child, it contributes nothing to the economy. If that same parent hires a baby-sitter so he or she can take a job caring for other people's children that counts as an economic contribution.
- Oil spills and terrorist bombings both generate new economic activity and therefore add to GNP.

The growth myth has another serious flaw. Since 1950, the world's economic output has increased 5 to 7 times. That growth has already increased the human burden on the planet's regenerative systems—its soils, air, water, fisheries, and forestry systems—beyond what the planet can sustain. Continuing to press for economic growth beyond the planet's sustainable limits does two things. It accelerates the rate of breakdown of the earth's regenerative systems—as seen so dramatically in the case of many ocean fisheries—and it intensifies the competition between rich and poor for the resource base that remains.

The disparities in this competition have become truly obscene. There are now 358 billionaires in the world with a combined worth of $760 billion—equal to the total annual income of the world's poorest 2.5 billion people—almost half of the world's population.

In case after case we find that development projects—many funded with loans from the World Bank and other multilateral development banks—are displacing the poor so that the lands and waters on which they depend for their livelihoods can be converted to uses that generate higher economic returns— meaning converted to use by people who can pay more than those who are displaced. In all too many instances what growth in GNP really measures is the rate at which the economically powerful are expropriating the resources of the economically weak in order to covert them into goods and services that all too quickly become the garbage of the rich.

The Myth of Free Unregulated Markets It is almost inherent in the nature of markets that their efficient function depends on the presence of a strong government to set a framework of rules for their operation. We know that free markets create monopolies, which government must break up to maintain the conditions of competition on which market function depends. We also know that markets only allocate efficiently when prices reflect the full and true costs of production. Yet in the absence of governmental regulation, market incentives persistently push firms to cut corners on safety, pay workers less than a living wage, and dump untreated toxic discharges into a convenient river.

Take the example of the Benguet Mining Company in the Philippines documented by Robin Broad and John Cavanagh in their book *Plundering Paradise*. In the quest for gold, Benguet Mining cut deep gashes into the mountains, stripped away trees and top soil, and dumped enormous piles of rock and soil into local rivers. With their soils and water sources depleted, the indigenous people in the area can no longer grow rice and bananas and have to go to the other side of the

mountain for drinking water and to bathe. The cyanide used by the Benguet corporation to separate the gold from the rock poisons the local streams, kills cattle
that drink from the streams, and reduces rice yields of people in the lowlands
who use the water for irrigation. When the tailings and cyanide empty into the
oceans they kill the coral reefs and destroy the fishing on which thousands of
coastal people depend.

The company reaps handsome profits. The local people bear the costs.
Economists applaud the company's contribution to national output and export
earnings. And the winners in the global economy are able to buy their gold trin-
kets at a more attractive price. The one thing at which free, unregulated markets
are truly efficient is in transferring wealth from the many to the few.

The Myth of Free Trade   Many so-called trade agreements, such as NAFTA and
GATT, are not really trade agreements at all. They are economic integration agreements intended to guarantee the rights of global corporations to move both
goods and investments wherever they wish—free from public interference and
accountability. GATT is best described as a bill of rights from global corporations.

The Myth that Economic Globalization Is Inevitable   Many of the people who
claim globalization is a consequence of inevitable historical forces are on the payrolls of the global corporations that have invested millions of dollars in advancing
the globalization policy agenda and hiring PR flacks to tell the public it is
inevitable. Economic globalization is inevitable only so long as the world's largest
corporations are allowed to buy politicians and write laws.

The Myth that Corporations Are Benevolent Institutions   The corporation is an
institutional invention specifically and intentionally created to concentrate control over economic resources while shielding those who hold the resulting power
from liability for the consequences of its use. The more national economies
become integrated into a seamless global economy, the further corporate power
extends beyond the reach of any state and the less accountable it becomes to
any human interest or institution other than a global financial system that is now
best described as a gigantic legal gambling casino.

The Myth that Foreign Investment Creates Local Prosperity   Foreign investment
is attracted by perceived opportunities to turn a quick profit—not to benefit
some needy local community. Though they do have real world consequences,
most "international capital flows" are little more than movements of electronic
money from one computer account to another in a high-stakes poker game.

From 1990 through 1994 Mexico became touted as an international economic
miracle by attracting $70 billion in foreign money with high interest bonds and a
super heated stock market. As little as 10 percent of this foreign money went into
real investment. Most of it financed consumer imports and debt service payments or ended up in the private foreign bank accounts of wealthy Mexicans—
including the accounts of the 24 Mexican billionaires the inflows helped to
create. The bubble burst in December of 1994 and the hot money flowed out
even faster than it flowed in. Mexico's stock market and the value of the peso

plummeted. Mexican austerity measures and a sharp drop in US exports to Mexico resulted in massive job losses on both sides of the border.

Suggested Actions

The following are actions we might consider if we were serious about advancing economic justice, environmental sustainability, and political participation throughout the world—starting in the United States and other industrial countries.

- Transform the North's inequitable and unsustainable economies to provide the world a new model for sustainable lifestyles and economic justice and eliminate the need to extract resources from low income countries that they could be using to meet the needs of their own people.
- Convene an international conference to eliminate the foreign debts of Southern countries by: 1) creating a new democratically accountable agency under the United Nations with a mandate to support Southern countries in legally repudiating odious debts; and 2) introducing a 0.5 percent tax on international financial transactions to finance the pay down of remaining Southern international debt under agreements that preclude recreating it. If our concern is to help the poor and the environment, eliminating their international debts should be a top priority. Currently, the main useful function of foreign aid is to partially offset payments on international indebtedness the aid system helped create. While eliminating aid without eliminating this debt would be unconscionable, eliminating the debt would eliminate the major need for the aid system.
- Phase out the multilateral development banks—the World Bank and the regional development banks. By their nature as lending institutions, they add to the debts of Southern countries with nearly every action they take. It is not evident they have useful roles in creating just and sustainable societies.
- The United States could benefit the poor and the environment by eliminating $11.0 billion from the current US foreign aid budget of $15.2 billion. Of the remaining funds, $2.4 billion should be allocated among: 1) qualified UN agencies dealing effectively and creatively with critical needs—such as UNIFEM and UNFPA; and 2) public development foundations—such as Appropriate Technology International and the existing Latin American, African and Asian regional development foundations—that support civic engagement in advancing structural changes toward the creation of just, democratic and sustainable societies. The remaining $1.8 billion could be allocated to a fund for humanitarian assistance programs implemented through the United Nations and qualified NGOs. The remaining programs now funded under the foreign aid account should be eliminated or funded under more appropriate budget accounts that make no pretense that they represent assistance to needy people and countries.

- Eliminate military and security related economic assistance and initiate negotiations on an international convention to end the global arms trade.

One of the major goals of reforms called for here is to convert or reverse the enormous damage that the present discredited aid system has already caused. It is well within our means to replace this system with forms of international cooperation and mutual self-help that work for the creation of a just and sustainable world for all people. The longer we wait, the worse the mess we will eventually face.

Appendix

Key Institutional Players in Foreign Aid

International and Regional Organizations

USAID
320 Twenty-first Street NW
Washington, DC 20523-0056   (202) 647-4200
e-mail: pinquiries@usaid.gov (public inquiries)
web site: www.usaid.gov

World Bank
1818 H Street
Washington, DC 20433   (202) 477-1234
e-mail: comments@www.worldbank.org
web site: www.worldbank.org

African Development Bank
BP 1387, 01
Abidjan, Ivory Coast

Asian Development Bank
6 ADB Avenue, Mandaluyong
0401 Metro Manila, Phillippines   (632) 632-4444
e-mail: www@mail.asiandevbank.org
web site: www.asiandevbank.org

Caribbean Development Bank
PO Box 408
Wildey, St. Michael, Barbados

Inter-American Development Bank
1300 New York Avenue NW
Washington, DC 20577   (202) 789-5925
web site: www.iadb.org

International Monetary Fund
700 Nineteenth Street NW
Washington, DC 20431   (202) 623-7000
e-mail: webmaster@imf.org
web site: www.imf.org

United Nations
UN Plaza
New York, NY 10017   (212) 963-1234
e-mail: webmaster@un.org
web site: www.un.org

Food and Agriculture Organization (FAO)
Villa delle Terme di Caracalla
00100 Rome, Italy   (396) 579-3434
e-mail: Webmaster@fao.org
web site: www.fao.org

International Fund for Agricultural Development (IFAD)
Via del Serafico 107
00142 Rome, Italy   (396) 54591
e-mail: w.admin@ifad.org
web site: www.ifad.org

United Nations Children's Fund (UNICEF)
3 United Nations Plaza
New York, NY 10017   (212) 326-7000
e-mail: chein@unicef.org (information assistance)
web site: www.unicef.org

United Nations Development Programme (UNDP)
1 United Nations Plaza
New York, NY 10017   (212) 906-5000
e-mail: webmaster@undp.org
web site: www.undp.org

United Nations Environment Programme (UNEP)
PO Box 30552
Nairobi, Kenya   (254) 333-930
e-mail: eisinfo@unep.org
web site: www.unep.org

United Nations High Commissioner for Refugees (UNHCR)
PO Box 2500
1211 Geneva 2
Switzerland   (22) 739-8502
e-mail: webmaster@unhcr.ch
web site: www.unhcr.ch

United Nations Population Fund (UNFPA)
220 East Forty-second Street
New York, NY 10017   (212) 297-5020
e-mail: ryanw@unfpa.org
web site: www.unfpa.org

World Food Programme (WFP)
Villa delle Terme di Caracalla
00100 Rome, Italy   (396) 579-3030
e-mail: webadministrator@wfp.org
web site: www.wfp.org

World Health Organization (WHO)
20 Avenue Appia
CH-1211 Geneva 27
Switzerland   (22) 791-2111
e-mail: postmaster@who.ch
web site: www.who.ch

NGOs

ACCION International
120 Beacon Street
Somerville, MA 02143   (617) 492-4930
web site: www.accion.org
Supports microenterprise in developing countries by providing loans ($330 million in loans since its founding in 1961) that achieve a payback rate of 98 percent. Has affiliates in fourteen countries and has recently begun a program of microlending in low-income communities in the United States.

Bread for the World
1100 Wayne Avenue, Suite 1000
Silver Spring, MD 20910   (301) 608-2400
web site: www.bread.org
Christian faith-based lobby of approximately 44,000 members organized by congressional districts to advocate on behalf of the poor in the United States and in developing countries. The Bread for the World Institute publishes research and education material on policies related to hunger and development.

CARE
151 Ellis Street, NE
Atlanta, GA 30303   (404) 681-2552
web site: www.care.org
One of the largest relief and development organizations in the world. Programs are focused around the following areas: health, population, emergency aid, food security, agriculture, and natural resource management. Receives a substantial portion of its close to half billion dollar budget from the United States government in the form of commodities and funds.

Catholic Relief Services
209 West Fayette Street
Baltimore, MD 21201   (410) 625-2220
web site: www.greenmoney.crs.org
Works in over seventy-nine countries providing assistance ranging from emergency relief to enterprise development, with a staff of over 1,400. Provides assistance "on the basis of need, not creed."

Church World Service
475 Riverside Drive
New York, NY 10115   (212) 870-2257
web site: www.nccusa.org/cws/
Is the relief, development, and refugee assistance arm of the National Council of Churches, composed of thirty-three Protestant and Orthodox communions across the United States. Works with churches and organizations in seventy developing countries, focusing on grassroots development.

Development GAP
927 15th Street NW, 4th Floor
Washington, DC 20005   (202) 898-1566
web site: www.igc.org/dgap/
Officially called the Development Group for Alternative Policies. Is a center for analysis, advocacy, and action motivated by the mission to close the gap between third-world local realities and the perception of Northern policy makers.

Ford Foundation
320 East Forty-third Street
New York, NY 10017   (212) 573-5000
web site: www.fordfound.org
Its philanthropic work addresses problems in the United States and developing countries, organized under seven categories: urban poverty, rural poverty, rights and social justice, governance and public policy, education, international affairs, and reproductive health and population. In 1995, it provided more than $300 million in grants and loans.

Friends of the Earth
1025 Vermont Avenue NW, Suite 300
Washington, DC 20005   (202) 783-7400
web site: www.essential.org/foe.html
Advocacy organization dedicated to protecting the planet from environmental degradation. Promotes grassroots environmental activism and presses for environmentally responsible policies by the United States and other governments and aid-providing institutions.

Heifer Project International
PO Box 808
Little Rock, AR 72203   (501) 576-6836
web site: www.intellinet.com/heifer/
Provides more than twenty-two types of food- and income-generating animals to needy families in developing countries. Trains and teaches environmentally sound sustainable agriculture. HPI requires recipients to "pass on the gift" of one or more of their animal's offspring to another family in need.

InterAction
1717 Massachusetts Avenue NW, Suite 801
Washington, DC 20036   (202) 667-8227
web site: www.interaction.org
A coalition of more than 150 U.S.-based PVOs working in the areas of relief and development throughout the world. Interaction coordinates and promotes members' activities and sets ethical standards to ensure accountability and professional competence.

Interfaith Hunger Appeal
475 Riverside Drive, Suite 1630
New York, NY 10115   (212) 870-2035
· web site: www.ihaglobal.org
A partnership of four international development organizations (Catholic Relief Services, Church World Service, Lutheran World Relief, and the American Jewish Joint Distribution Committee). Works with undergraduate faculty toward the goal of more and better teaching about development.

International Committee of the Red Cross
Case Postale 276
1211 Geneva 19
Switzerland   (22) 345580
web site: www.icrc.org
Directs and coordinates the international work of the International Red Cross and Red Crescent Movement in helping victims of war and internal violence and promotes international humanitarian law. Works independently of all governments and international organizations and maintains a strict policy of neutrality in providing assistance.

Lutheran World Relief
390 Park Avenue South
New York, NY 10016   (212) 532-6350
web site: www.lwr.org
Works with partner Southern NGOs in forty-four countries in areas such as agriculture, microenterprise, and reconciliation. Provided $20 million in aid in 1996.

Overseas Development Council
1875 Connecticut Avenue NW, Suite 1012
Washington, DC 20009   (202) 234-8701
web site: www.odc.org
Conducts analyses, congressional briefings, symposia, and educational activities in five policy areas: U.S. foreign policy and developing countries, international finance and the debt crisis, international trade, development strategies and cooperation, and environment and development.

Oxfam America
26 West Street
Boston, MA 02111   (617) 482-1211
web site: www.reliefnet.org/met/stoxfam.html
One of nine autonomous Oxfams throughout the world. Funds self-help and disaster relief through indigenous organizations in developing countries. Produces development education and awareness materials and programs targeted toward an undergraduate audience.

Oxfam UK and Ireland
274 Banbury Road
Oxford OX2 7DZ
United Kingdom   01-865-312603
web site: www.oneworld.org/oxfam
Another autonomous Oxfam (the other seven are in Australia, New Zealand, Canada, Quebec, Hong Kong, Holland, and Belgium). Like Oxfam America, it focuses on programs designed to foster self-reliance. Also has a strong advocacy program that currently is campaigning for an international ban on land mines.

Results
236 Massachusetts Avenue NE, Suite 300
Washington, DC 20012   (202) 543-9340
web site: www.results.action.org
Conducts advocacy campaigns directed at the public, policy makers, and the media with the goal of encouraging citizen involvement and appropriate legislative action to end hunger. Has over one hundred membership groups in the United States.

TechnoServe
49 Day Street
Norwalk, CT 06854   (203) 838-6717
web site: www.technoserve.org
Provides technical assistance and business training to rural community-based enterprises. Works in twenty countries in Latin America and Africa (and Poland since 1991).

Trickle Up
54 Riverside Drive
New York, NY 10024   (212) 362-7958
web site: www.interaction.org/ia/mb/trickle.html
Provides conditional grants for entrepreneurs in developing countries, as well as nonformal business training. Operational in 108 countries.

U.S. National Committee for World Food Day
1001 Twenty-second Street NW
Washington, DC 20437   (202) 653-2404
*Committee of 450 member organizations cooperating to promote understanding of
and action on hunger and poverty issues on World Food Day (October 16). Conducts
annual nationwide teleconference for campuses and communities throughout the
United States and abroad.*

World Neighbors
4127 NW 122 Street
Oklahoma City, OK 73120   (800) 242-8387
web site: www.halcyon.com/kroger/wn.html
*Provides assistance to remote rural communities in the areas of animal husbandry,
agroforestry, and preventive health. Established in 1951, WN works in nineteen countries in the global South. Takes U.S. groups on development-study trips to programs in
Asia, Africa, and Latin America.*

World Resources Institute
1709 New York Avenue NW
Washington, DC 20006   (202) 638-6300
web site: www.wri.org
*An independent center for policy research and technical assistance on global environ-
mental and development issues. Disseminates its research, policy, and information to
policy makers, NGOs, and educators. Program areas include climate, population, biological resources, and environmental education.*

World Vision
919 West Huntington Drive
Monrovia, CA 91016   (818) 357-7979
web site: www.wvi.xc.org
*Christian relief and development organization that conducts large-scale programs in
child sponsorship, emergency relief, community development, and Christian leadership
development. Has programs in 103 countries.*

Glossary

absolute poverty. Income level below which a minimally nutritionally adequate diet plus essential nonfood requirements are not affordable.

ADB. Asian Development Bank.

ADF. African Development Fund.

adult literacy rate. Percentage of persons aged fifteen and over who can read and write. One of the indicators used to measure human development.

AfDB. African Development Bank.

APWA. All Pakistan Women's Association.

balance of payments. The difference between a country's receipts and payments. Consists of two main accounts: a current account, which includes balance of trade, and a capital account, which includes investments. A balance-of-payments deficit occurs when a country's payments exceed receipts.

basic human needs approach. Strategy adopted in the 1970s that focused development assistance on programs that were targeted at meeting the basic needs of the poorest segments of a population. Basic needs were identified as sufficient nutritious food and clean water, adequate shelter, protection from disease, and access to elementary education.

bilateral aid. Transfer of funds, goods, or services directly from a donor government to a recipient government.

BRAC. Bangladesh Rural Advancement Committee.

Bretton Woods Conference. Negotiations held in Bretton Woods, New Hampshire, in 1944, attended by forty-five states and leading world economists to design the post–World War II economic order. The goals were to ease the reconstruction of Europe and to foster international trade and economic integration. Among the outcomes of the talks was the creation of Bretton Woods Institutions: the World Bank, the International Monetary Fund (IMF), and the General Agreement on Tariffs and Trade (GATT).

CARE. Cooperative for American Relief Everywhere.

cash crop. Agricultural product grown for the purpose of being sold, usually in international markets, rather than for consumption, as in subsistence farming. Typical cash crops include tobacco, cotton, coffee, and cocoa.

CBI. Caribbean Basin Initiative.

CDB. Caribbean Development Bank.

cold war. Military rivalry and tension that existed between the United States and the former Soviet Union and their respective allies from 1945 to 1990.

COLUFIFA. Committee for the Fight for the End of Hunger (Senegal).

commodity. Raw materials or primary products traded on the international market. These goods come directly from the ground, without the added value of industry—such as agricultural goods or mineral products that are mined or extracted from the earth—and they often constitute the bulk of developing nations' exports. Commodity goods are subject to wide price variations, leaving Southern economies vulnerable to market shifts.

concessional terms. Conditions of a loan that provide lower interest rates or longer payback periods than do commercial loans.

conditionality. The attachment of conditions or requirements to loans by aid donors, aimed at encouraging policy reforms in developing countries. For example, recipient countries are often required to reduce government spending or end human rights violations.

CRS. Catholic Relief Services.

current account. The account that measures a country's international trade in goods and services over a given period. Current accounts also measure private transfers and official transfers, such as a country's payments to international organizations and interest payments on a nation's foreign debt.

DA. Development Assistance. One component of U.S. foreign aid.

DAC. Development Assistance Community of the Organization of Economic Cooperation and Development (OECD). DAC was established in 1961 as a seventeen-member committee to provide a forum for donor governments to consult and cooperate with one another on aid policies. Today, DAC is made up of twenty-two members: Australia, Austria, Belgium, Canada, Denmark, Finland, France, Ireland, Italy, Germany, Japan, Luxembourg, the Netherlands, New Zealand, Norway, Portugal, Spain, Sweden, Switzerland, the United Kingdom, the United States, and the Commission of European Communities.

DAWN. Development Alternatives with Women for a New Era (Barbados).

debt crisis. Emergency in the world's financial system in the 1980s and 1990s brought about when Southern nations were unable to repay debts to Northern governments and lending institutions.

debt forgiveness. Cancellation of all or part of the obligation to pay a debt.

debt service. Sum of current interest plus the scheduled repayment of principal on a loan.

deforestation. Depletion of forest or woodlands mainly by logging, overgrazing, or clearing. The threat of deforestation is most severe in tropical forests, particularly in South America.

devaluation. Lowering of the value of a country's currency relative to the currency of other countries. Devaluations can be caused by trends in the international currency market or by a governmental policy required under the terms of a structural adjustment program.

developed countries. Countries with relatively high per capita incomes and characterized by high productivity, low illiteracy rates, low birth rates, strong infrastructure, and market economies.

developing countries. This term is often used interchangeably with less developed countries, third world countries, and the global South. Refers to roughly 130 countries in Africa, Asia, and Latin America where all or some of the following characteristics are found: majority of the population living in poverty, little or no industry, high birth rates, low life expectancy, malnutrition, and poor housing.

development banks. International banks that provide loans and technical assistance to developing countries to assist with their development. Examples include large international institutions such as the World Bank and smaller regional banks such as the Caribbean Development Bank.

development education. Domestic education, formal and informal, designed to educate the public about global issues, challanges, and connections.

ECA. United Nations Economic Commission for Africa.

economic development. Increase in a country's economic growth rate or gross national product caused by the use, production, and distribution of more resources, goods, and services.

ECOSOC. Economic and Social Council of the United Nations.

EEC. European Economic Community.

ESF. Economic Support Funds. A significant component of the U.S. bilateral aid program that is most commonly provided to strategically important countries experiencing balance-of-payment difficulties.

FAO. Food and Agriculture Organization of the United Nations.

FMS. Foreign Military Sales. A U.S. foreign aid program.

food aid. Assistance in the form of commodities such as cereal, wheat, oil, or milk powder provided to a developing country for relief and development efforts.

free-market economy. An economy in which market forces dictate prices and production levels. It contrasts with a centrally planned economy, in which major economic decisions are made by the state.

free trade. Trade that is not subjected to any restrictions, such as quotas or tariffs.

GAO. General Accounting Office.

GATT. General Agreement on Tariffs and Trade. A multilateral trade agreement that dictates the rules for international trade. It promotes equal treatment for all trading nations, negotiated tariff reductions, and an elimination of import quotas.

GDP. Gross domestic product. Total value of goods and services produced within a nation in a given year.

GNP. Gross national product. A broader measure of an economy's performance than GDP, it includes the total value of all goods and services produced by a nation in a given year and income from foreign operations. It excludes similar payments made to nonresidents who contribute to the economy. Per capita GNP refers to the gross national product of a nation divided by its population.

grant element. Portion of a loan that is interest free. IDA loans, for example, have grant elements of nearly 90 percent.

HDI. Human Development Index. Ranking formulated by UNDP that measures a country's development based on health conditions, literacy, and access to goods and services.

IAF. Inter-American Foundation.

IBRD. International Bank for Reconstruction and Development. Commonly known as the World Bank, IBRD channels private funds and provides loans and technical assistance to developing nations.

IDA. International Development Association. The concessionary arm of the World Bank, IDA provides loans to the lowest-income countries on more favorable terms than those offered by IBRD. Loans, or credits, have a service charge but are usually interest free and allow a ten-year grace period.

IDB. Inter-American Development Bank.

IDCA. International Development Coordinating Agency.

IFAD. International Fund for Agricultural Development.

IFC. International Finance Corporation. Affiliate of the World Bank created to encourage private enterprise and investment in developing countries. IFC offers loans to both governments and private companies.

ILO. International Labor Organization.

IMET. International Military Education and Training. A U.S. grant program.

IMF. International Monetary Fund. Established in 1945 to promote stability in the international monetary system, IMF offers loans on the condition that the receiving country adopt measures to correct the deficit. Loans are conditioned on the agreement of the debtor country to adopt IMF-approved economic reforms.

Imperialism. Political and economic domination of a distant nation. Imperialism is usually associated with European overseas expansion between 1500 and 1900, when Spain, France, England, Germany, and other countries controlled many parts of today's global South. Native cultures were often suppressed by the imperial power, and the occupying powers sometimes subjected indigenous peoples to enslavement and exploitation. Also called colonialism.

indigenous peoples. Ethnic groups who have resisted assimilation and extermination and maintained the integrity of their culture and way of life. Worldwatch Institute describes them as "the keepers of human variety," and the UN estimates that there are approximately 300 million indigenous people. Also called Indians, aborigines, autochthonous peoples, natives, or first nations.

INEDER. Educational Institute for Rural Development (Bolivia).

infant mortality rate. Annual number of deaths among children under the age of one per thousand live births.

inflation. Percentage increase in prices in an economy, usually measured by an index of consumer prices. Inflation tends to be highest during times of economic turbulence, such as energy shocks, debt crises, or wars.

informal economy. Part of the economy that is not recognized by the government; also referred to as the black market. It operates parallel to the official economy and arguably contributes greatly to a country's balance of payments, national income, and employment.

infrastructure. Basic facilities and services that are essential to the functioning and development of an economy, such as transportation, communications systems, water, and power facilities. Can also refer to social infrastructure such as schools, health facilities, and housing.

least developed countries. Term used by the United Nations to refer to the poorest of the poor countries, which fulfill the following criteria: GDP of less than a certain figure (in 1994, $300), manufacturing represents less than 10 percent of GDP, and adult literacy rate of less than 20 percent. Of the forty-seven nations officially labeled LDCs, thirty-one are in Africa.

long-term debt. Debt that is not due (does not reach maturity) for at least one year.

LWR. Lutheran World Relief.

maldevelopment. Term used to describe those aspects of development that have had an extremely negative effect on developing economies. Mega-projects, such as dam building, that dislocate populations and worsen social inequality are examples of maldevelopment.

malnutrition. Physical and/or mental health impairment caused by the failure to obtain required nutrients. Malnutrition can be caused by inadequate food intake or a shortage or imbalance of key nutrients.

MAP. Military Assistance Program. A component of U.S. foreign aid.

market economy. Economy in which decisions on the allocation of resources, production, investment, and distribution are made by supply and demand. Market economies are usually based on a system of private ownership.

Marshall Plan. Formally known as the European Recovery Program. Launched by the United States in the aftermath of World War II, the plan dispensed over $13 billion between 1948 and 1952 and is widely hailed as a key factor in Europe's rapid return to economic security.

microenterprises. Small economic ventures owned and operated by one entrepreneur and employing fewer than five people.

MIGA. Multilateral Investment Guarantee Agency.

MPP. Mouvan Peyizan Papaye (Peasant Movement of Papaye, Haiti).

MSA. Mutual Security Administration. Successor to the Marshall Plan.

multilateral aid. Financial or material assistance from several countries to an international intermediary institution, such as the World Bank or a regional multilateral development bank, which then allocates the aid to recipient countries.

multinational corporation. Company with operations, investments, or subsidiaries in more than one country.

nationalization. The process of government takeover of private business and industry. Although nationalization of key industries was a popular development strategy several decades ago, most economists now believe that market forces manage businesses better than governments do.

New Directions. Legislation enacted by the 1973 Foreign Assistance Act that emphasized U.S. aid to the poor in developing countries, especially via smaller development projects that promised self-reliance and empowerment.

NGO. Nongovernmental organization. NGOs are independent, nonprofit charitable organizations involved in aid giving and regional development. The term PVO, which stands for private voluntary organization, is interchangeable with NGO and is used more frequently in the United States.

NICs. Newly industrialized countries. Nations whose economies have shifted from primarily agricultural to a more industrial export base. Many of these nations have industrialized with aggressive export-led strategies. Examples of NICs are South Korea and Taiwan.

NIS. Newly independent states.

North-South. Describes the economic division of the world between the developed countries of Europe, North America, and the Far East and the developing countries of Africa, Asia, and Latin America.

ODA. Official development assistance. Term used by DAC to refer to grants or loans provided by the official sector of donor nations, with the promotion of economic development and welfare as the main objective. ODA funds must be concessional, containing a grant element of at least 25 percent, and must be administered to a country on the OECD list of less developed countries or to a multilateral institution.

ODI. Overseas Development Institute.

OECD. Organization for Economic Cooperation and Development. Made up of most of the world's twenty-seven developed and industrialized nations, OECD's purpose is to further economic growth and encourage cooperation among its members.

OPEC. Organization of Petroleum Exporting Countries. OPEC was established by major oil-exporting countries in 1961 and acts as a cartel to promote its members' joint economic interests. OPEC members include Algeria, Ecuador, Gabon, Indonesia, Iran, Iraq, Kuwait, Libya, Nigeria, Qatar, Saudi Arabia, the United Arab Emirates, and Venezuela.

ORT. Oral rehydration therapy. Simple, low-cost treatment for diarrhea consisting of salt, water, and sugar. Diarrhea causes dehydration, which is the single biggest killer of children.

PL 480. Public Law 480, also known as the Peace Act of 1954. The law provides food aid to selected countries as relief or at reduced cost and includes concessional loans for the purchase of U.S. agricultural commodities. Billions of dollars of food aid have been shipped under the act, which has achieved important humanitarian ends but has also been widely criticized for its negative economic effects on donor nations and local food producers.

policy-based lending. Loans granted under the provisions of macroeconomic reforms in developing countries.

primary health care. Low-cost, simple health services that include family planning, clean water supply, sanitation, immunization, and nutrition education. The focus is on disease prevention and detection rather than treatment.

privatization. The sale of government-owned companies or industries. In recent years, often at the insistence of IMF or the World Bank, many nations have privatized key industries, raising public revenues by selling businesses to private concerns.

program assistance. Aid that goes toward particular economic sectors, such as agriculture, with the goal of remedying broad economic problems. It is usually provided in the form of foreign exchange and import funding.

project assistance. Assistance provided for specific activities with a predetermined outcome as the goal, such as construction or engineering projects.

protectionism. Trade barriers imposed to restrict the inflow of imported goods from another country.

PVO. Private voluntary organization. See NGO.

recession. Period of reduced economic activity marked by a decline in productivity and employment that, if prolonged, can lead to a depression. A recession is defined by two consecutive quarters of decline in major economic indicators.

refugee. A person outside of her or his home country who has a well-founded fear of persecution because of race, religion, nationality, political opinion, or membership in a particular social group if she or he were to return.

repatriation. Sending refugees and other migrants back to their home countries.

Sahel. The semiarid zone south of the Sahara, from the Atlantic coast of Mauritania and Senegal to Sudan and Chad. The Sahel was struck by devastating famine from 1968 to 1974 and continues to be the region most threatened by drought and desertification.

SEED. Support for East European Democracy Act.

SEWA. Self-Employed Women's Association (India).

short-term debt. Debt that is fully due (reaches its maturity) within one year.

social indicators. Statistics that measure the social welfare of a population. The principal social indicators are the adult literacy rate, population increase rate, mortality rate, and average life expectancy. Others indicators include school enrollment ratios and access to water.

soft loan. Low-interest loans that are repayable over a long period of time; also called concessional loans.

SSM. Sarvodaya Shramadana Movement (Sri Lanka).

structural adjustment. A cluster of policy prescriptions usually aimed at developing countries, often as a condition of a loan. Structural adjustment demands that governments spend within their means, keep exchange rates competitive, let markets determine prices, withdraw from regulation and subsidy, and privatize industries that had previously been nationalized.

subsidy. Payment by a government to producers or distributors to either ensure the economic viability of an industry or prevent an increase in prices.

subsistence farming. Small-scale agriculture practiced by individuals or families to provide for immediate food needs.

sustainable development. Defined by the Brundtland Commission as development that meets the needs of the present without compromising the ability of future generations to meet their own needs. Sustainable development combines environmental protection with economic objectives of growth into a common framework.

TCA. Technical Cooperation Administration. Part of President Truman's Four-Point Plan.

third world. Coined in the 1950s by a French economist to describe those countries that rejected alignment with both the first world of the West and the second world of the East. Although the political, nonalignment connotations of the term remain, it has taken on a broader meaning. Today, *third world* refers to all developing countries and encompasses all of Latin America; Africa except for South Africa; and all of Asia except for Japan, Singapore, Hong Kong, and Israel. Many development specialists reject the term on the grounds that it implies inferiority to the countries of the first world. Thus the term *South* is more commonly used to refer to the less developed countries of the world.

UN. United Nations.

UNDP. United Nations Development Programme. A specialized agency of the United Nations, UNDP is the world's largest source of grant funding for development cooperation.

UNEP. United Nations Environment Programme. Mandated by the United Nations to coordinate and provide policy guidance for sound environmental action throughout the world.

UNFPA. United Nations Population Fund.

UNHCR. United Nations High Commissioner for Refugees.

UNICEF. United Nations Children's Fund. Works around the world to improve the lives of children in developing countries by providing community-based service.

USAID. U.S. Agency for International Development. The principal bilateral development assistance agency of the U.S. government.

WARMI. Women's Organization of Independencia (Peru).

WFP. World Food Programme. Sponsored jointly by the Food and Agriculture Organization (FAO) and the United Nations, WFP is the largest source of food assistance.

WHO. World Health Organization. A UN agency founded in 1948 with the mandate to assist people to reach the highest possible level of health.

WID. Women in development.

World Bank Group. International financial institutions comprising the International Bank for Reconstruction and Development (IBRD), the International Development Association (IDA), the International Finance Corporation, the Multilateral Investment Guarantee Agency, and the International Centre for the Settlement of Investment Disputes. IBRD is the main lending organization, providing loans and technical assistance to countries with relatively high per capita incomes. IDA offers loans, or credits, to countries that cannot afford IBRD loans.

Bibliography

Antrobus, Peggy. "Funding for NGOs: Issues and Options." *World Development* 15 Supplement (1987): 95–102.

Bandow, Doug. "Economic and Military Aid." In *Intervention in the 1980s: U.S. Foreign Policy in the Third World*, edited by Peter J. Schraeder. Boulder, Colo.: Lynne Rienner, 1989.

Bandow, Doug, and Ian Vasquez, eds. *Perpetuating Poverty: The World Bank, the IMF, and the Developing World*. Washington, D.C.: Cato Institute, 1994.

Bebbington, Anthony, and Graham Thiele. *NGOs and the State in Latin America: Rethinking Roles in Sustainable Agricultural Development*. London: Routledge Press, 1992.

Bello, Walden. *Dark Victory: The United States, Structural Adjustment and Global Poverty*. Oakland, Calif.: Institute for Food and Development Policy, 1994.

Bertini, Catherine. "Feeding the Poor: Are We Facing a Global Crisis?" Speech delivered at Chicago Council on Foreign Relations, June 7, 1995.

Black, Jan Knippers. *Development in Theory and Practice: Bridging the Gap* Boulder, Colo.: Westview Press, 1991.

Buvinić, Mayra, and Margaret A. Lycette. "Women, Poverty, and Development in the Third World." In *Strengthening the Poor: What Have We Learned?* edited by John P. Lewis. New Brunswick, N.J.: Transaction Books, 1988.

Cassen, Robert, and associates. *Does Aid Work? Report to an Intergovernmental Task Force* 2nd ed. New York: Oxford University Press, 1994.

Charleton, Sue Ellen M. *Women in Third World Development*. Boulder, Colo.: Westview Press, 1984.

Clark, John. *Democratizing Development: The Role of Voluntary Organizations*. West Hartford, Conn.: Kumarian Press, 1991.

Cline, William. "Managing International Debt: How One Big Battle Was Won." *Economist*, February 18, 1995, 17–9.

Cohen, Marc J. "But the Cupboard Is Bare: The Crisis of Aid." In *Hunger 1996: Countries in Crisis*. Silver Spring, Md.: Bread for the World Institute, 1995.

———. "The Road Not Taken—The U.S. Government and Hunger." In *Hunger 1994: Transforming the Politics of Hunger*. Silver Spring, Md.: Bread for the World Institute, 1993.

Cohen, Marc, and Don Reeves. "Development Aid and International Institutions." In *Hunger 1997: What Governments Can Do*. Silver Spring, Md.: Bread for the World Institute, 1996.

Cuny, Frederick. "Refugees, Displaced Persons and the UN System." In *U.S. Foreign Policy and the UN System*, edited by Charles William Maynes and Richard Williamson. New York: W. W. Norton, 1996.

De Waal, Alex, and Rakiya Omaar. "Doing Harm by Doing Good? The International Relief Effort in Somalia." *Current History* 92 (1993): 198–202.

Dichter, Thomas W. "The Changing World of Northern NGOs: Problems, Paradoxes and Possibilities." In *Strengthening the Poor: What Have We Learned?* edited by John P. Lewis. New Brunswick, N.J.: Transaction Books, 1988.

Drabek, Anne Gordon. "Development Alternatives: The Challenge for NGOs—An Overview of the Issues." *World Development* 15 Supplement (1987): ix–xv.

Driscoll, David D. *The IMF and the World Bank. How Do They Differ?* Washington, D.C.: International Monetary Fund, 1989.

Durning, Alan. "Ending Poverty." In *State of the World's Children 1990*. New York: Oxford University Press, 1990.

Eberstadt, Nicholas. *American Foreign Aid and American Purpose*. Washington, D.C.: American Enterprise Institute for Public Policy Research, 1988.

Edwards, Michael, and David Hulme. "Scaling up the Development Impact of NGOs: Concepts and Experiences." In *Making a Difference*, edited by Michael Edwards and David Hulme. London: Earthscan Publications, 1992.

Elliott, Charles. "Some Aspects of Relations between the North and South in the NGO Sector." *World Development* 15 Supplement (1987): 57–68.

Fisher, Julie. *The Road from Rio: Sustainable Development and the Non-Governmental Movement in the Third World*. Westport, Conn.: Praeger Publishers, 1993.

———. *Nongovernments: NGOs and the Political Development of the Third World*. West Hartford, Conn.: Kumarian Press, 1997.

Forsythe, David. "Humanitarian Assistance in U.S. Foreign Policy, 1947–1987." In *The Moral Nation*, edited by Bruce Nichols and Gil Loescher. Notre Dame, Ind.: University of Notre Dame Press, 1989.

Fox, Thomas F. "NGOs from the United States." *World Development* 15 Supplement (1987): 11–19.

Gordon, David. "Economic Freedom and Development Aid." Testimony before the Senate Committee on Foreign Relations, September 19, 1996.

Hancock, Graham. *Lords of Poverty: The Power, Prestige, and Corruption of the International Aid Business*. London: Macmillan, 1989.

Hellinger, Doug. "NGOs and the Large Aid Donors: Changing the Terms of Engagement." *World Development* 15 Supplement (1987): 135–43.

Hellinger, Stephen, Douglas Hellinger, and Fred M. O'Regan. *Aid for Just Development: Report on the Future of Foreign Assistance*. Boulder, Colo.: Lynne Rienner, 1988.

Hook, Steven W. *National Interest and Foreign Aid*. Boulder, Colo.: Lynne Rienner, 1995.

———. ed. *Foreign Aid toward the Millennium*. Boulder, Colo.: Lynne Rienner, 1996.

Jepma, Catrinus. *The Tying of Aid*. Paris: OECD, Development Centre Studies, 1991.

Jolly, Richard. "Adjustment with a Human Face: A UNICEF Record and Perspective of the 1980s." *World Development* 19, no. 12 (1991): 1807–21.

Korten, David C. "Third-Generation NGO Strategies: A Key to People-Centered Development." *World Development* 15 Supplement (1987): 145–59.

Korten, David C., and L. David Brown. "Working More Effectively with Nongovernmental Organizations." In *Nongovernmental Organizations and the World Bank*, edited by Samuel Paul and Arturo Israel. Washington, D.C.: World Bank, 1991.

Kutzner, Patricia L. "Thirty Years of Anti-Hunger Advocacy." In *Hunger 1994: Transforming the Politics of Hunger*. Silver Spring, Md.: Bread for the World Institute, 1993.

Laatikainen, Katie Verlin. "The Disillusionment of Nordic Aid." In *Foreign Aid toward the Millennium*, edited by Steven W. Hook. Boulder, Colo.: Lynne Rienner, 1996.

Lancaster, Carol. "Governance and Development: The Views from Washington." *IDS Bulletin* 24 (January 1993): 9–15.

Lappé, Frances Moore, Joseph Collins, and David Kinley. *Aid as Obstacle: Twenty Questions about Our Foreign Aid and the Hungry*. San Francisco: Institute for Food and Development Policy, 1980.

Lewis, John P., ed. *Strengthening the Poor: What Have We Learned?* New Brunswick, N.J.: Transaction Books, 1988.

Lumsdaine, David Halloran. *Moral Vision in International Politics: The Foreign Aid Regime, 1949–1989*. Princeton, N.J.: Princeton University Press, 1993.

Marcussen, Henrik Secher. "Comparative Advantages of NGOs: Myths and Realities." In *Foreign Aid towards the Year 2000: Experiences and Challenges*, edited by Olav Stokke. Portland, Ore.: Frank Cass, 1996.

Maren, Michael. *The Road to Hell: The Ravaging Effects of Foreign Aid and International Charity*. New York: Free Press, 1997.

Mathews, Jessica. "Power Shift." *Foreign Affairs* 76, no. 1 (1997): 50–66.

McConahay, Mary Jo. "Wise Women of the Rainforest." *Choices* 4, no. 2 (August 1995): 18–23.

McGuire, Mark F., and Vernon Ruttan. "Lost Directions: U.S. Foreign Assistance Policy Since New Directions." *Journal of Developing Areas* 24 (1993): 127–79.

Minear, Larry. "The Other Missions of NGOs: Education and Advocacy." *World Development* 15 Supplement (1987): 201–11.

Morrison, Elizabeth, and Randall Purcell, eds. *Players and Issues in U.S. Foreign Aid: Essential Information for Educators*. West Hartford, Conn.: Kumarian Press, 1988.

Nowels, Larry Q., and Curt Tarnoff. "Foreign Assistance as an Instrument of U.S. Leadership Abroad." National Policy Association Report no. 285 (Washington, D.C.: NPA, 1997).

OECD. *Development Assistance Committee 1993 Report*. Paris: OECD, 1993.

———. *Development Assistance Committee 1995 Report*. Paris: OECD, 1995.

———. *Development Assistance Committee 1996 Report*. Paris: OECD, 1996.

———. *Twenty Five Years of Development Cooperation—A Review, 1985 Report*. Paris: OECD, 1985.

O'Hanlon, Michael, and Carol Graham. *A Half Penny on the Federal Dollar: The Future of Development Aid*. Washington, D.C.: Brookings Institution Press, 1997.

Omestad, Thomas. "Foreign Policy and Campaign '96." *Foreign Policy* 105 (winter 1996–97): 37–54.

Overseas Development Institute. "Poor Country Debt: A Never Ending Story." *ODI briefing paper*. London: ODI, March 1995.

———. "Rethinking the Role of the Multilateral Development Banks." *ODI briefing paper*. London: ODI, November 1996.

Paul, Samuel. "Governments and Grassroots Organizations: From Co-Existence to Collaboration." In *Strengthening the Poor: What Have We Learned?* edited by John P. Lewis. New Brunswick, N.J.: Transaction Books, 1988.

Pradervand, Pierre. *Listening to Africa: Developing Africa from the Grassroots*. New York: Praeger Publishers, 1989.

Program on International Policy Attitudes (PIPA). "Americans and Foreign Aid: A Study of American Public Attitudes." March 1, 1995.

Raffer, Kunnibert, and H. W. Singer. *The Foreign Aid Business: Economic Assistance and Development Co-operation*. Brookfield, Vt.: Edward Elgar Publishing, 1996.

Rau, Bill. *From Feast to Famine: Official Cures and Grassroots Remedies to Africa's Food Crisis.* London: Zed Books, 1991.

Rich, Bruce. *Mortgaging the Earth: The World Bank, Environmental Impoverishment, and the Crisis of Development.* Boston: Beacon Press, 1994.

Richardson, Richard, and Jonas Harlaz. *Moving to Market: The World Bank in Transition.* ODC Policy Essay no. 17. Baltimore: Johns Hopkins University Press, 1995.

Riddell, Roger C. *Aid in the 21st Century.* Discussion Paper Series no. 6. New York: Office of Development Studies, United Nations Development Programme, 1996.

———. *Foreign Aid Reconsidered.* Baltimore: Johns Hopkins University Press, 1987.

Rieff, David. "Charity on the Rampage." *Foreign Affairs* 76, no. 1 (1997): 132–8.

Sachs, Jeffrey. "Beyond Bretton Woods." *Economist*, October 1, 1994, 23–7.

———. "Growth in Africa." *Economist*, June 29, 1996, 19–21.

———. "Making the Brady Plan Work." *Foreign Affairs* (summer 1989): 87–104.

Savitt, William, and Paula Bottorf. *Global Development: A Reference Handbook.* Denver: ABC-CLIO, 1995.

Sen, Gita, ed. *Development, Crises, and Alternative Visions: Third World Women's Perspectives.* New York: Monthly Review Press, 1987.

Sewell, John W., and Christine E. Contee. "U.S. Foreign Aid in the 1980s: Reordering Priorities." In *U.S. Foreign Policy and the Third World: Agenda 1985–86*, edited by John Sewell, Richard Feinberg, and Valeriana Kallab. New Brunswick, N.J.: Transaction Publishers, 1985.

Smillie, Ian. "Changing Partners: Northern NGOs, Northern Governments." In *Non-Governmental Organisations and Governments: Stakeholders for Development*, edited by Ian Smillie and Henny Helmich. Paris: Development Centre of the Organization for Economic Co-operation and Development, 1993.

———. "Mixed Messages: Public Opinion and Development Assistance in the 1990s." In *Public Support for International Development*, edited by Colm Foy and Henny Helmich. Paris: Development Centre of the Organization for Economic Co-operation and Development, 1996.

———. "NGOs and Development Assistance: A Change in Mind-Set?" *Third World Quarterly* 18, no. 3 (1997): 563–78.

Stewart, Frances. "The Many Faces of Adjustment." *World Development* 19, no. 12 (1991): 1847–64.

Stokke, Olav. "Foreign Aid: What Now?" In *Foreign Aid towards the Year 2000: Experiences and Challenges*, edited by Olav Stokke. Portland, Ore.: Frank Cass, 1996.

Sullivan, Denis J. "The Failure of U.S. Foreign Aid: An Examination of Causes and a Call for Reform." *Global Governance* 2, no. 3 (1996): 401–15.

Tarnoff, Curt, and Larry Q. Nowels. "U.S. Foreign Assistance: The Rationale, the Record, and the Challenges in the Post-Cold War Era." National Planning Association Report no. 275 (Washington, D.C.: NPA, 1994).

Theunis, Sjef, ed. *Non-Governmental Development Organizations of Developing Countries: And the South Smiles.* Dordrecht: Martinus Nijhoff Publishers, 1992.

UNDP. *Human Development Report 1992.* New York: Oxford University Press, 1992.

———. *Human Development Report 1993.* New York: Oxford University Press, 1993.

———. *Human Development Report 1994.* New York: Oxford University Press, 1994.

UNICEF. *The State of the World's Children 1987*. New York: Oxford University Press, 1987.

————. *The State of the World's Children 1990*. New York: Oxford University Press, 1990.

Uvin, Peter. "Fighting Hunger at the Grassroots: Paths to Scaling Up." *World Development* 23 (1995): 934.

Welland, Kate, and James Copestake. *NGOs and the State in Africa: Rethinking Roles in Sustainable Agricultural Development*. London: Routledge Press, 1993.

Wedel, Janine R. "Aid and Reform in the Former Second World." In *Foreign Aid toward the Millennium*, edited by Steven W. Hook. Boulder, Colo.: Lynne Rienner, 1996.

Willetts, Peter. "Consultative Status for NGOs at the United Nations." In *"The Conscience of the World": The Influence of Non-governmental Organizations in the UN System*, edited by Peter Willetts. Washington, D.C.: Brookings Institution Press, 1996.

Wood, Robert E. "Rethinking Economic Aid." In *Foreign Aid toward the Millennium*, edited by Steven W. Hook. Boulder, Colo.: Lynne Rienner, 1996.

World Bank. *How the World Bank Works with Nongovernmental Organizations*. Washington, D.C.: World Bank, 1990.

Yudelman, Sally. "The Integration of Women into Development Projects: Observations on the NGO Experience in General and in Latin America in Particular." *World Development* 15 Supplement (1987): 179–87.

Zimmerman, Robert F. *Dollars, Diplomacy and Dependency: Dilemmas of U.S. Economic Aid*. Boulder, Colo.: Lynne Rienner, 1993.

Zimmerman, Robert F., and Steven W. Hook, "The Assault on U.S. Foreign Aid." In *Foreign Aid toward the Millennium*, edited by Steven W. Hook. Boulder, Colo.: Lynne Rienner, 1996.

Index

About the Author

PAULA HOY is the associate director of Interfaith Hunger Appeal (IHA), a nonprofit organization dedicated to raising awareness of global hunger and development issues. She is the director of IHA's education programs, which promote more and better teaching of global issues through faculty network building, curriculum development, and dissemination of pedagogical publications. This volume draws on her experience in working with development educators of all levels, as well as with the partner agencies of IHA: Catholic Relief Services, Church World Service, Lutheran World Relief, and the American Jewish Joint Distribution Committee. Her committment to global education comes in large part from her years spent in Mexico and the lessons she learned from unforgettable educators in commmunities such as Coyul, Cuernavaca, and Dungas in Niger. Hoy is also coauthor (with William Savitt) of *Global Development: A Reference Handbook* (ABC-CLIO, 1995). She lives with her husband in New York City.

Books of related interest
from Kumarian Press

Nongovernments:
NGOs and the Political
Development of the Third
World
Julie Fisher

This definitive work on nongovernmental organizations provides a
complete overview of the composition and the types of NGOs that
have emerged in recent years.
Julie Fisher describes in detail the
influence these organizations have
had on political systems throughout the world and the hope their
existence holds for the realization
of sustainable development.

US $24.95 Paper   1-56549-074-6
US $45.00 Cloth   1-56549-075-4

Beyond the Magic Bullet:
NGO Performance and
Accountability in the Post-
Cold War World
Michael Edwards, David Hulme

In this volume, experts review
the issues of NGO performance
and accountability in international
development assistance and provide guidance with respect to the
process of assessment. Case studies from Central America, Asia,
South America, East Africa and
North Africa.

US $18.95 Paper   1-56549-051-7
US $38.00 Cloth   1-56549-052-5

Achieving Broad-Based
Sustainable Development:
Governance, Environment, and
Growth With Equity
James H. Weaver, Michael T.
Rock, Kenneth Kusterer

This comprehensive and multidis-
ciplinary work provides an excellent overview of economic development and the results of growth.
The authors provide a model that
looks through economic as well as
social, political, and environmental
lenses.

US $26.95 Paper   1-56549-058-4
US $38.00 Cloth   1-56549-059-2

Governance, Administration
and Development:
Making the State Work
Mark Turner, David Hulme

Provides a comprehensive introduction to public policy and management in developing countries
and transitional economies. The
book assesses both traditional and
new models of public administration with particular emphasis on
the challenge to the centrality of
the state in development and current debates about the conditions
of effective governance.

US $24.95 Paper   1-56549-070-3
US $48.00 Cloth   1-56549-071-1

**Management Dimensions of
Development:
Perspectives and Strategies**
Milton J. Esman

The author critiques the thinking
of the founding development administration practitioners and emerging generations and demonstrates
how to go beyond early development approaches. Esman builds a
case for multiorganizational strategies sensitive to all players within a
society—government, private enterprise, and voluntary organizations.

US $16.95 Paper   0-931816-64-5
US $30.00 Cloth   0-931816-65-3

**Promises Not Kept:
The Betrayal of Social Change
in the Third World,
Fourth Edition**
John Isbister

This book develops the argument
that social change in the Third
World has been blocked by a series
of broken promises, made explicitly or implicitly by the industrialized countries and also by Third
World leaders themselves.

The fourth edition takes into
account the success stories in the
Third World, particularly in East
Asia, asking why those experiences have not been more widespread.

US $18.95 Paper   1-56549-078-9

Kumarian Press, Inc.
14 Oakwood Avenue
West Hartford, CT 06119-2127
USA

Inquiries: 860-233-5895
Fax: 860-233-6072
Order toll free: 800-289-2664

e-mail: kpbooks@aol.com
internet: www.kpbooks.com

 Kumarian Press is dedicated to publishing and distributing books and other media that will have a positive social and economic impact on the lives of peoples living in "Third World" conditions no matter where they live.

As well as books about International Development, Kumarian Press also publishes books about the Environment, Nongovernmental Organizations, Government, Gender, Peace, and Conflict Resolution.

To receive a complimentary catalog or to request writer's guidelines, call or write:

Kumarian Press, Inc.
14 Oakwood Avenue
West Hartford, CT 06119-2127 USA

Inquiries: 860-233-5895
Fax: 860-233-6072
Order toll free: 800-289-2664

e-mail: kpbooks@aol.com
internet: www.kpbooks.com